Springer Series in Transitional Justice

Volume 6

Series Editor

Olivera Simić

For further volumes:
http://www.springer.com/series/11233

Peter D. Rush · Olivera Simić
Editors

The Arts of Transitional Justice

Culture, Activism, and Memory after Atrocity

Springer

Editors
Peter D. Rush
Faculty of Law
University of Melbourne
Carlton, VIC
Australia

Olivera Simić
Griffith Law School
Griffith University
Gold Coast, QLD
Australia

ISBN 978-1-4614-8384-7 ISBN 978-1-4614-8385-4 (eBook)
DOI 10.1007/978-1-4614-8385-4
Springer New York Heidelberg Dordrecht London

Library of Congress Control Number: 2013946409

Printed on acid-free paper

Springer is part of Springer Science+Business Media (www.springer.com)

Preface
After Atrocity: Foreword to Transition

Peter D. Rush

Transitional justice is an established enterprise. According to its historians, it emerged in the 1980s in response to a set of practical dilemmas that beset the social and political transformations underway in South Africa, the countries of the Southern Cone, as well as in the Central and Eastern European states with the collapse of communism. In dealing with the recent and ongoing past of atrocities and human rights violations, the transformations were framed, narrated, in terms of a shift from authoritarian regimes to democratic social forms in which negotiated settlements foregrounded a commitment to the rule of law and legal justice. As Paige Arthur perceptively puts it in her "conceptual history":

> The field of "transitional justice"—an international web of individuals and institutions whose internal coherence is held together by common concepts, practical aims, and distinctive claims for legitimacy—began to emerge as a response to these new practical dilemmas and as an attempt to systematize knowledge deemed useful to resolving them. The field of transitional justice, so defined, came directly out of a set of interactions among human rights activists, lawyers and legal scholars, policymakers, journalists, donors and comparative politics experts concerned with human rights and the dynamics of "transitions to democracy," beginning in the late 1980s.[1]

Eventually, in a more subdued tone, the United Nations would consolidate the institutional life of transitional justice as a normative process of dealing with the past and setting right standards for the future. According to its 2004 Report, transitional justice is best defined as "the full range of processes and mechanisms associated with a society's attempts to come to terms with a legacy of large-scale abuses in order to ensure accountability, serve justice and achieve reconciliation".[2] Moreover, the rule of law provides the emphatic terms of reference for the enterprise. The rule of law

P. D. Rush
Institute for International Law and the Humanities, Faculty of Law
University of Melbourne, Melbourne Australia

[1] Paige, Arthur. 2009. How "transitions" reshaped human rights: a conceptual history of transitional justice. *Human Rights Quarterly* 31(2):321–367, 324.

[2] United Nations Security Council. 2004. The rule of law and transitional justice in conflict and post-conflict societies, report of the secretary general, 5. http://www.un.org/en/ruleoflaw/index.shtml

> refers to a principle of governance in which all persons, institutions and entities, public and private, including the State itself, are accountable to laws that are publicly promulgated, equally enforced and independently adjudicated, and which are consistent with international human rights norms and standards. It requires, as well, measures to ensure adherence to the principles of supremacy of law, equality before the law, accountability to the law, fairness in the application of law, separation of powers, participation in legal decision making, avoidance of arbitrariness and procedural and legal transparency.[3]

Transitions then are social transformations in process, and transitional justice is an enterprise that governs the directionality of the transformation—coming to terms with a legacy of atrocity as well as setting right standards for the future. And the justice of that directionality—its coming to terms, as much as its future—is measured by its commitments to the rule of law, its structure of procedure (due process) and its social legitimacy (democracy). Of course, in the aftermath of atrocity, what remains is a melancholy justice. It is forever deferred to an indefinite future, somewhat like Shelley's 'lone and level sands' that 'stretch far away' beside the ruins of Ozymandias.[4]

Such might be the settled state of transitional justice. Yet the self-understanding of transitional justice has been going through a reassessment of and reflection on its own commitments, regulative ideals and sites of criticism and evaluation. Its histories are being reconstructed; Arthur's essay quoted above is part of this trend, and to it we can add the thematic 'genealogy' of Ruti Teitel and the taking stock of the extant transitions by Fletcher, Weinstein and Rowen.[5] In part, the effort of this historical revaluation of the scholarship, its dilemmas and its institutional actors has been to question the prominence of the discourses of sociology and political

---

[3] United Nations Security Council. 2004. The rule of law and transitional justice in conflict and post-conflict societies, report of the secretary general, 4. http://www.un.org/en/ruleoflaw/index.shtml. The report was updated subsequently in United Nations Security Council. 2011. The rule of law and transitional justice in conflict and post-conflict societies, report of the secretary general. http://www.un.org/en/ruleoflaw/index.shtml. For attention to its rhetoric and a critique of this account of reconciliation, see Eric, Doxtader. "A critique of law's violence yet (never) to come: United Nations transitional justice policy and the (fore)closure of reconciliation", Alexander Hirsch (ed) *Theorizing Post-Conflict Reconciliation: Agonism, Restitution and Repair*, (Routledge, 2012), Chapter 3.

[4] Percy, B. Shelley. 1977. Ozymandias. In *Selected Poems*, ed. P. B. Shelley and Webb T, 11. London: Everyman.

[5] Ruti, G. Teitel. 2003. Transitional justice genealogy. *Harvard Human Rights Journal* 16: 69–94. Constructing the history as a conditioned but patterned dynamic rather than as progress; Laurel, E. Fletcher, Harvey, M. Weinstein. and Jamie, Rowen. 2009. Context, timing and the dynamics of transitional justice—a historical perspective. *Human Rights Quarterly* 31(1):163–220, providing thumb-nail sketches of transitions.

science, social policy and law.[6] Similarly, a constellation of topics drawing on the categories of diverse disciplines have provided a variegated lexicon when reading post-conflict transitions: dealing with the past, memory, trauma, witnessing and testimony, accountability, war crimes and human rights, nation-building, truth and reconciliation, responsibility, survivors, to mention a few. And the technologies, providing both the tool box for intervention as well as the referents of academic and policy debates, have expanded and been pluralised: not only criminal prosecution and trials; not only truth commissions authorised by the state mostly through constitutional settlements and legislative mandates and sometimes judicial litigation (on the latter, the recent Canadian experience is illustrative); but also reparations, amnesties, truth trials and apologies. The reassessment then has been of its intellectual, disciplinary and institutional commitments and affiliations.

In this book, we contribute to this revaluation of transitional justice by turning its approach and lexicon in the direction of artistic practices and their discourses of aesthetic judgment. The chapters deal with theatre and performance practices, public art installations, photography, narrative fiction, literature and criticism, poetry, body art, film, as well as museums and public architecture. The readings are authored—sometimes jointly in conversation across disciplines, others singly in an interdisciplinary vein—by artists and activists, dramaturges and policy researchers, scholars and literary critics, transitional justice experts and legal academics. Without downplaying the differences and disagreements in approach, what holds the various contributions together is the reconstruction of our attachment to the *cultural forms and forces through which practices of representation give value and meaning to the enterprise of transitional justice—as a system of knowledge, an institutional craft and as the subject-matter and material of social policy*. Some chapters turn their attention to the actual contributions of specific artistic, activist and cultural practices to transitional justice in specific local, regional and diasporic contexts. Others discern an untapped—and sometimes foreclosed—potential of cultural works in generating and maintaining the imagination of justice in transition. Yet others provide trenchant critiques of the denialism and ideology of transitional justice in specific national projects.

After atrocity, the disputes of transitional justice can only be mediated by history and by visceral notions of personal and collective responsibility. We could think of this as affective justice—not so much an emotion, as a bodily feeling, a corporeal sonority, a rhythm that places bodies on the line, an obligation that haunts and unsettles the narratives of transitional justice. It is the justice, beyond

---

[6] From a legal perspective, see Christine, Bell. 2009. Transitional justice: interdisciplinarity and the State of the 'field' or 'non field'. *International Journal of Transitional Justice* 3: 5–27. For evaluation, see the chapter by Eugene McNamee in this book. From a literary-critical perspective, see Siphiwe, Dube. 2011. Transitional justice beyond the normative: towards a literary theory of political transitions. *International Journal of Transitional Justice* 5:177–197. And from a critical theory perspective, see Hannah, Franzki. and Maria, Carolina. Olarte. 2013. "Understanding the political economy of transitional justice: a critical theory perspective" (forthcoming 2013, copy on file with author).

all visions of right and good, that Charlotte Delbo, a survivor, poet and playwright, heard in the cries, the grieving, of the Madres de La Plaza de Mayo at the height of the dirty war in Argentina. The last stanza of her poem *Les Folles de Mai* (The Madwomen of May) exhorts the Madres[7]:

Go round madwomen of May
round and round on the Plaza de Mayo
cry women of Buenos Aires
cry till the ghosts of your tortured rise
like so many staring eyes
staring into ours and accusing us
incandescent stares that burn
burning the skin from our souls
and causing us to scream from your pain
cry until the world
bursts with shame.

The first four chapters of this collection can be read as setting the scene on which the arts of transitional justice are staged and sometimes performed. Eugene McNamee (Chap. 1) takes up the literary and theatrical practices of the *Field Day* group of poets, dramaturges, academics and critics and explores its project of re-inventing the cultural imaginary of Ireland. Its purchase on transitional justice, as I read it, is not only in foregrounding the translations and idioms necessary to the formation of cultural intervention, but also providing a critical re-evaluation of the peace process and constitutional settlement in Northern Ireland. Here, transition emerges not so much as social transformation as the invention of cultural intervention.

The chapter argues that transitional justice scholarship, as much as the Belfast/Good Friday Agreement, draws its force and form from a cultural imaginary which has yet to be acknowledged. More generally, as a literary-critical reading of transitional justice, McNamee establishes the importance of the imaginary and rhetorical dimension of the transitional justice enterprise—a question and theme that is pursued in most of the chapters throughout the book. Specific works of art are read as exercises of the imagination, and hence their potential for transformation (transition as cultural change, a change of position and standpoint). In other chapters, the imaginary appears under the auspices of ideology critique as the loss of imagination, the dominance of the symbolic and its instrumentalised narratives of justice. And in yet other chapters, the cultural imaginary is embodied in detailed readings of the form or genre through which specific works of art emerge. In McNamee's chapter, the accent falls more on justice, than transition. If the form of justice is cultural, then its force is not so much normative as affective.

In Chap. 2, Laura McLeod engages in a conversation with a documentary photographer (Biliana Rakočević) and a body artist (Jovana Dimitrijević) that draws out the lineaments of transitional justice concerns in Serbia. This is the first of a number of chapters which reconstruct relations between artistic practices and

[7] Charlotte, Delbo. 1990. *Days and Memory*, 85. London: Marlboro Press.

activism: Rakočević has documented the activism of Women in Black, a feminist and anti-war organisation that engaged in public protests during and after the Yugoslav wars; Dimitrijević's performances have engaged the visceral dimensions—thematised here as both homosexual orientation and laceration of the body—of conflict and transitional justice.

The growth of human rights films; the use of image galleries (often rows of portraits) on websites—I am thinking here of the documentation of the *desaparecidos* as well as the testimonial archive of the stolen generations in Australia[8]; the use of digital imaging systems in reconstructing the geomorphology of an area to find the location of mass graves, the importance of visual evidence (both the display of physical objects and illustrative mapping) in criminal prosecution—all these require us to reconstruct the rhetoric of the image that shapes responses to historical injustice and mass atrocity. Much of this imagery works as illustration, witnessing and promotion. The next two chapters—Chap. 3 by Maria Elander and Chap. 4 by Fayen d'Evie—establish the importance of performance in shaping both the responses to transition and our visions of justice. Performance is used in a double sense as staging and as performativity. Maria Elander provides a close reading of the Tuol Sleng photographs, not only for what they depict, but more importantly for their generic conventions: mug shot, portrait, artwork and so on. It is these generic conventions that do much of the didactic work of the photographs and their representations of atrocity, responsibility and legal justice. Where Elander's chapter focuses on the museum as a public and legal institution, Fayen d'Evie's chapter turns to public art installations—and specifically the *Fragments* event that was part of the *Nuit Blanche* Festival in Canada. Where country studies are prominent in transitional justice scholarship, her chapter takes up the importance of transitional justice concerns for *diasporic* communities. She argues that the installation—through its participatory practice and staging—manages to index experiences of atrocity that are sub-national (personal narratives) and supranational (human solidarity). The indexical quality is here carried by the dramaturgy of the installation as much as by the displays of artefacts contributed to the work by diasporic communities of survivors. (On the legal destruction of artefacts, see also Chap. 9).

So far the chapters have offered up a conceptual matrix of terms (cultural imaginary, performance, genre or form, and experience) and productive readings of specific works of art that revise our understanding of the creation and limits of transitional justice. The next three chapters focus on various traditions of a single literary form—namely, theatre. Padraig McAuliffe presents Ariel Dorfman's play

---

[8] See for example: the testimony website that weaves together sound and image in an autobiographical presentation of the stolen generations in Australia at http://stolengenerations-testimonies.com/index.php; *Project Disappeared*, a project by human rights organisations and activists, that strives to keep the memory and truth of state terrorism and *los desaparecidos* at http://www.desaparecidos.org/main.html and the photographic exhibit of transition of the Latin American Network of International Sites of Conscience on the Memoria Abierta website at http://www.memoriaabierta.org.ar/eng/index.php.

Death and the Maiden as a staging of transitional justice debates before they had congealed into a systematic discourse of knowledge. In fact, for McAuliffe, the play is both a performance of the early dilemmas[9], as much as a critique of transitional justice. The play's the thing. Akin to McNamee's argument in Chap. 1, McAuliffe's analysis can be read as a reconstruction and intervention in the self-understanding of transitional justice: in the beginning, there was theatre. The next two chapters pursue a similar leitmotif, albeit at the level of transitional justice policy and transitional justice activism. Chapter 7 by Nadia Siddiqui, Hadi Marifat and Sari Kuovo describes—with numerous examples—the policy roles that community theatre has played in Afghanistan transitional justice institutions. The potential of theatre, they argue, is that it provides a forum for the participation of the victims and survivors of conflict. Whereas Siddiqui et al. draw on the traditions of the Theater of the Oppressed and of Playback Theatre, the work of Bertolt Brecht provides the inspiration for the activist theatre of the Dah ensemble in Serbia in Chap. 6. The chapter is co-authored by one of its founding members (Dijana Milošević) and, as with Chap. 2, arises out of a dialogue between an artist—specifically, a dramaturge and theatre director—and an academic (Olivera Simić). Drawing a distinction between the drama of courts and the performance of theatre, Dah presents its plays as dealing with the past and also breaking with it; it generates cultural change not only by "lend[ing] our beings and our voices to the people whose voices we do not hear" but also by creating a dramatic space where consciousness is transformed through the meeting of different and dissenting points of view. In all this, it rejoins the classical tradition of theatre as catharsis or cure, and the audience plays the role of chorus.

The medium of theatre is performance and its privileged modality is time. As Dianne Taylor remarked in the context of the theatre of public protest associated with the Madres de la Plaza de Mayo, performance is a 'restored' or 'twice behaved behaviour'.[10] Atrocities are events that overwhelm and defy are cognitive understanding, and return in visceral parts and images. It would be surprising then if transitional justice was not a discourse marked by temporal dilemmas. Transitions are liminal, in a time between a before and an after. And justice too—or at least legal-political justice—is the very matter of dealing and breaking with the past: of facing a history of injustice, backing into the future. These temporal slippages and complexities are explored through activist art in Chap. 2.[11] In the final three chapters, they are developed in terms of narrative and memory.

---

[9] It is thus usefully read alongside Paige Arthur's conceptual history, supra n. 1.

[10] Dianne, Taylor. 1997. *Disappearing Acts*. Durham: Duke University Press. 184–185.

[11] For an interesting development of the questions of time in the context of transitional justice, see Berber, Bevernage. 2013. *History, Memory and State-Sponsored Violence: time and justice*. London: Routledge. Juxtaposing the time of history and the time of legal justice (as retributive justice), he measures the institutional discourses of transitional justice against the irrevocable time of the catastrophic.

Chapter 8 by Ajla Demiragić and Edin Hodžić reconstructs the literary narratives of the genocide at Srebrenica. The focus is on the literature of trauma and its representation of "the survivors—those located between, even defining the space between, the past and the future". The dilemmas of the sequencing of the narratives provide one way into the narrative form, but the overall focus in the chapter concerns the thematic patterning of the narratives in line with dominant cultural and political discourses of the genocide. This leads them to pose the lapidary question: "Can transitional justice for Srebrenica begin in fiction?" and their chapter ends by indicating what they see as the main contours of a paradigm shift that would usher in literary transitional justice. The penultimate chapter—by Olivera Simić—suggests a practical and tragic limit to such an endeavour. It concerns the destruction of some 1,000 artefacts from the graves of Srebrenica by the International Criminal Tribunal for the former Yugoslavia (ICTY). The chapter phrases this destruction of physical evidence in terms of a dialectic of memory and forgetting. Law comes down on the side of forgetting. The activism of the Mothers of Srebrenica struggles to hold onto a memory preserved in the artefacts. As Hatidža Mehmedović remarks in Chap. 9, "the house of justice … committed genocide of memories".

The preservation of memory is also the concern of the final chapter by Despina Angelovska. The case study is the redevelopment of public space by the Macedonian government under its Skopje 2014. The government programme has seen the proliferation of memorials and monuments, museums and statues, public buildings and thoroughfares. Subjecting the programme to a critique of ideology, the politics of memory is understood as part of an effort by post-communist elites to create a narrative of nation-building which cynically uses and abuses memory projects as symbolic reparations for the victims of the communist era. Against the cynicism of the state and its top-down approach, the chapter argues that the legitimacy and effectiveness of transitional measures depend on local ownership and genuine participation.

Narrative memory then provides one vector for the critique of transition as social transformation and cultural change. There are others. Consider again the rhythm of the Madres going round and round and the exhortation to cry cry cry in Delbo's poem. After atrocity, in the performance of public protest, the arts and activism of transition, it remains possible to hear a demand for affective justice. Is this not a justice that 'bursts' the world …

Contents

Figures

Contributors

Despina Angelovska is an Associate Professor at the University of Audiovisual Arts, ESRA, Skopje, Republic of Macedonia, e-mail: despina.angelovska@gmail.com

Fayen d'Evie is an artist, Researcher and Independent Publisher in Muckleford, Australia, e-mail: fayendevie@gmail.com

Ajla Demiragic is a lecturer in the Department of Comparative Literature of the Faculty of Philosophy, University of Sarajevo, e-mail: demiragic.ajla@gmail.com

Jovana Dimitrijević is a contemporary artist, activist, performer and movie director in Serbia, e-mail: nikodbabenemadzabe@yahoo.com

Maria Elander is a teaching fellow and PhD candidate in the Faculty of Law, University of Melbourne, Australia, e-mail: elanderm@unimelb.edu.au

Edin Hodžić is Head of the Public Law Program at Analitika-Center for Social Research, Sarajevo, e-mail: edin.hodzic@analitika.ba

Sari Kuovo is a founding member and co-director of Afghan Analysts Network, Afghanistan, e-mail: sari@afghanistan-analysts.org

Hadi Marifat is a founding member and director of Afghanistan Human Rights and Democracy Organization, Afghanistan, e-mail: hadimarifat@gmail.com

Padraig McAuliffe is a lecturer in the School of Law, University of Dundee, Scotland, e-mail: p.g.mcauliffe@dundee.ac.auk

Laura McLeod is a Research Associate if the School of Social Sciences, Faculty of Humanities, University of Manchester, England, UK, e-mail: laura.mcleod@manchester.ac.uk

Eugene McNamee is Head of Law School, University of Ulster, Belfast, UK, e-mail: E.McNamee@ulster.ac.uk

Dijana Milošević is a theatre director, cofounder and artistic director of Dah Theatre in Belgrade, e-mail: dijana.mlsvc@gmail.com

Biliana Rakočević is a photographer living and working in Belgrade, e-mail: biliana11@gmail.com

Peter D. Rush is Director of the International Criminal Justice program in the Institute for International Law and the Humanities, and Associate Professor in the Faculty of Law, University of Melbourne, Australia, e-mail: prush@unimelb.edu.au

Nadia Siddiqui is manager of grants development at the International Center for Transitional Justice and previously part of the Center's Afghanistan and International Policy Relations programmes, e-mail: nsiddiqui@ictj.org

Olivera Simić is a lecturer in the Law School, Griffith University, Australia, e-mail: o.simic@griffith.edu.au

Chapter 1
Fields of Opportunity: Cultural Invention and 'The New Northern Ireland'

Eugene McNamee

If ever a time and place called out for the solace and rigour and passionate rejoinder of great drama, it is here and now. There is a whole culture to be achieved. The politicians, visionless almost to a man, are withdrawing into their sectarian stockades. It falls to the artists to construct a working model of wholeness by which this society can begin to hold up its head in the world...[1]

Introduction

Culture these days, in the instability of the distinction between culture as life and culture as art, seems to be everywhere and nowhere.[2] This instability of meaning dictates that 'culture' is often at its most resonant when, as in the quote above, it is

---

[1] Stewart Parker, Northern Irish playwright, author of numerous stage and television dramas through the 1980s, including commissioned work for *Field Day* Theatre Company, speaking in 1986. Died at the age of 47 in 1989. For quote and discussion see: Marilynn J. Richtarik, *Acting Between the Lines: the Field Day Theatre Company and Irish cultural politics* 1980–1984 (Oxford: Clarendon Press, 1994), 7. Parker, probably because of his tragically early death, is one of the largely unsung heroes of Northern Irish cultural life and his contribution to the themes of this essay deserve detailed treatment in its own right. See generally Marilynn J. Richtarik, *Stewart Parker: a life* (Oxford: OUP, 2012).

[2] Homi Bhabha in the opening lines of *The Location of Culture* (London: Routledge, 1994) puts the point in the following terms: 'It is the trope of our times to locate the question of culture in the realm of the *beyond*.'

E. McNamee (✉)
Head of Law School, University of Ulster, Jordanstown Campus, Belfast BT37 0QB, UK
e-mail: E.McNamee@ulster.ac.uk

P. D. Rush and O. Simić (eds.), *The Arts of Transitional Justice*,
Springer Series in Transitional Justice 6, DOI: 10.1007/978-1-4614-8385-4_1,

'to be achieved'.[3] In Northern Ireland, as the recent 'flag' protests demonstrate,[4] the contestations of culture still have the power to constitute grand social upheaval, even fifteen years after a constitutional settlement was supposed to have settled such matters through institutionalizing the idea of 'parity of esteem' for unionist and nationalist cultural traditions; the institutional language has not fully taken root, and there is still much 'to be achieved'. And if the current mobilization of many thousands of protestors in the purported defence of 'culture' (in the shape of the flying of the Union flag) might seem on one level a cause for celebration in that it marks an explosion of energy and colour from a Unionist working class quarter that had seemingly lost its political voice, the attendant violence and the fact that defending one culture seems to imply denigrating another marks a troubling unsustainability: this is not culture that can be endured.[5] The question re-emerges of the viability of current political arrangements and of the ongoing 'Peace Process', as this 'cultural' backlash sets in. This essay, by turning back to the high point of the conflict in Northern Ireland and tracing certain elements of the cultural interventions (where 'culture' bears a different but related meaning) from that point forward, argues a reversal of a certain priority in the standard literature, which would have the political (institutional and legal) as the leading edge of conflict transformation.[6] In this reading, cultural shifts (in this context meaning the opening up of certain imaginative possibilities which resonated with emotional sensibility *and* which regarded the re-working of questions of national identity and belonging) provided the conditions of possibility for political change.[7] In other words that, as in the opening quote, the artists (here the focus is on literary artists and critics surrounding the *Field Day* group) did indeed provide a 'working model of wholeness' that opened up a political space.

This speaks to current debates on the nature and limits of transitional justice as a field of scholarship, in particular to the necessary centrality (or not) of law (both

[3] For a situated discussion which complexifies the usual bi-lateral 'two cultures' analysis of the Northern Ireland social situation see Joseph Ruane and Jennifer Todd, *The Dynamics of Conflict in Northern Ireland* (Cambridge: Cambridge University Press, 1994).

[4] Prompted by the decision to remove the Union (UK) flag from flying above Belfast City Hall on all but certain designated occasions (a decision made by the city councilors on the grounds of promoting 'inclusivity' of different traditions) street protests and riots, in the name of 'defending our culture' have continued around Northern Ireland for two weeks at the time of writing; 18th December, 2012.

[5] The 'flag protests' have been dealt with at great length in various local and national newspapers, in particular the daily Belfast Telegraph (which maintains a general online archive of its journalism) http://www.belfasttelegraph.co.uk/

[6] See, for example, Paul Bew, *The Making and Remaking of the Good Friday Agreement* (Dublin: Liffey Press, 2007); Eamonn Mallie and David Mc Kittrick, *The Fight for Peace: the secret story behind the Irish Peace Process* (London: Heinemann, 1996); George Mitchell, *Making Peace* (London: Heinemann, 1999); Jonathan Powell, *Great Hatred, Little Room: making peace in Northern Ireland* (London: Bodley Head, 2008).

[7] For a related argument specifically focused on poetry and biopolitics see Eugene McNamee, "The Government of the Tongue", *Law and Literature* 14.3 (2002); 427–461.

in terms of legal analysis and of normative proposition).[8] Likewise, it contributes to debate on the value of bringing to bear forms of literary analysis (comfortable with questions linking texts and affect) when considering 'justice' within a paradigm such as transitional justice that is self-consciously transformative (and therefore necessarily fluid in its meaning structure).[9] This in turn sheds light on questions about the generalizability of local solutions that, in this analysis, would require consideration as matters of both transition and translation.[10]

Structurally, the essay begins with *Field Day* and the ideas it promoted, moves to its enriching encounters with certain intellectual antagonists (notably prominent critic Edna Longley) and argues that in this productive antagonism were generated certain rich ideas which took root in the political soil. The essay then ponders the question of how such riches were partly squandered in Northern Ireland in the translation of cultural ideas into pragmatic political programmes and professional 'post-conflict' scholarship. There follows a related reflection on 'the state of the field' of transitional justice scholarship, focused on the eponymous article by Professor Christine Bell, wherein she ponders the dynamics and culture of the field of transitional justice, and the degree to which it might be shaped. This step allows for the locally generated arguments from the Northern Irish case to be linked to a level of general theoretical application.

---

[8] This debate has been current for several years now in the pages of the *International Journal of Transitional Justice* and is particularly notable in the numerous editorials dealing either directly or indirectly with the issue (see Rama Mani *IJTJ* 2 (2009): 253–265; Kimberly Theidon, *IJTJ* 3 (2009) 295–300; Juan E. Mendez *IJTJ* 3 (2009) 157–162; Harvey M. Weinstein *IJTJ* 5 (2011) 1–10; Lucy Hovil and Moses Okello *IJTJ* 5 (2011) 333–344. For a limited selection of important contributions at other sites, see Paige Arthur, "How transitions re-shaped Human Rights: a conceptual history of TJ" *Human Rights Quarterly* 31 (2009): 321–367; Kieran McEvoy, "Beyond Legalism: towards a thicker conception of TJ" *Journal of Law and Society* 34.4 (2007): 411–440; David P. Forsythe, "Transitional Justice: the quest for theory to inform policy" *International Studies Review* 13 (2011): 554–578. See in particular Christine Bell, "Transitional Justice, Interdisciplinarity and the State of the 'Field' or 'Non-Field'" *The International Journal of Transitional Justice* 3 (2009): 5–27; this work will be discussed in more detail below.

[9] The notion of necessary circularity in transitional justice is phrased as follows by Ruti Teitel in her seminal text *Transitional Justice* Oxford University Press, Oxford, 2000 p6: 'In its ordinary social function, law provides order and stability, but in extraordinary periods of political upheaval, law maintains order even as it enables transformation… law is alternately constituted by and constitutive of, the transition'. For insightful comment on literary justice see Siphiwe Dube 'Transitional Justice beyond the Normative: towards a literary theory of political transitions', *IJTJ*, 2011.

[10] See note 8 above, particularly Theidon's editorial and the collection of articles in that issue of *IJTJ*. See also Hovil and Okello editorial, and Forsythe, "Transitional Justice: the quest for theory to inform policy".

Field Day and the 'Fifth Province of the Imagination'

The origins of the *Field Day* project can be dated precisely to the 1979 meeting of minds between the young actor Stephen Rea and the internationally renowned playwright Brian Friel that they should form a theatre company to produce radical social change through cultural intervention.[11] There was and remains a strong Irish tradition of culture-as-politics that could ground such apparent immodesty. The 'Celtic Revival' movement, for example, promulgated by Yeats and Lady Gregory in the early nineteenth century, centred around Dublin's Abbey Theatre, is recognized as key to the upsurge in Irish nationalist sentiment that culminated in the 1916 'rising' against the British rule, the war of independence, and the eventual foundation of the Irish state in 1922.[12] Joyce, while often parodying such nationalist sentiment, did not shy from the idea of the artist as central to the creation of a public consciousness. Through his alter ego Stephen Dedalus in *A Portrait of the Artist as a Young Man,* he claimed as his own task that of 'forging in the smithy of my soul the uncreated conscience of my race'. Paul Muldoon, in his review of the canon of Irish literature, identifies this urge to public pronouncement (and the related condition of 'a quite disproportionate sense of his or her own importance') as a defining feature of Irish writers, given 'the role of the Irish writer as it has evolved over the centuries'.[13]

If the 'Celtic Twilight' revivalism of Yeats and Lady Gregory had sought inspiration in the heroic ancient myths of Ireland, and Joyce had mythologized the everyday, the *Field Day* inheritors of the culture-as-politics mantle were far from such notions in the wellspring of their creativity.[14] *Field Day*'s eventual body of

---

[11] 'Field Day' is in part a pun on the surnames of Friel and Rea; for an account of the foundation of *Field Day* see Richtarik *Acting Between the Lines,* 10. Friel, through such plays as *Philadelphia Here I Come, Faith Healer* and *Aristocrats* had, by the time of *Field Day*, already earned a reputation as 'The Irish Chekhov'. For discussion of his career see Scott Boltwood *Brian Friel, Ireland, and The North* (Cambridge: Cambridge University Press 2007).

[12] The classic analytic text on the entwining of Irish culture, politics and literary form is Declan Kiberd *Inventing Ireland: The Literature of the Modern Nation* (London: Vintage, 1996). For a further introduction to relevant literature on the 'Celtic Twilight' and its influence on Irish nationalism, see David Dwan, *The Great Community: Culture and Nationalism in Ireland,* (Dublin: Field Day, 2008).

[13] Paul Muldoon *To Ireland, I* (Oxford: OUP, 2000) 4.

[14] For an interesting analysis of Yeats' Modernism and his vision of Irish exceptionalism in this regard (ie; remaining essentially uncorrupted and pre-Modern) see Dwan, *The Great Community*. In the introduction to *Our Irish Theatre* (London: Capricorn, 1965) an essay written in 1913 reviewing the early progress of Yeats' and Gregory's project of a national theatre, Lady Gregory recalls the initial mission statement; 'We propose to have performed in Dublin in the spring of every year certain Celtic and Irish plays, which whatever their degree of excellence will be written with a high ambition, and so build up a Celtic and Irish school of dramatic literature. We hope to find in Ireland an uncorrupted and imaginative audience trained to listen by its passion for oratory, and believe that our desire to bring upon the stage the deeper thoughts and emotions of Ireland will ensure for us a tolerant welcome…'.

work indicates that they had drawn from Yeats but had also processed the cultural weight of the anti-heroic post-Yeatsian traditions of Joyce and Beckett, not to mention the leavening of such weighty (and urban) fare with the more irreverent and folkloric touches of Flann O'Brien and Patrick Kavanagh.[15] The result was the accumulation of a kind of fractured ironic distance from the Yeatsian cultural nationalist paradigm, and even from the anti-Yeatsian Modernism of Joyce.[16] Friel can be identified as the guiding light of the *Field Day* creative project, and there was in his work no quest for rediscovery of a glorious past as a model of aspiration nor indeed a Joycean turn to the everyday as epic, but rather a more prosaic and elegiac recognition of the emotional realities of the human condition as fallen and 'astray' in the world, with a gravitational pull to the sensations and emotions of home and hearth.[17] Already lauded as 'The Irish Chekhov' before his association with *Field Day* because of his focus on emotional subtleties generated in everyday interactions, for Friel, the route to national re-invention was now, in his *Field Day* work, re-figured as passing through forms of self-recognition on the local level with cross-cutting universalist themes. As he put it, 'we are talking with ourselves as we must, and if we are overheard in America, or England, so much the better'.[18] Self-recognition was, in other words, not to be predicated on aiming for a somehow truer, better, higher self, but on the recognition of an emotionally authentic, at-home self.[19]

By the time of the staging of *Field Day*'s first play, the originators of the theatre company had been joined, at their invitation, by several other board members: Seamus Heaney, Tom Paulin (both poets), David Hammond (a producer with BBC Northern Ireland) and Seamus Deane. If the most famous of the Directors was Seamus Heaney, then Deane (an old schoolmate of Heaney's) was to become the

15 See Richtarik, *Acting Between the Lines*. See also Richard Kirkland, *Literature and Culture in Northern Ireland Since 1965: Moments of Danger* (London: Longman, 1996), especially Chap. 5 'Nothing Left but the Sense of Exhaustion: Field-Day and Counter-hegemony'. See further Kiberd *Inventing Ireland*, especially section 11 'Recovery and Renewal'.

16 For discussions on Irish writing and ironic distance see Seamus Heaney, *The Place of Writing*, (Atlanta: Emory University Scholars Press, 1989).

17 The proximity (and links) of Friel's writing to Heideggerean linguistic and ontological philosophy is explored in Richard Kearney *Transitions* (Dublin: Wolfhound Press, 1988) Chap. 6 'The language plays of Brian Friel'.

18 Richtarik, *Acting Between the Lines*, 12. Interesting cross-themes of homeliness could be drawn out from works on transitional justice from below; see, for example, Ciaran McEvoy and Lorna McGregor, *Transitional Justice from Below: grass-roots activism and the struggle for change* (Oxford: Hart, 2008); McEvoy "Beyond Legalism".

19 Various writers have noted the links between the ideas expressed in Friel's 'Translations' and the work of George Steiner, particularly in *After Babel: Aspects of Language and Translation* (Oxford: OUP, 1975). See, for example, Helen Lojek "Brian Friel's Plays and George Steiner's Linguistics: Translating the Irish", *Contemporary Literature* 35.1(1994); 83–99, Francis C. McGrath "Irish Babel: Brian Friel's 'Translations' and George Steiner's 'After Babel'" *Comparative Drama* 23.1 (1989) 31–49.

most influential in the eventual development of *Field Day*.[20] Deane, a sometime poet, critic and academic was, in all of these roles, a steadfast adherent to the notion of post-colonial theory as a prism through which to read the Irish situation, and this became gradually identified as a general *Field Day* position.[21] The Marxian influenced economic analyses married to the emphasis placed on the colonization of consciousness which could account for seemingly free peoples' self-destructively aping the manners of the colonizer was for Deane the key to unlocking the variant mysteries of the dysfunctional territories in both the north and the south of Ireland (the north convulsed in fratricidal violence, and the south socially atrophied at the knee of the Catholic Church). The particular extremities of the turmoil in the North were seen as the sharpest expression of the general condition of all-island post-colonial malaise. For Deane, there was no question but that interventions through cultural forms, particularly the theatre which had already served it's apprenticeship as the flag-carrier of the Yeatsian Celtic Revival, were directly political because culture itself, in both narrative and formal terms, was irreducibly political. Thus, Deane served as a catalyst to the production and dissemination, through manifold essays and articles, of much more explicit expressions of what *Field Day* was trying to do, and eventually he became recognized as the person most willing to articulate a *Field Day* line.[22]

The first play staged by *Field Day* was Friel's 'Translations' which premiered in Derry/Londonderry in 1980. This play has come to be regarded as the prime exemplar of a whole series of ideas of what the company stood for, and in this light invites scrutiny in some depth.[23] In 'Translations' the action is set against the background of the mapping of a part of Ireland by the Ordnance Survey team in the 1830s. The mapping exercise, undertaken in part by military personnel

---

[20] Heaney was awarded the Nobel Prize for literature in 1995 (for 'works of lyrical beauty and ethical depth...') but already in 1980 was extremely well-known throughout the English-speaking world. His first collection *Death of a Naturalist* (London: Faber) was published to wide critical acclaim in 1966. Deane came to general public prominence largely through his work with *Field Day*, and went on to write the 1996 Booker Prize shortlisted novel *Reading in the Dark*. Paulin went on to become Professor of Poetry at Oxford. Rea went on to enjoy a very successful international stage, television and cinema career.

[21] Edward Said, Frederic Jameson and Terry Eagleton all wrote pamphlets for the group (respectively 'Yeats and Decolonisation', 'Modernism and Imperialism' and 'Nationalism, Irony and Commitment'), which were published together as the volume *Nationalism, Colonialism and Literature* (Minneapolis: University of Minnesota Press, 1990).

[22] Whether or not, as has been claimed, Deane became the chief ideologue of the group in the sense that he dictated its overall direction, or whether he simply assumed a mantle of spokesperson that none of the other directors cared to don (and perhaps over-reached himself in presenting himself as the voice of a collective that was always more internally disparate in its views) is a moot point. The point is well discussed in 'Prologue: The Beginnings' in Carmen Szabo, *Clearing the Ground: The Field Day Theatre Company and the Construction of Irish Identities*, (Cambridge: Cambridge Scholars Publishing, 2007).

[23] Richard Kearney, for example, analyses *Translations* together with *Faith Healer* and *The Communication Cord* as Friel's coming to terms with 'the twin modern crises of *identity* and *language*.' Kearney, *Transitions*, 123.

(hence, 'Ordnance Survey'), brings Yolland, an idealistic young lieutenant in the British Army, to lodge in the village of Baile Beag (in English 'Small Town') as a guest of his local accomplice Owen, who is tasked with helping him render local Irish place names into English. Owen's father Hugh is the 'hedge-school' Master (the 'hedge schools' being improvized local classrooms, a reaction to the lack of a national educational system) and his brother Manus is his father's classroom helper and an aspirant teacher in his own right. Owen, Hugh and Manus can all speak English, but Manus refuses to do so to mark his objection to the translation and mapping exercise. All the rest of the villagers speak only Irish (in performance, everyone speaks English and the audience is asked to accept the conceit that most are speaking Irish—leading to on-stage confusions that serve the narrative arc).

The action develops to play out the tensions between the brothers, one accepting the need to move with the changing linguistic times and the other refusing to do so. Their father, an improbable classical scholar and a perennial drunk, plays a courtly fool, speaking the truth of ancient wisdoms to the power of the affable but clueless Lieutenant Yolland, and stoically remaining above the political glowering between his sons. A romance develops between Yolland and a local Irish-speaking girl Máire, the romance flowering in the music of their incantatory exchange of the Irish place names that have come to enchant him even as he plans their destruction. As Yolland falls more deeply in love, Owen, the accomplice in the translation process, is ever more troubled at his role in serving up rough English renderings of what he more and more recognizes as his own emotional core of homeliness in the language of his birth and his locality. As the mapping progresses, the play takes on a frantic energy; something has to give in the conflict between continuity and change. The play closes on multiple forms of irresolution: Yolland has disappeared (perhaps murdered by mysterious anti-British locals who exist only as a menacing off-stage presence) and threats have been made by his superior that if he is not found, the village will be razed; Manus (the linguistic refusnik brother) has fled, fearing implication in the disappearance; Owen (the translation accomplice) ponders his future and his past, perhaps turning against his own erstwhile views of progress and towards an idea of fighting to resist change; Hugh, (the hedge-school classicist) is oddly—given his lampooning of the uncultured English during the play—turning in the other direction; reflecting on the survey process that 'We must learn those new names… we must learn where we live. We must learn to make them our own. We must make them our new home'.[24] The question of whether this is possible hangs in the air as the curtain falls.

The play, which has enjoyed a long international career of outings in translation and English language revivals since its first showing, has been heavily criticized in some quarters as a travesty of history, presenting the mapping and naming project as an exercise in colonial domination when it was in fact an exercise in preserving some remnant of the dying Gaelic culture, undertaken with meticulous concern for

[24] Quoted in Richtarik, *Acting Between the* Lines, 32.

local history.[25] Certainly, the play has been frequently claimed as a lament for culture lost and as such an exercise in historical blame-laying.[26] Friel was always much more circumspect than this, claiming that the play was 'a play about language and only about language', and in this way converting the objections about historical inaccuracy into an indication that he was after the deeper fictional truth of emotional reality that required the distortion and foreshortening of history.[27] There is perhaps a deliberate disingenuity here, in that the play investigates how language is inseparable from issues of identity, place, memory and loss. These are emotional conditions that, the play suggests, are experienced in and through language.

To read the play, however, as abstracting language into some idea of 'flat' and direct meaning so that these possible interpretations could be definitively fixed through a political (or analytic philosophical) interrogation would ignore the essential pliability and performativity of language which theatre as a form lends. In other words, if some critical reaction to the play would tend to reduce it to political simplicity, this ignores certain primary formal and thematic aspects that resist easy political readings.[28] For example, the sharing of priority in the play amongst a generous list of characters produces the effect of complexifying both the political and emotional territories. The fact that each of the characters shows something of a conflict within themselves redoubles this complexity, and the play is structured so as to close on irresolution rather than resolution, shifting the obligation to provide meaning from the playwright onto the audience. The overall themes of language, memory and loss are played out in an emotional register, rather than in a political one that might indicate some kind of authorial policy of necessary resistance in the face of the movements of history and the processes of change. Reading a direct political message thus entails refusing emotional sympathies being encouraged by character development, and in this the play exemplifies the *Field Day* project of precisely complicating the field of potential emotional and political identifications in such a way as to create a mesh of history in place of a simple linear narrative, implicating history as an item of 'point of view' rather than objective trajectory.[29] Insofar as this constitutes a grand thesis of the nature of history, it is in direct counterpoint and should be regarded as refuting the Yeatsian heroic mission of reclaiming a truer historical trajectory through recourse to long-gone mythical ages

---

[25] Richtarik, *Acting Between the* Lines, 38–50.

[26] Richtarik, *Acting Between the* Lines, 40.

[27] Such an approach links in particular to the ongoing debates on 'justice' and/versus 'reconciliation'. See, for example, the series of essays in Scott Veitch, ed., *Law and the Politics of Reconciliation* (Aldershot: Ashgate, 2007).

[28] See for example Edna Longley's critique in "Poetry and Politics in Northern Ireland", *The Crane Bag* 9 (1985) 26–41.

[29] In another of his most renowned works 'Faith Healer', Friel has the memory of the same sequence of events related by the three central characters present. Each produces an account barely recognisable to that of the others. Brian Friel, *Faith Healer* (London: Faber and Faber, 2001).

and to the 'terrible beauty' of revolutionary martyrdom.[30] It is rather a thesis that carries a strong emotional undercurrent of pathos; the need to adapt and adjust to the vagaries of history as opposed to the power to define it, but nonetheless balanced by the need to ethically and actively respond to this potentially overwhelming condition; there is still the chance to build a new home in the new language.

In the programme notes to the first production of 'Translations', Seamus Deane refracted and made an explicit political point of the emotional tone of the play detailed immediately above. He attacked the empty 'aestheticism' of the existing theatre in Northern Ireland (as exemplified by the Lyric Theatre in Belfast) a theme to which he returned with renewed vigour in the programme notes to the second *Field Day* play, a translation by Friel of Chekhov's 'Three Sisters', where he accused the lyric of 'coterie drama', while to the left, 'community theatre' came in for ridicule as the 'plebification of drama'. Field Day was to walk a fine line 'in the interval between these, while recognizing that it will every so often touch one of them.[31]' Deane here is re-iterating and re-enforcing the original Friel and Rea's idea of creating work that would demand audience engagement and in so doing re-invent the standard notion of audience both within and beyond the theatre walls: the idea was to create a theatre to create a people, to engender democracy through art.[32] Such democracy-as-process ideas complement *avant la lettre* Habermasian deliberative democratic ideas with the idea that certain cultural forms at certain times bear a greater power than standard political discourse to make politics emotionally real and vital. In so doing, it also rehearses the paradox of justice from below or from above; the twisted hierarchy of high cultural (or elite knowledge) prompts to popular activism.[33]

Theatre was not the only avenue of cultural intervention for *Field Day*. In the early 1980s, under the energetic stewardship of Deane, it reached out into other forms to further articulate and advance its ideas. Taking its cue from the core theme of 'Translations' the first further venture was a series of three pamphlets issued in 1983, each of them in some degree dealing with 'the language question' raised in the play. In 'A New Look at the Language Question', Tom Paulin took up the theme laid out by Hugh at the close of 'Translations' that 'we must make these

---

[30] W.B. Yeats in reference to the Easter I916 'Rising' (violent insurrection) wrote: 'All changed, changed utterly/A terrible beauty is born…' from "Easter 1916" in *W.B. Yeats: Selected Poems* (London: Penguin, 2000).

[31] Quoted in Szabo *Clearing The Ground*, 10.

[32] There are interesting comparisons here to the arguments on courts (with attendant iconography and iconology) as participative democratic spaces presented in Judith Resnik and Denis Curtis, *Representing Justice: Invention, Controversy, and Rights in City-States and Democratic Courtrooms* (New Haven: Yale University Press, 2011).

[33] Here there are evident links to the theorization (and practical study) of 'transitional justice from below': see, for example: Anna Erikkson, "A Bottom-Up Approach to Transformative Justice in Northern Ireland" *International Journal of Transitional Justice* 3 (2009) 301–320; McEvoy and McGregor *Transitional Justice from Below*.

words our own, we must learn to live in these places…', with an investigation of the desirability and possibility of a coherent 'Irish-English' idiom, in the mould of 'American-English' or 'Caribbean-English'. The essay opens with the line 'the history of a language is often a story of possession and dispossession, territorial struggle and the establishment or imposition of a culture…' and closes on the melancholy reflection that what can be recognized of a specific Irish-English idiom is 'a living but fragmented speech, untold numbers of homeless words, and an uncertain or a derelict prose.' The metonymic association of the language to the culture is generally automatic. The second essay is by Seamus Heaney 'An Open Letter' and chronicles in verse, in the form of a letter to the editors, his somewhat irate (yet such ire expressed in almost mannered courteousness) reflections on his inclusion without prior consultation in a Penguin Volume of Contemporary *British* Poetry. The essay contains the lines 'be advised my passport's green/No glass of ours was ever raised/To toast the Queen.[34]' The final pamphlet in the trilogy was Deane's analysis of a fundamental distinction that he identified at the core of British-Irish relations down the long duree of history and right through to the present, that of 'Civilians and Barbarians'. Deane conducts his analysis in terms of the distinction as based on an idea of 'lawful' v 'lawless' but spreading out in reach as a culturally animating metaphor to the extent of structuring consciousness itself.[35] He closes with the reflection that 'of all the blighting distinctions which govern our responses and limit our imaginations at the moment, none is more potent than this…'. A second series of pamphlets issued in the following year took up where this notion of structuring metaphor left off, to examine Irish-English relations in terms of (in turn) writing style, myth and attitude.[36] A third series issued in 1985 examined the issue of Protestant and Unionist identity (or identities) in Ireland and their intersection with the national and linguistic questions.[37] The continuing themes are language, belonging and identity.

Taken in its entirety, the output of *Field Day* up until this point of about 1985 might be taken as an overall project to create as a supplement to the four provinces

---

[34] A wonderful historical irony is that on the visit of Queen Elizabeth II to Dublin in 2011 Heaney was seated at her left hand and, at least on this occasion, did indeed raise his glass to toast the Queen.

[35] The distinction maps more or less onto the 'savages' and 'saviours' of Makau Mutua, "Savages, Victims and Saviours: The Metaphor of Human Rights", *Harvard International Law Journal*, 42, (Winter 2001): 21. See also for comparison Bradin Cormack, *A Power to do Justice: Jurisdiction, English Literature and the Rise of the Common Law,* 1509–1625 (Chicago: Chicago University Press, 2007), especially Chap. 3 "Inconveniencing the Irish: custom, allegory and the Common Law in Spencer's Ireland."

[36] The first six pamphlets mentioned here are collected in the volume *Ireland's Field Day*, Hutchinson, London 1985; the 4th, 5th and 6th pamphlets are 'Heroic Styles: the tradition of an idea' by Seamus Deane, 'Myth and Motherland' by Richard Kearney, and 'Anglo-Irish Attitudes' by Declan Kiberd.

[37] Field Day Pamphlets: No. 7, "The Whole Protestant Community" by Terence Brown; No. 8 "Watchmen in Sion" by Marianne Elliot; No. 9 "Liberty and Authority in Ireland" by Robert McCartney.

of Ireland a ‘fifth province of the imagination’ (an idea which harks back to an ancient Irish notion of the mystical fifth province of Ireland that hinged the other four).[38] In more prosaic terms, the idea was that there did not have to be an identification with a physical territory, but rather with a cultural or imaginative idea, in order for people to feel ‘at home’, so long as this cultural idea was sufficiently robust and well grounded—hence the multi-modal exploration and building of this idea through numerous edited collections, essays, plays and media interventions. Of particular importance and to stand at the centre of the overall enterprise, there was projected the preparation of a ‘Field Day Anthology of Irish Literature’, to place the power of authority over the canon (modestly such a word was always rejected) firmly on Irish soil; a kind of physical instantiation of the fifth province idea, a repository of memory on which to base an imagination of culture and nation. Thus, through the vehicle of theatre that both in terms of theme and form articulated a different conception of audience as a different form of citizen; *Field Day* was to attempt the re-vivification of politics through culture, attempting to create a participative, democratic community almost by stealth. In its other cultural contributions, it was to set out a resource bank for a new cultural and social imagination, based on the recovered cultural history of Ireland, dragged from the bog where it had been cast by colonialism. The working assumption was that social upheaval and constitutional reform would surely follow.

A Field Too Green? Refusing *Field Day*

Not everyone was comfortable with this utopic vision. As the reputation and reach of the *Field Day* enterprise grew, with a landmark play produced and being registered as a great cultural event each year (critics now flew in from London and New York for the Derry/Londonderry premieres) and with the periodic release of the pamphlets and essays mentioned above, even so grew the storm clouds of dissent. An intellectual counterbalance to *Field Day* emerged around the figure of the prominent literary and cultural critic Edna Longley.[39] Right through the latter years of the 1980s and into the early years of the 1990s, a period in which the *Field Day* brand first waxed and then later waned as its own energies sagged and the

[38] The modern incarnation of the phrase dates to the opening editorial of *The Crane Bag*. In some ways a fore runner/fellow-traveller to *Field Day*, this was a cultural journal published in Dublin between 1977 and 1985 under the editorship of Mark Patrick Hederman and Richard Kearney and with definite editorial notions of the political import of culture. First five volumes published as a collected volume *The Crane Bag Book of Irish Studies* 1977–1981 (Dublin: Blackwater Press, 1982); second four volumes published as *The Crane Bag Book of Irish Studies* 1982–1985 (Dublin: Blackwater Press, 1985).

[39] See Richtarik, *Acting Between the Lines,* 239–255 for reference to other prominent writers adopting similar argumentative positions, for example John Wilson-Foster, Gerard Dawe, Frank McGuinness and Fintan O’Toole.

criticisms began to bite, Longley kept up a kind of cultural guerrilla campaign against the group primarily through the pages of literary magazines such as *The Honest Ulsterman* published in Belfast and *The Crane Bag,* published in Dublin.[40] In 1994 (by which stage there had been a definite shift of character within *Field Day* towards a critical group with periodic theatre productions, rather than a theatre company with ancillary critical commentary), she published a kind of 'look back in anger' collection of essays that refined and collated her earlier thoughts and which had at its core a virulent attack on the *Field Day* enterprise.[41]

Longley rubbished the idea that *Field Day* had managed to transcend Yeatsian myth through its recourse to post-colonial analysis. The myth behind their purported myth-debunking was for her an unreconstructed idea of the naturalness of an all-island nation that, in the weft and warp of its images, ideas and literary figures was overly determined by a Northern Catholic bias. She notes that she had previously questioned the *Field Day* agenda on two main grounds: 'firstly, that their chosen political model appeared to simplify the state of literary play, to ignore the cultural negotiations at work in poetry in the North and to foreclose on the new politics they might symbolize; secondly, that a distinctively Northern Nationalist formation was claiming a wider validity than it had earned, not only with respect to the North but also with respect to the whole island.[42]' The rejection of the Yeatsian visions she analyses as not alone animated by a distrust of the myths of ancient heroism, but by a distrust of the Protestantism identified with Yeats, and with this a rejection of the genius of (Irish) Protestantism itself. For her, *Field Day* was a group, under the guise of historical illumination, dedicated to replacing myth with myth of their own perhaps subconscious choosing or as she quotes approvingly the novelist Colm Tóibín, 'a number of men [who] have come to believe in their own dreams'. Yeats, in contrast, was reclaimed as the poet (as in the title of her book) of 'the living stream'; if making myth then at least doing so self-consciously as a wilful transcendent politics. Furthermore, *Field Day*, by virtue of having virtually no women authors represented in its supposedly definitive Anthology of Irish Literature, had exposed itself to claims of macho bias, a theme that Longley had rehearsed in an earlier essay.[43]

---

[40] For a series of references see Richtarik *Acting Between the Lines,* 244–255, and Szabo *Clearing the Ground*, "conclusion".

[41] Edna Longley, *The Living Stream; literature and revisionism in Ireland,* (Newcastle: Bloodaxe Books, 1994).

[42] Longley, *The Living Stream,* 23. The self-reference is to her earlier essay "Poetry and Politics in Northern Ireland".

[43] In the essay *From Cathleen to Anorexia: The Breakdown of Irelands* (Dublin: Attic Press, 1990) Longley's attack on *Field Day* is in part structured around an idea of feminism in contrast to the perceived 'macho' qualities of Field Day. Field Day in fact acknowledged the error of omission of women's voices and set about the task of producing complementary volumes which eventually emerged in 2005: Angela Bourke ed. *The Field Day Anthology of Irish Writing Volumes IV and V: Irish Women's Writing and Tradition: v.* 4 *and* 5 Cork: Cork University Press, 2005.

The Longley attacks were certainly powerful, and by this stage (1994), the group in its original incarnation (centred around Friel and Rea) was collapsing under the weight of that inevitable internal condition 'artistic differences'.[44] However, to retrospectively note change is not to diminish the force of the cultural impact at the time, and the critical engagement with *Field Day* need not be regarded as a zero-sum game leading to nothing gained. The attack by Longley (and in this, she was representative of a good many others) was not a rejection of the idealism of the 'fifth province' idea, or even a rejection of Irish nationalism, or of the need for and value of cultural production and criticism as directly politically contributory and confrontational.[45] It was rather, an outflanking of *Field Day* as having reduced itself to imagining a fifth field which would necessarily be *green*. She recognized that there was at work a politics of the imaginary, but contested its qualities: it was not sufficiently rigorous, since it was not subtle enough to get to grips with a distinctive Protestant and/or Unionist imaginary, and not generous enough to find a way to converse with those that did, being more interested in reaching out to an imagined band of post-colonial brothers, or as Longley has it, engaging in 'intellectual holiday romances in a post-colonial never-never land'. For her, the *Field Day* Anthology (published in 1991) was an attempt at producing a 'master version' of history in its choices, exclusions, categorizations and editorial comments (not to mention in its implicit sexism). It was a version she rejected not only as insufficiently inclusive as history, but also as insufficiently subtle as a form of literary appreciation/criticism. *Field Day*, in other words, was despite itself lapsing into dewy-eyed sentimentalism about some kind of pure Irishness, and using this projected image (largely created by the prism of borrowed post-colonial theory) to attempt to fashion a future. Longley's move then was in no way a denial of the political nature of culture, or a denial of the value of an attempt to deliberately approach political issues through cultural forms, but rather a deepening of the terms of engagement and a claim that a politics of the Irish imaginary demanded more than it was offered by the *Field Day* group. In effect then what is constituted in the engagement between *Field Day* and Longley is itself a productive antagonistic cultural politics that, as in 'Translations', is ultimately characterized by its lack of resolution. Each side is animated by the same ideal that culture matters very deeply, to the point where important poems and plays (neither side shies from an idea of cultural standards) deserve the same detailed critical attention as do foundational legal and political documents, precisely because they are equally socially constitutive.[46]

---

[44] Friel's play Dancing at Lughnasa was offered to The Abbey theatre Dublin rather than Field Day and premiered in 1990. Friel formally resigned from the Field Day Board in 1994.

[45] This is clear from Longley's essay, "Poetry and Politics in Northern Ireland".

[46] This is a neat inversion of the animating argument of the Law and Literature movement that legal (and political) texts deserve analysis as forms of literature. For a recent major contribution in this field see Desmond Manderson, *Kangaroo Courts and the Rule of Law: The Legacy of Modernism* (London: Routledge, 2012). See also Cormack, *A Power to do Justice*.

Fast forward only four years from Longley's *The Living Stream* (as noted above a kind of paperweight to a long-term engagement with these themes) and fourteen from the publication by *Field Day* of Deane's engagement with Yeats in his 'Heroic Styles' pamphlet (which had particularly raised Longley's ire and sparked the decade-long *Field Day*/Longley debate) and this notion of imaginary politics is right at the heart of the eventual constitutional settlement, the 'Belfast/Good Friday Agreement' of April 1998, that marked the conversion of violent conflict into non-violent political confrontation.[47] The Agreement in effect provides for an agreement to disagree on the constitutional 'ownership' of Northern Ireland, this copper fastened by the 'principle of consent'; that should the majority of the citizens of Northern Ireland wish to rupture the Union with the Great Britain this would be made possible, but until that point, the territory would remain as a devolved part of the United Kingdom. There was also, to facilitate the ongoing recognition at the heart of the Agreement that some citizens principally identified as 'Irish' and others as 'British', an understanding that the individual subject/citizen might identify culturally where they chose within a structure of governance where 'both traditions' would be accorded equal status. The 'equal status' is not a declaration with no practical import, but rather a commitment to supporting cultural expression in multiple forms and to neutralizing those elements considered most culturally one-sided and therefore offensive. In this latter category, for example, there was a systematic re-naming exercise in relation to government functions and departments to remove designations of connection to the British Crown and to replace them with more neutral and local nomenclature; paradigmatic here was the re-naming of the 'Royal Ulster Constabulary' to the 'Police Service of Northern Ireland'. On the positive side of cultural recognition was the notion incorporated into the Agreement of 'parity of esteem' for the principal cultural traditions. As an example, in linguistic terms, this translated into a commitment to promote the Irish and Ulster-Scots languages (and associated cultural forms) through capital and programme development funds, and also to the extent that government information would be provided in all three languages (English, Irish, Ulster-Scots).[48]

While such a sense of productive irresolution definitely recalls (and I would argue echoes) the *Field Day*/Longley debates, writing on the genesis of the Agreement generally ignores this cultural theme, and privileges the more obviously political. The route to the Agreement is generally traced back to the 1981

[47] The Belfast Agreement (also known as 'Good Friday Agreement' after the signing date) is a composite name for the 'British-Irish Agreement' and the 'Multi-Party Agreement' (the former in effect assenting to and institutionalizing in international law the latter agreement between local politicians). The Agreement therefore, while undoubtedly constitutional, is not a constitution since Northern Ireland does not have the quality of a State. For an account of the legal delicacies (that reflect political ones) see Austen Morgan, *The Belfast Agreement: a practical legal analysis* (London: The Belfast Press, 2000). Insofar as the Agreement sets in place mechanisms of review (and thus is self-consciously 'transitional') it bears comparison to the Interim Constitution of South Africa of 1993.

[48] This emphasis on language and the symbolic centrality of naming recalls the *Field Day* focus, particularly as expressed in 'Translations', discussed above.

hunger strikes in the Maze prison, during the course of which Bobby Sands, the first hunger striker, was put forward for election and elected as an MP in a move designed to put pressure on the British government to agree to the demands for prisoner 'political status'. While the demands were not granted and Sands subsequently died (as did nine others in the same protest), the political narrative is often developed that the events of the hunger strike marked a shifting of the balance of power within the Republican movement away from those dedicated to armed insurrection and towards those who advocated 'a ballot box in one hand, and an Armalite in the other' (a process which culminated, over many years, in the dropping of the Armalite from the political equation).[49] What this version of a trajectory does not include is a pattern of understanding of how the political ideas themselves became fashioned around a notion of the politics of an imaginary, a decoupling of the idea of citizenship from the idea of defined territory.[50] Yet this is exactly the cultural imaginative work that had been done (and in almost exact temporal parallel given *Field Day*'s first production in late 1980 and the Hunger Strike in early 1981) by the Field Day group and its interlocutors like Longley; the figuring of a space of identity, betimes frictional and oppositional, yet located in an area beyond the field of territorial politics; a realization of a version of the fifth province through a re-constitutionalization of the fourth. The political discourse had become, in this close intertwining of all matters of past and future with questions of culture and identity, a kind of crude version of the grand cultural conversation that had run through the 1980s and early 1990s with *Field Day* at one pole and critics such as Longley at the other.[51]

Building Walls: Good Fences Make Good Neighbours?

If on one level, the new political discourse was a reproduction of the preceding cultural conversation, on another level, it quickly departed radically from it precisely in that it quickly lost the flavour of conversation at all, and took on the

[49] For an overview see Mallie and McKittrick, *The Fight for Peace,* 20–28. 'ArmaLite' is a brand named assault rifle. The quote is attributed to Danny Morrison, Sinn Fein director of publicity, speaking at the Sinn Fein Ard-Fheis (Annual Convention) 1981.

[50] For a related argument about a politics of the imaginary focused on memorialization see Eugene McNamee "Eye-Witness: memorializing humanity in Steve McQueen's Hunger" *International Journal of Law in Context* 5 (2009) 281–294.

[51] It would be certainly possible to attempt a sociological analysis of the direct links from *Field Day* (and Crane Bag) protagonists such as Friel, Deane, Heaney and Kearney to developments within the thought of John Hume as leader of the SDLP who 'brought in from the cold' Gerry Adams and the republican movement, to the reconceptualizations within republican thought which allowed for eventual political accommodation. For work in this vein see John Hume *Personal Views* (Dublin: Town House, 1996); Barry White *John Hume* (Belfast: Blackstaff, 1984). The aim here, however, is to remain at a more abstract level dealing with shifts in ideas rather than individual changes of mind.

contours of a dialogue of the deaf. The *Field Day* vs critics ongoing, if sometimes testy or even aggressive, engagement with notions of Irish identity and their link to cultural and linguistic issues always had the dynamic of a kind of Derridean *différance*; the deferral of final meaning in the recognition of difference as an active process rather than static encounter. Its success was always in its failure, since failure was built into the model, and so the lack of agreement and the ability to keep on finding ways to investigate the articulation of this lack was in a way its greatest triumph. Agreement, in other words, kills conversation, but *Field Day* was spiky, provocative, punkish, resolutely determined to attempt profound comment, and its opponents were no less so and no less able. In the translation of some of this cultural imagination onto the political plane, there was the betrayal of auto-interrogation and restlessness. In the Agreement of 1998, the conversation that was killed was the idea of a transcendent unity-in-disagreement of Northern Irish culture, in favour of a retreat into the safer territory of mutual respect but fundamental and enduring difference; the Agreement to disagree moved from ongoing discussion to tense silence on matters cultural and to a focus on the 'safe' ground of jobs, housing and health, where the political Unionist/Nationalist logic of 'one for you, one for me' became absolutely standard.

This pattern of ideas is at least in part structurally conditioned, in that political representatives at the local assembly have to designate themselves as 'Unionist', 'Nationalist' or 'Other' in order that a complex system of power-sharing between these two 'traditions' of 'Nationalist' and 'Unionist' can be facilitated. When this is coupled to the deeply ingrained atavistic habits of cultural identification predicated on notions of foundational difference, the picture is not promising. In effect what was allowed to emerge was a notion of culture defined by the same kind of tripartite structure as the 'Nationalist', 'Unionist' and 'Other' political designations, in the cultural sphere being 'Irish Language/Culture' (for which read broadly a perceived Catholic Nationalist Culture) 'Ulster-Scots Culture' (for which read broadly Presbyterian Unionist Culture) and 'Other Culture' (for which read broadly 'high culture') all under the promotional aegis of the 'Department for Culture, Arts and Leisure' or DCAL. There resulted the accommodation of the sectarianization of culture (with associated solid links to 'community' and 'tradition') and an acceptance of such a state of affairs as worthy of management rather than challenge.[52]

---

[52] A further dynamic of the political treatment of culture that has emerged since the Agreement plays to the cross-cutting theme of class within Northern Irish society, and that is the consolidation of a long term institutional and conceptual distinction between 'arts' and 'community arts'. Both these forms of art are government funded indirectly through the Arts Council of Northern Ireland, and sometimes directly in terms of specific programme grants (particularly for community arts and community festivals) and capital project allocation (particularly for the traditional arts infrastructural provision in terms of theatre and music venues) from DCAL. The community arts sector is supported through a number of local NGOs (the main umbrella group being 'The Community Arts Partnership') and the traditional arts sector populated by a wide variety of organizations, with the theatre sector particularly prominent, there being about a dozen Northern Ireland based professional theatre companies. There seems to have

In parallel to the manoeuvres outlined above, another large-scale impetus is identifiable as an intersection to the parcelling out of culture, and that is the commodification of culture as a spur to development. Certainly, this discourse spreads far beyond the shores of Northern Ireland, but it has been vigorously embraced here both by the government and to a certain extent, in a potential pact with the devil, by arts organizations themselves. Such organizations play for the politicians the sweet music of the 'cultural pound', that is the amount of revenue generated locally by arts organizations and events, in terms of local employment, the attraction of external revenues and the spur to the circulation of local monies not only into the primary sites such as theatres, music venues etc., but also into the secondary sites such as cafes, pubs, restaurants, etc. The politicians in turn provide, or have up until this point, capital funding for large-scale projects such as the construction of (large concert venue) 'The Waterfront Hall' and (large theatre/dance/visual arts space) the 'Metropolitan Arts Centre'. If there is a sub-division of culture at one level into areas of specific community-'owned' interest, the common denominator for culture becomes that of economic development, culture redefined as 'the creative industries'; as the Arts Council of Northern Ireland declares on its website 'Our mission is to put the arts at the centre of our social, economic and creative life'. The high point to this process is the designation of Derry/Londonderry as the UK City of Culture for 2013. The delicious irony here is that the criteria for selection were largely based on the notion of which city would most benefit from the regenerative effects of such an award, which would (the thinking goes) bring culture trailing in its wake and with culture money, rather than which was the most 'cultural' city to begin with.

Taking the above series of developments (the reification, sectarianization and commodification of culture) together, it is hard to maintain a sense that the profound mission that *Field Day* set itself of creating a new democratic politics through creating a new engaged cultural audience has met with much enduring success. Nevertheless, it is important to recall that the profile of its concerns set the scene in terms of identity and language for the political discussions, leading to the eventual political settlement, and the idea of the importance of facilitating cultural identification as a technique to defuse conflict over territory lies absolutely at the heart of the Agreement. It is true that many of the other dynamics as to a grand social re-imagination have been lost or diluted. The deliberate confrontation of sectarianism has been collapsed into a soft-soap governmental politics of 'Cohesion, Sharing and Integration', and this has been channelled down into support for the arts along lines which, under the guise of 'parity of esteem' for different 'cultures', 'communities' and 'traditions' accept the enduring status of those

(Footnote 52 continued)
been an implicit acceptance that this distinction between community arts and 'arts' is somehow fundamental and the institutional (and funding) structure has developed to support both, with the division rarely troubled from either side.

cultures and their necessary difference one from the other. In a comparison of the NI Assembly policy documents ‘A Shared Future’ from 2005 and ‘Cohesion, Sharing and Integration’ from 2010, Todd and Ruane note that:

> *Cohesion* sees ‘cultures’ and ‘identities’ as given and stable entities. In *Shared Future*, the vision was of constant cultural change and dynamism: with individuals making their cultural and identity choices in a context of social division, economic difficulty and permeable cultural boundaries, the strategic aim being to facilitate these choices through creation of a safe environment with mutual recognition state-neutrality between cultures… In *Cohesion*, in our view, the vision amounts to a ‘reification’ of cultures which pushes change into the future and loses sight of both its positive potential and of the dangers of the present.[53]

The *Field Day* railing against the empty aestheticism of ‘coterie drama’ to one hand and the ‘plebification of culture’ to the other, and the promotion of performative democracy has been dissolved by the acceptance that community arts are distinctly different to ‘high’ arts (their value being defined in terms of participation rather than quality of product) and both have been divorced from any grand political import except through vague processes of long-term change. Such change has been captured by discourses of economic development within the overall acceptance that the political core structure itself is not subject to any radical critique, and here Northern Ireland is little different to anywhere else in the developed West. Cultural politics has been quieted from a revolutionary notion to a series of programmes of action that have used entrenched ideas of fundamental difference and inevitable forms of order as their model. But none of these qualifications should minimize the remarkable success of making culture part of the skeleton of the political agenda in the first place, and recent events would tend to indicate that the day may once again have arrived for cultural issues to take centre stage as a matter of priority, and for ‘culture’ to once again be opened up for interrogation as some forward-looking species of unity in difference, rather than accepted as simply a matter of delineation and support of mutually exclusive ‘traditions’. The archive of concentrated artistic and related critical attention to questions of belonging, tradition, culture and the emotional weight of such questions (a portion of which has been sketched above) remains as a potentially fruitful resource, should the political ground shift.

---

[53] Jennifer Todd and Joseph Ruane, “From ‘A Shared Future’ to ‘Cohesion, Sharing and Integration’: An analysis of Northern Ireland’s Framework Documents” *Institute for British Irish Studies (IBIS), University College Dublin,* (2010), 3. ‘Cohesion, Sharing and Integration’ following adverse critical reaction, was re-opened for further consultation in 2010 and at the time of writing, December 2012, remains under review and unpublished in revised form.

Love is a Battlefield? The Dynamics of Transitional Justice Scholarship

Having entered the field of cultural politics in post-conflict Northern Ireland, the opportunity presents itself to cast a sideways glance to a related issue of transitional justice scholarship generally and its recent evolutions and self-interrogations. The argument presented here has been that certain cultural ideas (here associated with *Field Day* as case study) animated the Northern Irish political settlement. What followed could be described as the reverse colonization of this field of ideas by a political structure that managed to turn the open field into a series of well-tended sectarian monocultures. It might also be suggested that a parallel process happened, to some degree parasitic on the first, whereby the task of *thinking about* the dynamics of conflict (and post-conflict) was displaced from the broadly cultural arena, professionalized and re-located largely within the academic sphere.[54] Northern Irish academia is host to large numbers of scholars working on conflict and post-conflict issues, under a variety of rubrics and within a variety of departments, schools and faculties; 'peace studies', 'conflict studies', 'post-conflict studies', 'restorative justice programmes', 'peace and reconciliation studies' etc. Just as there is a large 'troubles industry' in reviewing and dealing with the past through government initiative, there is a vibrant sub-sector in the academy, providing the intellectual and policy foundations of such activity and doing their best to sell the idea of the comparative value of the Northern Irish case to international scholars and, in particular, fee-paying students. Each of the two law schools, for example, plays host to large-scale study programmes in 'transitional justice' and teaches this subject as a major part of their curriculum. This local development chimes with the seemingly exponential growth of this subject over the last ten years or so.[55]

Such general growth and the expansion into 'interdisciplinarity' have been recently examined as both local and global phenomenon and critically figured in terms of the notion of 'field' by Professor Christine Bell, who has commented in the following terms:

> I have argued that the narration of the field of transitional justice studies as interdisciplinary is not a romantic and innocent call to intellectual interchange. Rather it performs two political functions: it assists in consolidating and legitimating transitional justice as a field, and it enables an attack on the perceived colonization of the field by law.[56]

Professor Bell is an ex-director of the Transitional Justice Institute of the University of Ulster, and ex-inhabitant of the city of Derry/Londonderry from

---

[54] Not to say that political comment doesn't happen through culture, but the sense of direct link to political change has been lost in favour of the professional apparatus designed to operationalize change at the behest of government; the ground has been settled.

[55] Such growth is succinctly and powerfully reviewed in Bell, "State of the Field".

[56] Bell, "State of the Field", 24.

whence sprang the *Field Day* enterprise (she is currently Professor of Constitutional Law at the University of Edinburgh). In an at-times extremely elegant dissection of the current 'state of the field or non-field' of transitional justice scholarship, the overall enterprise is nevertheless rendered somewhat confusing by the implicit encouragement it provides to recursively apply to its own process a series of distinctions that it by turns posits as useful analytic devices and then dissolves; 'field/non-field', 'crisis/non-crisis', 'practice/scholarship', 'norm/narrative' etc. While such a technique has great illuminative effect in highlighting the huge dynamism in the scholarship and the concomitant difficulty in trying to create adequate heuristics to maintain a sense of coherence and utility, it is in danger of either falling prey to its own complications or opting for oversimplification in order to find a way through the morass. Professor Bell reaches just such a kind of simplifying 'truth' position in a rendering of the familiar Clausewitzian 'war as politics' dynamic. The proposition here is that all confusions can be resolved through an Ur-analytic of 'transitional justice studies as a battlefield'; in other words, when people say that they want to join the (interdisciplinary) conversation, what is really going on is that they want to discursively hack everyone else down. Joining the fray, Professor Bell attempts to cut her own swathe with a notional sword of the 'normative core content of justice' and seeks to define transitional justice as married to a 'deep justice project' predicated on negotiations between academics and practitioners who accept that 'justice has a normative core content' and that 'meaningful justice as an outcome can only be achieved through a combination of reason and passion in pursuit of changed power relationships'.[57]

The inherent paradoxes here are not only just practical (in what seems the reservation of passion to practitioners and reason to academics) but also metaphorical (conflict resolution dynamics figured as a battle?) and metaphysical (justice as normative content yet also as the will-to-peace of latter-day Joans of Arc). The reference to 'reason and passion' is in fact an auto-reference to a scheme of ideas developed in Bell's most recent book 'On the Law of Peace' (OUP, 2008) where the scheme is pushed even further through the mechanism of analogizing the need for reason and passion to Blake's idea of the need for a marriage 'of heaven and hell'.[58] It is perhaps beside the point to note that the examples provided (of peace agreement provisions and related negotiations and measures) would tend to indicate less of a marriage of heaven and hell than, well, a marriage; a series of compromises based on a long-term commitment to intimately living

---

[57] Bell, "State of the Field" 27.

[58] For the development of these ideas see Christine Bell, *On the Law of Peace*, (Oxford: Oxford University Press, 2008), especially Chaps. 12 and 14, 'The New Law of Transitional Justice' and '*Lex Pacificatoria:* marriage of heaven and hell' (the metaphor of 'marriage of heaven and hell' is borrowed from William Blakes eponymous work of 1790, itself usually read as a commentary on the flowering of the Enlightenment in the French revolution.) For a reading of the post-revolutionary restoration in France as a paradigm of historical transitional justice see Jon Elster, *Closing the Books: Transitional Justice in Historical Perspective,* (Cambridge: Cambridge University Press, 2004), Chap. 2, "The French restorations in 1814 and 1815".

together in harmony.[59] In this latest essay (which draws on the scheme of ideas laid out in the book), there is a plea for the reservation of 'transitional justice' studies to a relatively pure legal field as a guard against the dangers of slack, jumbled thinking animated by some romantic notion that mixing everything up is a good idea because people talking to each other is necessarily a good thing.

Professor Bell's caution here as to the necessarily good outcomes of allowing everyone their say with a naivete that all are participating on a 'level playing field' is well-advised. And yet, given the dominance and conditioning nature of her own chosen metaphors ('field', 'battlefield' 'heaven' 'hell'), one wonders just how secure such an attempt to insulate out and prioritize 'the legal' could ever be if even its leading exponent displays a counterloyalty to a pattern of anti-normative *literary* behaviour in the very act of expressing their love of law? In other words, the grain of Bell's argument as to the necessary centrality of law crashes beneath the weight of the metaphorical structure that she tries to construct for it. There is an unacknowledged tension in the work because it is not able in its own terms to create that meaningful relationship between reason and passion, precisely, I suspect, because it is too wedded to the dualism implied in that opposition. In other words, a deep justice project cannot bootstrap itself into discursive coherence by force of will because such willfulness brings with it the kind of abuse of language that constitutes a kind of linguistic injustice in an environment where words really matter. Justice scholarship should rather be deeply attentive to the processes of language and culture on multiple levels, including, and very basically, the level of metaphors brought to bear within any work that seeks to propose what is in effect a linguistic solution to a series of practical problems. This is the lesson of *Field Day* and the encounter with critics like Longley: language, particularly at certain constitutional moments, is a form of practice and it is worth every ounce of energy and attention that can be lavished on it. Transitional justice is not a battle, and (post-conflict) scholarship is not usefully figured as a battlefield.[60]

The implication of the above is that transitional justice is not necessarily defined by the fight to distinguish between 'legal' transitional justice and 'other' transitional justice, which is read as the struggle for an attachment to 'core normative content'. Rather it is more appropriately constituted precisely in the recognition of justice as a vector concept that functions simultaneously in law, politics and in what might be generally termed the realm of affect. *If law goes to accountability and politics to reconciliation, then affective justice is the sense, the feeling, that justice has been done.* Transitional justice should aim at a coherence

[59] For a helpful (in this context) historical sociology of love and marriage see Niklas Luhmann *Love as Passion: the codification of intimacy* (Stanford: Stanford University Press, 1999).

[60] There are some excellent (if rare) examples of work developing this theme of the law/literature intersection with specific reference to Transitional Justice. See, for example: Siphiwe Ignatius Dube "Transitional Justice Beyond the Normative" *International Journal of Transitional Justice* 5(2011) 177–197; Magdalena Zolkos "The Time That Was Broken, The Home That Was Razed: deconstructing Slavenka Drakulic's storytelling about Yugoslav war crimes" *International Journal of Transitional Justice* 2 (2008) 214–226.

of a specific kind that is not dependent on a master discourse, but is dependent on the ability of the doubled terms ('transition' and 'justice') to signify appropriately and positively in multiple arenas at the same time (a task ironically facilitated perhaps because 'transition' as a concept is so resoundingly empty wherever it is placed, while 'justice' is to a symmetrical extent resoundingly full; one tends to balance the other).

Literature provides valuable lessons in such delicate operations of co-ordination in that literary justice is precisely built around the recognition of the value of often paradoxical relationships between text and sub-text (the fact that the reader is invited to be more enlightened than the character) and the engagement of the senses. Literature is the master discourse of the affect, in the sense not of dominating or dictating meaning within a field of inquiry that must be taken to include anthropology, psychology and the social sciences generally, but in the sense of fashioning itself to include the insights of all these modes of inquiry in a form that is of the most affective. Therefore, the general case made here on the basis of a generalizable local example, is that transitional justice, precisely in acknowledging itself as a process inseparable from *feelings* of justice, is literally unthinkable without the lessons of literature and art.

Acknowledgments Thanks to Peter Rush, the anonymous reviewers, and to Fionnuala Ni Aolain and Bill Rolston for their helpful comments on an earlier draft.

Bibliography

1. Arthur, Paige, 2009. How transitions re-shaped Human Rights: A conceptual history of TJ *Human Rights Quarterly* 31:321–367. http://www.belfasttelegraph.co.uk/.
2. Bell, Christine. 2008. *On the Law of Peace*. Oxford: Oxford University Press.
3. Bell, Christine. 2009. Transitional Justice, Interdisciplinarity and the State of the 'Field' or 'Non-Field. *The International Journal of Transitional Justice* 3: 5–27.
4. Bhabha, Homi. 1994. *The Location of Culture* London: Routledge.
5. Boltwood, Scott. 2007. *Brian Friel, Ireland, and The North* Cambridge: Cambridge University Press.
6. Cormack, Bradin. 2007. *A Power to do Justice: Jurisdiction, English Literature and the Rise of the Common Law, 1509–1625* Chicago: Chicago University Press.
7. Deane, Seamus. 1996. *Reading in the Dark* London: Jonathan Cape.
8. Dube, Siphiwe Ignatius. 2011. Transitional Justice Beyond the Normative *International Journal of Transitional Justice* 5: 177–197.
9. Dwan, David. 2008. *The Great Community: Culture and Nationalism in Ireland* Dublin: Field Day.
10. Elster, Jon. 2004. *Closing the books: Transitional justice in historical perspective.* Cambridge: Cambridge University Press.
11. Eagleton, Terry, Said, Edward, and Jameson. 1990. Frederic *Nationalism, Colonialism and Literature* Minneapolis: University of Minnesota Press.
12. Erikkson, Anna. 2009. A bottom-up approach to transformative justice in Northern Ireland. *International Journal of Transitional Justice* 3: 301–320.
13. Friel, Brian, 2001. *Faith Healer* London: Faber and Faber.
14. Friel, Brian, 1981. *Translations* London: Faber and Faber.

15. Field Day Theatre Company *Ireland's Field Day*, 1985. London: Hutchinson.
16. Forsythe, David P. 2011. Transitional Justice: the quest for theory to inform policy. *International Studies Review* 13: 554–578.
17. Gregory, Augusta. 1965. *Our Irish Theatre* London: Capricorn.
18. Heaney, Seamus. 1966. *Death of a Naturalist* London: Faber.
19. Hederman, Mark Patrick., and Kearney, Richard. eds. 1982. *The crane bag book of Irish studies* 1977–1981 Dublin: Blackwater Press.
20. Hederman, Mark Patrick., and Kearney, Richard. eds. 1985. *the crane bag book of Irish studies* 1982–1985 Dublin: Blackwater Press.
21. Hovil, Lucy and Okello, Moses. eds. 2011. *The International Journal of Transitional Justice* 5:333–344.
22. Kearney, Richard. 1988. *Transitions: Narratives in modern Irish culture* Dublin: Wolfhound Press.
23. Kiberd, Declan. 1996. *Inventing Ireland: The Literature of the Modern Nation* London: Vintage.
24. Kirkland, Richard. 1996. *Literature and culture in Northern Ireland Since 1965: Moments of danger* London: Longman.
25. Lojek, Helen 1994. Brian Friel's plays and george steiner's linguistics: translating the Irish, *Contemporary literature* 35.1:83–99.
26. Longley, Edna. 1985. Poetry and politics in Northern Ireland. *The Crane Bag* 9: 26–41.
27. Longley, Edna. 1990. *From cathleen to Anorexia: The breakdown of Irelands* Dublin: Attic Press.
28. Longley, Edna. 1994. *The living stream; literature and revisionism in Ireland.* Newcastle: Bloodaxe Books.
29. Mallie, Eamonn and Mc Kittrick,David. 1996. *The fight for peace: the secret story behind the Irish Peace Process* London: Heinemann.
30. Manderson, Desmond. 2012. *Kangaroo courts and the rule of law: The legacy of modernism* London: Routledge.
31. Mani, Rama. 2009. *Editorial The International Journal of Transitional Justice* 2: 253–265.
32. McEvoy, Ciaran. 2007. Beyond legalism: towards a thicker conception of transitional justice. *Journal of Law and Society* 34(4): 411–440.
33. McEvoy, Ciaran and McGregor, Lorna. 2008. *Transitional Justice from Below: grass-roots activism and the struggle for change* Oxford: Hart.
34. McGrath, Francis C. 1989. Irish Babel: Brian Friel's 'Translations' and George Steiner's 'After Babel'. *Comparative Drama* 23(1): 31–49.
35. McNamee, Eugene. 2002. The government of the Tongue. *Law and Literature* 14(3): 427–461.
36. McNamee, Eugene. 2009. Eye-Witness: memorializing humanity in Steve McQueen's Hunger. *International Journal of Law in Context* 5: 281–294.
37. Mendez, Juan E. 2009. *Editorial The International Journal of Transitional Justice* 3: 157–162.
38. Mitchell, George. 1999. *Making Peace* London: Heinemann.
39. Mutua, Makau. 2001. Savages, Victims and Saviours: The Metaphor of Human Rights, *Harvard International Law Journal*, 42, (Winter): 201–245.
40. Powell, Jonathan. 2008. *Great Hatred, Little Room: making peace in Northern Ireland* London: Bodley Head.
41. Resnik, Judith and Curtis, Denis. 2011. *Representing Justice: Invention, Controversy, and Rights in City-States and Democratic Courtrooms* New Haven: Yale University Press,
42. Richtarik, Marilynn J. 1994. *Acting between the lines: the Field Day theatre company and Irish cultural politics* 1980–1984 Oxford: Clarendon Press.
43. Richtarik, Marilynn J. 2012. *Stewart Parker: a life* Oxford: OUP.
44. Ruane, Joseph. 1994. *and Todd, Jennifer.* The Dynamics of Conflict in Northern Ireland Cambridge: Cambridge University Press.
45. Steiner, George. 1975. *After babel: aspects of language and translation.* Oxford: OUP.

46. Szabo, Carmen. 2007. *Clearing the ground: The Field Day Theatre Company and the Construction of Irish Identities* Cambridge: Cambridge Scholars Publishing.
47. Theidon, Kimberly. 2009. *Editorial The International Journal of Transitional Justice* 3: 295–300.
48. Veitch, Scott ed. 2007. *Law and the Politics of Reconciliation* Aldershot: Ashgate.
49. Weinstein, Harvey M. 2011. *Editorial The International Journal of Transitional Justice* 5: 1–10.
50. Yeats W.B., *W.B. Yeats.* 2000. *Selected Poems* London: Penguin.
51. Zolkos, Magdalena. 2008. The time that was broken, the home that was razed: deconstructing Slavenka Drakulic's storytelling about Yugoslav war crimes. *International Journal of Transitional Justice* 2: 214–226.

Chapter 2
Artistic Activism, Public Debate and Temporal Complexities: Fighting for Transitional Justice in Serbia

Laura McLeod, Jovana Dimitrijević and Biliana Rakočević

A critical element of the transitional justice process is the public debate about the extent of guilt and/or responsibility borne by a state. In Serbia, this public debate has been marked by a resistance towards acknowledging Serb-committed atrocities during the wars in ex-Yugoslavia. This resistance ranges from an uncritical and complete denial that crimes were committed, to a sense of uncertainty about the 'truth', to attempts to explain away or justify Serbia's involvement in the wars.[1] Arguably, these debates about Serbia's relationship to the past are not just about the past, or a social memory of the past, but also about the present and the future, how the past is recalled in the future and the future direction of Serbia. That is, public debates about transitional justice involve a sense of temporal complexity.

This chapter, a collaborative piece between a British academic and two artists living in Serbia, explores the role of art within the public debate about transitional justice in Serbia, picking up on the theme of temporal complexity. Both Biliana Rakočević and Jovana Dimitrijević have undertaken a number of artistic projects aiming to stimulate public debate about the memory of the wars in ex-Yugoslavia and the future direction of Serbia. In this chapter, we focus on two particular

[1] Discussion of attitudes about Serbia's relationship to the wars is widespread. See Jelena Obradovic-Wochnik 'Knowledge, Acknowledgement and Denial in Serbia's Responses to the Srebrenica Massacre' *Journal of Contemporary European Studies*, Vol. 17, No. 1 (2009): 61–74; Jelena Subotić *Hijacked Justice: Dealing with the Past in the Balkans* (Ithaca: Cornell University Press, 2009), 38–82 and Daša Duhaček 'The Making of Political Responsibility: Hannah Arendt and/in the Case of Serbia' in *Women and Citizenship in Central and Eastern Europe* ed. Jasmina Lukić et. al. (Aldershot: Ashgate, 2006), 205–221.

L. McLeod (✉) · J. Dimitrijević · B. Rakočević
School of Social Sciences, University of Manchester, Oxford Road,
Manchester M13 9PL, UK
e-mail: laura.mcleod@manchester.ac.uk

J. Dimitrijević
e-mail: laura.mcleod@manchester.ac.uk

B. Rakočević
e-mail: laura.mcleod@manchester.ac.uk

P. D. Rush and O. Simić (eds.), *The Arts of Transitional Justice*,
Springer Series in Transitional Justice 6, DOI: 10.1007/978-1-4614-8385-4_2

projects. The first, which is an element of Biliana's artistic engagement, is documentary photography of the activities of the feminist–pacifist organization, Women in Black (Belgrade). Women in Black insist upon the necessity of facing the past and assert the need to accept collective responsibility and guilt for the war crimes committed by the Serbian state and society during the 1990s. The second project, 'Section 175', relates to a 2009 exhibition developed by Jovana. In this exhibition, she aimed to highlight the connections between denial of Serbia's criminal past and negative attitudes towards homosexuality. Through a personal reflection by the artists about the projects they have worked on, this chapter seeks to consider how their works have sought to engage with the public debate about the process of transitional justice in Serbia, highlighting the temporal complexities that are inherent in the process. Through their artistic engagement, both Biliana and Jovana disrupt the linear narrative often presented about transitional justice. This disruption opens possibilities for alternative ways of thinking about transitional justice.

It is difficult to define the rapidly expanding concept of transitional justice[2], but arguably, it is conventionally understood by international actors as a predominantly legal process of facing past human rights abuses, incorporating practices such as tribunals and international criminal courts. Certainly, this is the case in Serbia, where international transitional justice efforts have concentrated upon Serbia's cooperation with the International Criminal Tribunal for Former Yugoslavia (ICTY), which, as Jelena Subotić argues, has meant that 'Serbia [has] managed to get away with domestic politics as usual, limiting or blocking serious consideration of crimes of the past and individual and societal complicity in them'.[3] While we do not wish to detract from the importance of the legal process, we argue that transitional justice needs to be located within a broader social and political context. This echoes the point made by Bell and O'Rourke that the scope for a feminist consideration of transitional justice lies 'in terms of a broader feminist theory of transition'.[4] Paying attention to the broader context in Serbia would, for instance, notice the oppression of homosexuals and/or public resistance to transitional justice. Creating space for the consideration of alternative approaches to transitional justice highlights the need for a broader conceptualization that notices the social and political context. We argue that these alternative approaches can be viewed through artistic practices as art exposes the temporal complexity of transitional justice.

We aim to highlight ways in which art can act as a critical intervention in processes of transitional justice, rather than merely a means of helping the survivors of an atrocity. As Vikki Bell suggests, artworks tend to be 'poorly

---

[2] Christine Bell 'Transitional Justice, Interdisciplinarity and the State of the 'Field' or 'Non-Field'' *The International Journal of Transitional Justice,* Vol. 3 (2009), 7.

[3] Subotić, *Hijacked Justice,* 39–45, 47, 81.

[4] Christine Bell and Catherine O'Rourke, 'Does Feminism need a Theory of Transitional Justice? An Introductory Essay' *The International Journal of Transitional Justice*, Vol. 1, No. 1 (2007), 42.

understood as facilitative or therapeutic visual accompaniment', where artistic engagement is thought to be 'merely illustrative or a witnessing of social and political issues'.[5] For us, art can be utilized to explore alternative processes of transitional justice, opening up public debates about the best way to achieve transitional justice via exposing the temporal complexity of the process. Through understanding art as a critical intervention, Jovana and Biliana offer a critique of a purely legal aspect to transitional justice, highlighting the importance of social change alongside the legal and institutional changes. In calling for an alternative vision of transitional justice, we do not intend to fix the precise configuration of that alternative. Attempts to reconceptualize concepts, processes and practices carry the danger of reproducing problems inherent in current conceptualizations.[6] Furthermore, as Jovana suggests, some alternative visions are potentially elitist and exclusionary. However, we suggest that art stimulates the exploration of alternatives and provides a space for reflection and consideration.

This chapter opens with an overview of the transitional justice debate in Serbia and a discussion of temporal complexity. Attention will then turn to a detailed reflection from Jovana and Biliana on their artistic activities before concluding with a consideration of the ways in which art can play a part in the disruption of a coherent and linear narrative about transitional justice. All three authors recognize that transitional justice is not merely about the past, or facing the past, but also about the future and future social memory. Understanding the temporal complexity of transitional justice opens possibilities for alternative ways of framing the issue in a society marked by a cultural resistance and denial of the war crimes committed.

Debating Transitional Justice in Serbia and Temporal Complexity

Serbia has a knotty relationship to the wars and conflicts that characterized the disintegration of Yugoslavia during the 1990s. Officially, the Serbian state did not go to war, and there was little war-related fighting on Serbian soil. However, Milošević's Serbia was seen as the protagonist of violence in Bosnia-Herzegovina, Croatia and Kosovo. It is likely that the Milošević-controlled Yugoslav army actively aided the military machinery of the Bosnian and Croatian Serbs.[7] Contemporary Serbian politics is characterized by a number of highly competing

[5] Vikki Bell 'Contemporary Art and Transitional Justice in Northern Ireland: The Consolation of Form' *Journal of Visual Culture* Vol. 10, no. 3 (2011), 325.

[6] Laura J. Shepherd *Gender, Violence and Security: Discourse as Practice* (London: Zed Books, 2008), p. 172.

[7] Nenad Dimitrijevic 'Serbia After the Criminal Past: What Went Wrong and What Should Be Done' *The International Journal of Transitional Justice*, Vol. 2, No. 1 (2008), 19.

narratives about the extent to which the Serbian state and society can be said to be responsible for the atrocities committed during the wars in Croatia, Bosnia-Herzegovina and Kosovo. These debates continue to inform many policy decisions in Serbia[8] and shape 'the way Serbia is seen by others, and the way Serbs see themselves'.[9]

A particular point of contention centres on the events that took place in Srebrenica, eastern Bosnia-Herzegovina, on 11 July 1995. The Srebrenica massacre is viewed as one of the worst atrocities of the war in Bosnia-Herzegovina, where at least 7,000 Bosnian Muslim men and boys went missing, presumed executed.[10] Surveys suggest that around 50 % of the (Serbian) population doubt if Srebrenica ever happened and query the circumstances surrounding these events.[11] These doubts may be a result of complete denial of events, or reflect 'the lack of readiness to publically acknowledge facts that were privately known', or interpretative denial.[12] In 2010, social and political tensions regarding the memory of Srebrenica were reasserted as the National Parliament passed a declaration condemning the crimes in Srebrenica.[13] The months before the declaration was passed were marked by discussions about how to interpret the events that took place in Srebrenica during July 1995: Was Srebrenica genocide, a war crime or a forgery?[14] Another point of contention relates to the extent of Serbia's cooperation with the ICTY, in particular the state's willingness to hand over indicted persons. While high-profile suspects such as Randovan Karadžić and Ratko Mladić were arrested (in 2008 and 2011, respectively), views about the ICTY remain very negative within Serbian domestic politics.[15]

---

[8] Laura McLeod 'Configurations of Post-conflict: Impacts of Representations of conflict and Post-Conflict upon the (Political) Translations of Gender Security within UNSCR 1325' *International Feminist Journal of Politics*, Vol. 13, No. 4 (2011), 605–622.

[9] Dimitrijevic 'Serbia After the Criminal Past', 6.

[10] The most relevant ICTY decision to date about Srebrenica relates to Radislav Krstić. See http://www.icty.org/x/cases/krstic/cis/en/cis_krstic.pdf (accessed 10 July 2012).

[11] Obradovic-Wochnik 'Knowledge, Acknowledgement and Denial' 62.

[12] Dimitrijevic 'Serbia After the Criminal Past', 5–6 and Obradovic-Wochnik 'Knowledge, Acknowledgement and Denial'.

[13] 'The Declaration of the National Parliament of the Republic of Serbia Condemning the Crimes in Srebrenica' Official Gazette of the Republic of Serbia (No. 20/10).

[14] For instance, Milan Bačević, the chair of the executive of the Serbian Progressive Party, suggested that Srebrenica was not a genocide and was a forgery made by the Hague. B92 'SNS: U Srebrenici nije bilo genocida' (retrieved www.b92.net on 17 October 2011). In contrast, Slobodan Vuksanović of the Democratic Party of Serbia described Srebrenica as a war crime, rather than genocide. B92 'DSS: Srebrenica—ratni zločin' (retrieved www.b92.net on 17 October 2011).

[15] Jelana Obradović-Wochnik, and Alexander Wochnik, 'Europeanising the 'Kosovo Question': Serbia's Policies in the context of EU Integration' *West European Politics* Vol. 35, No. 5 (2012), 1176; Marlene Spoerri and Annette Freyberg-Inan, 'From Prosecution to Persecution: Perceptions of the International Criminal Tribunal for the Former Yugoslavia (ICTY) in Serbian Domestic Politics' *Journal of International Relations and Development* Vol. 11, No. 4 (2008), 350–384.

The ferocity of these debates about Srebrenica and Serbia's cooperation with the ICTY means that civil society groups and non-governmental organization (NGOs) in Serbia seeking to publically assert the necessity of political and social responsibility and the importance of facing the past often face abuse—as documented by Biliana Rakočević in her photography (discussed below). NGOs are generally viewed negatively in Serbia for a range of reasons: they are thought to be unnecessarily critical of the government and too politicized.[16] The concerns held by certain groups, like Women in Black, about 'facing the past' mean that there is a generalized public perception that the campaigns of these NGOs are 'condescending or confrontational'.[17] This suggests that it is difficult for activists concerned with transitional justice to feel that their voice is accepted, and there is a sense of frustration amongst activists that their views about the necessity of facing the past are—generally—not considered to be legitimate or valid notions in Serbia. In this particular social and political context, Jovana and Biliana are working to resist denial, or rationalization of the Srebrenica massacre. Through their artistic projects, they seek to create a space for public discussion about Serbia's transitional justice agenda.

Art can play a role in transitional justice processes aimed at confronting the culture of silence, denial or rationalization.[18] Art can provoke public debate, as intended by the photographic exhibitions of Ron Haviv, whose 'Blood and Honey' exhibition explores the wars that took place in ex-Yugoslavia.[19] The exhibition travelled around Serbia in 2002, finishing in Novi Sad, a city north of Belgrade in September 2002.[20] When the photographs were exhibited in Novi Sad, the organizers wanted to create a space to enable public discussion of the photographs.[21] To achieve this, the photographs were initially displayed without any titles or explanations: instead, a blank piece of paper and a pencil were placed next to each photograph and visitors were encouraged to record their responses.[22] The

---

16 Åse Berit Grødeland 'Public Perceptions of non-governmental organisations in Serbia, Bosnia & Herzegovina, and Macedonia' *Communist and Post-Communist Studies* Vol. 39 (2006), 232–236.

17 Jelena Obradovic-Wochnik 'Serbian Civil Society as an Exclusionary Space: NGOs, the Public and 'Coming to terms with the Past'' in *Civil Society and Transition in the Western Balkans* ed. Vesna Bojcic-Dzelilovic, James Ker-Lindsay and Denisa Kostovicova (Basingstoke: Palgrave McMillan, forthcoming 2013).

18 See James Weaver and Jeanne Colleran, 'Whose Memory? Whose Justice? Personal and Political trauma in Ariel Dorfman's *Death and the Maiden*' *Performance Research: A Journal of the Performing Arts* Vol. 16, No. 1 (2011), 32; Rosemarie Buikema'Performing Dialogical Truth and Transitional Justice: The Role of Art in the Becoming Post-Apartheid of South Africa' *Memory Studies* Vol. 5, No. 3 (2012): 283.

19 Ron Haviv 'Blood and Honey' can be viewed at http://photoarts.com/haviv/bloodandhoney/ (retrieved 6 December 2011).

20 Marija Gajicki 'Case Study' in *Documents on Ron Haviv's Exhibition 'Blood and Honey' in Novi Sad* (Novi Sad: Vojvodjanka-Regional Women's Initiative, 2003), 17.

21 Gajicki 'Case Study', 21.

22 Gajicki 'Case Study', 21–22.

responses reveal the tensions that shape the transitional justice debate in Serbia. For instance, one set of photographs shows Serbian paramilitary soldiers (known as 'Arkan's Tigers' after the unit's leader, Željko Ražnatović-Arkan) attacking and killing three civilians in Bijeljina, north-eastern Bosnia-Herzegovina.[23] Some of the comments written by visitors to the exhibition in Novi Sad suggest that the photograph is doctored or that the photographer is presenting a one-sided story.[24] In contrast, one comment states that 'those who did this... they are war criminals'.[25] While this discussion further highlights the range of positions adapted towards transitional justice in Serbia, we can also draw out the notion that art has a role to play in the public debate about transitional justice processes, aiming to draw out a sense of truth and acknowledgement about the violence committed.

The organizers of the 'Blood and Honey' exhibition in Novi Sad were seeking to stimulate discussion about truth and memory of the recent past. Transitional justice is frequently framed in terms of 'facing the past': the process is said to be about the 'attempt to deal with past violence in societies undergoing or attempting some form of political transition'.[26] 'Facing the past' is generally about the creation of a social memory that is deemed to be truthful. The role of memory and truth is viewed as a critical element of facing the past, as Elizabeth Porter explains: 'choices about what is remembered and forgotten, and stories told truthfully and those covered over or suppressed have massive moral implications for individuals, groups, communities and politicians and influence the direction in which a country moves'.[27] In relation to Haviv's exhibition in Novi Sad, the blank sheets of paper were intended to provoke a discussion that would draw out a discussion about 'the truth' of the wars in ex-Yugoslavia. For the organizers of the Haviv's exhibition, this was a 'brutal project' which was 'very painful, but we thought it was the only way to overcome our problems'.[28] That is, the process of 'facing the past' involves remembering 'the truth' as a means of dealing with contemporary social problems.

Campaigns to reconsider 'the truth' about the past utilize a rationality suggesting that dealing with 'the past' will enable the achievement of a positive future which is deemed morally acceptable. In this respect, an intrinsic connection is forged between 'the past' and 'the future' in the rhetoric of transitional justice, producing a coherent and linear narrative. However, transitional justice is a complex normative process involving perceptions and beliefs about what it means to come to terms with the past. As such, transitional justice has a greater degree of temporal complexity than it might initially appear, as all temporal moments—past,

---

[23] *Documents on Ron Haviv's Exhibition 'Blood and Honey' in Novi Sad* (Novi Sad: Vojvodjanka-Regional Women's Initiative, 2003), 118.

[24] *Documents on Ron Haviv's Exhibition, 119*–122.

[25] *Documents on Ron Haviv's Exhibition,* 120.

[26] Bell 'Transitional Justice, Interdisciplinarity', 7.

[27] Elizabeth Porter *Peacebuilding: Women in International Perspective* (London: Routledge, 2007), 126.

[28] Interview, Marija Gajicki coordinator of VIVISECT, Novi Sad: 13 May 2008.

present and future—are infused with *interrelated* normative claims and ambitions. Hopes and ambitions about the future direction of that community are related to perceptions about the past and political debates about how to deal with past human wrongs. Utilizing the notion of 'transitional justice' belies narrative coherence borne out of the desire to 'rationalise a set of diverse bargains in relation to the past as an integral endeavour, so as to obscure the quite different normative, moral and political implications of the bargains'.[29] Thus, the temporal complexity of transitional justice in part arises from our 'moral agency [which] determines how we deal with the past'.[30] We argue that art can play a role in disrupting the coherent narrative of temporality invoked by revealing the politicized normative claims of transitional justice.

Artistic Engagement

To consider the possibilities of artistic engagement in a public debate, Biliana and Jovana reflected upon their projects and considered how their works have sought to engage with the public debate about the process of transitional justice in Serbia. The process was as follows: Laura wrote some initial questions that guided a draft reflective account, which formed the basis of discussion in a recorded face-to-face meeting in Belgrade during September 2011 and follow-up email communication. Working with the transcripts[31] of these recordings, Laura edited the reflective accounts for clarity. These reflective accounts were finalized by Jovana and Biliana.

These processes of reflection are a useful way of highlighting the temporalities embedded in our narratives about transitional justice. Our aim is to draw attention to the temporal complexity of transitional justice disrupting the linear narrative (that progress can be secured via legal judgements about the past) we often present. This disruption opens opportunities for alternative visions of transitional justice to complement the legal process. In reflection, our temporalities are exposed as we attempt to explain our actions and beliefs. These reflections highlight the political and politicized nature of Biliana's and Jovana's artistic activities, stressing our perspective that art can be taken as a political statement as the artistic endeavour is taking place within, and responding to, a particular context. The controversy surrounding transitional justice processes in Serbia means that these artistic engagements are a political and politicized statement aiming to contribute to and stimulate public debate about transitional justice.

[29] Bell, 'Transitional Justice, Interdisciplinarity', 6.

[30] Porter, *Peacebuilding*, 128.

[31] We would like to thank Adam Hardie for transcription of the recordings.

Biliana and Documenting the Public Activities of Women in Black

In 2005, Biliana started taking photographs of the street actions and performances enacted by activists of Women in Black, a feminist–pacifist NGO that has fought for political responsibility for the past 20 years. Women in Black insist that transitional justice is a critical element of their pacifist position.[32] Since the fall of the Milošević regime, Women in Black have sought to reject the social and political denial of Serbian responsibility and guilt through street actions, public campaigns, visiting the sites of crimes committed in the name of Serbia (such as Srebrenica).[33] A central aspect of the group's position on transitional justice is the necessity of facing the past and accepting responsibility and guilt for the war crimes committed during the 1990s. In this section, Biliana reflects upon her use of documentary photography to record the activities of NGOs working for transitional justice through a poem.

For Biliana, her own documentary photography opened up a range of new questions regarding how to capture her sense of frustration about the (growing) difference between popular public opinion in Serbia that preferred to deny the necessity of transitional justice and the campaigns pursued by NGOs that insist upon facing the past (which include, amongst others, Women in Black). She documented a number of Women in Black campaigns during 2008 and 2009, not only photographing the activists, but also the resistance faced by activists. Biliana has captured the various types of resistance and oppression in response to the public campaigns of Women in Black: from the heavy police presence that is deemed necessary to protect their street actions, to the violent chants of the far-right organization Obraz,[34] to the drawing of a swastika on the window of Belgrade's philosophy department by students on anti-fascism day 9 November 2009. These photographs are powerful reminders of how resistance to transitional justice processes is embedded in all aspects of society: for Biliana, her photographs capture hatred.

In her reflection, Biliana explores how engaged documentary photographs can play a role in transitional justice processes, suggesting that photographs are simultaneously records of the past and records of today. That is, there is a sense of temporal complexity in photographs, as they tell a story about how people are reacting to the process of 'facing the past', they simultaneously capture the problems of the present about Serbia's future direction. Via her photographs, Biliana aims to show us how to see, encouraging us to identify the problems and take action to improve the lives of people. These points are reinforced when

---

[32] Stašta Zajović *Transitional Justice: A Feminist Approach* (Belgrade: Women in Black, 2007), 61.

[33] Zajović, *Transitional Justice,* 64–70.

[34] Obraz is a Serbian far-right, nationalist, neo-nazi, clerofascist organization who swear allegiance to the Serbian nation and Serbian orthodox religion. In June 2012, the Serbian Constitutional Court ruled to ban the actives of Obraz.

Biliana suggests that documentary photography can be a means of educating young people in Serbia about the wars and Serbia's role in these wars. These pictures, 'worth a thousand words', demonstrate how the transitional justice process is fraught with temporal complexities. Biliana reflected upon her experiences of documentary photography via a poem that she wrote in December 2011. An extract appears below.

What is Transitional Justice? Another big word?
I am tired of words, I want Action!
Transitional Justice as a notion, an Idea of transitional way passing through the Past to the Future, without being secure and certain of Today.

Engaged I became in 2005 when I started to work for Women in Black and other feminist and women's NGOs.
I wanted so badly my photography to be useful, to be used for some purpose and then I Saw.
… Nobody cared! I was so shocked with what I SAW!
How to reconcile all these deaths in Life of the Present … Srebrenica … Vukovar … Višegrad …
What I have seen I photographed. I saw more, but was crying more.

How to reconcile Art and Life … How to use Art in Life to Show.
Words are a tool, but too long words make us tired.
Visual is more practical.
My Tool is my Photography. I need to reach public. I need to show my Photographs, the records of the Past, the records of ToDay.
Needing to show you more of I have SeeN, through my engaged photography. It is not Art you will see but the Emotions of Life.

There are so many photographs of before. Of before war. Of wars before.
In Documenting all the Political Transitional Life of Serbia.
I have seen all these activists on the Left… behind the Death in this Life of TODAY.
Do I need so much this Past to live in my Present?
I see. I record. I show You to See.
Do You SEE? If you see why don't you react?

What is the truth when we organize activities for 8th March, International Women's Day, and we have a cordon of policemen around us?
For protection or are we, Women in Black, the worst part of this Serbian Society?
Remember the past to live in your present. But my present is also a problem.
We have choices about what to remember and what is forgotten.

I will never forget the International Day of Human Rights in 2008.
On one side you have the Citizens of Belgrade and NGOs and on the other side Obraz.
Obraz are full of hate, nationalistic and Nazi oriented, and they were showing us the Finger.
Is this supposed to be normal?
On the Day of Human Rights?
How do you feel when you see young students drawing a swastika in the heat of their breath on the window of the Philosophical Faculty of Belgrade?
I am shocked!

How to teach the war of yesterday, the wars in Bosnia and Croatia?
Most of young people do not understand the real issue here.
Mostly they were told and they believe.
The education of young people is necessary to preserve normal life for them.
We must show the truth.

The only way for me is to show you my photographs. You will see. You will feel something.
They said that a picture is worth a thousand words. So please look. See. Watch. Here are the proofs.
Here are the witnesses.
Here are the Photographs.
And you are my public.

In her poem, Biliana describes her frustration about public resistance towards transitional justice campaigns, exploring her strategy of capturing and recording the opposition faced by Women in Black activists. Her insistence that there are choices to be made in what we forget and remember highlights that individuals are responsible for their understandings of transitional justice. Biliana's worry about how to teach the wars is a reminder of the politicized nature of memory: best described as a worry about the practice of memorialization. Memorialization can be described as the 'various processes and forms of collective remembrance… a process fundamental to recovering from trauma and atrocity'.[35] In a study of youth responses to sites of memorialization, it was found that such sites could promote new knowledge and understandings, contributing to an increased emotional understanding of the human consequences of atrocity.[36] Through their performances, Women in Black are aiming to increase knowledge and understanding of Serbia's roles in the wars: Biliana's visual record of the resistance faced by activists is indicative of the opportunity that exists to rethink collective and individual memories. The temporal perspective reinforced here serves to remind us

[35] Brandon Hamber, Liz Ševčenko and Ereshenee Naidu, 'Utopian Dreams or Practical Possibilities? The Challenges of Evaluating the Impact of Memorialization in Societies in Transition' *The International Journal of Transitional Justice*, Vol. 4, No. 4 (2010), 398.

[36] Hamber et al. 'Utopian Dreams or Practical Possibilities?', 397–420.

that processes of transitional justice inevitably involve a reshaping and recrafting of memory. The politicized nature of this process is not merely a debate about *how* to remember the past: it is also debate about future ambitions, about the way in which the past is configured in the future, about the frustrations of the present. Through encapsulating the opposition faced by Women in Black, Biliana's photographs challenge the linear narrative about transitional justice, highlighting the difficulties, if not the impossibility of collective agreement about how the past can be thought about in the present and the future.

Jovana and 'Section 175'

Jovana's reflection focuses on a December 2009 exhibition that she designed, called 'Section 175' held at the Student Cultural Centre, Belgrade. Jovana seeks to make connections between past human rights abuses, transitional justice processes and social violence against homosexuals. Jovana's personal narrative (below), written in September 2011, highlights possibilities for thinking about alternative processes for conducting our daily lives.

> I live in post-war Serbia, and we love to say that there was never a war in Serbia. True. Instead, Serbia took wars elsewhere and caused four civil wars in one decade on the territory of what was known as Socialist Federal Republic of Yugoslavia. These wars politicised the position of homosexuals in Serbian society—and continue to do so. If you say that you are homosexual, many say that you are not Serbian, and you are told to 'go to Croatia': you are unwanted. It is seen as anti-Serbian to be homosexual. These wars have continued to shape the political reality in which I live, where elite politicians are not interested in thinking about the deeper structural violences that their policies cause. Serbia is corrupt as our political elites refuse to face the past because they fear for their own future. As they see it, any mention of Srebrenica might decrease their popularity with voters. So, they make corrupt compromises and avoid public statements about war crimes to retain power. I have taken much of my political inspiration from the radical ideas of Women in Black, a network of feminist-pacifists that I joined in 2004, and believe that transitional justice is an inevitable link to the future, and the future exists in the present. Even after the fall of the Milosevic regime in October 2000, the refusal to accept political responsibility remained and in some respects we became our own threat. Srebrenica victims remained invisible to many Serbs for quite some time—even 10 years after the massacre. I first learnt about the horrors of Srebrenica after a trip to Holland in 2002.
>
> In this context I started developing a series of performances called Section 175, named after a paragraph in the 1871 German Criminal Code, which was used by Nazi Germany to persecute, arrest, and kill homosexuals. While on a trip to Berlin, I saw a monument to the homosexual victims of the Holocaust, and at this moment I was excited: I was so excited that I couldn't wait to come home and do something with it. I felt that we in Serbia could learn from the experiences and understanding developed in Germany about how to respond to collective guilt and responsibility. Like in Nazi Germany, homosexual people have faced oppression in Serbia. To achieve a transitional justice that includes social reconciliation, it is critical to ensure homosexual rights. In December 2009, I wanted to carry this idea further, and held an exhibition in central Belgrade. My project, 'Section 175' is a very personal story, offering another way of thinking about living in Serbia.

As you entered the gallery space of the 'Section 175' exhibition you were faced with blood-red, worn-out shoes placed on top of shiny silver stickers that had 'Srebrenica' printed on them in white capital letters. I wanted to create this idea of inviting people inside and asking them to look at themselves. The stickers which had 'Srebrenica' printed on them were designed in 2008 by Boban Stojanović, the director of Queeria, a homosexual rights organisation. The shiny surface reflects your face as you look down at the stickers: you are meant to see yourself and realise that you are responsible too for the atrocities that took place at Srebrenica. The shoes that were placed on these stickers had been painted blood-red. Through my activism with Women in Black, I wore out my shoes, and I wanted to show that there was an effort being made by some Serbians to stress the necessity of transitional justice. We were not all completely deaf and blind to the issues: there were women who walked the streets, stood in the streets because they believed in something: the necessity of facing the past.

Apart from symbolising the efforts made by activists to raise awareness of importance of transitional justice, the shoes are also symbolic of different moments of time in the transitional justice process. Shoes hint at those lives that have been lost, provoking us to reflect on these lives. But, by placing them around the gallery, I expressed how the trails of the future are already there and we can see some future genocide because there is one thing that remains after every trial: an error. We are in a constant trial and error process. All of my blood-red shoes displayed in the 'Section 175' exhibition were later part of the 'One Pair of Shoes, One Life' street performance held by Women in Black to mark the anniversary of Srebrenica on 15 July 2010. The 'One Pair of Shoes, One Life' ultimately aims to collect 8,372 pairs of shoes to reflect each person killed by genocide at Srebrenica, to remind others of the lives lost and to insist upon the acceptance of political responsibility from the Serbian government, whose officials and military officers gave the orders for the massacre.[37] I felt that these shoes belonged to this campaign. The intention of Women in Black is to build a monument that would somehow incorporate the shoes. I am proud that my work will become a part of that monument.

As part of the exhibition, I wore a white silk gown and painted my face white with dark black eyebrows. As people watched, I would then whip myself with roses and used a razor blade to carve the Star of David into my arm until my arm bled. I used the Star of David as a way of symbolising the concentration camps of the Holocaust, to make people think about the German experience, and the German process of transitional justice, and how it could be relevant to Serbia.

Performances are important to me. Performances are rituals. It's not impossible to buy or sell them, but if we begin to value this one moment more than anything our hands could hold, it might be a step out of the cycle, and make us think in alternative ways. So, to produce art, or to produce justice, is still just a means to go beyond production. I prefer recycling when it comes to materials. I never buy anything. Performance and hoarding are my methods. I could never say that I need a million dollars to make this or that. How can we expect justice in the world where art is expensive? Transitional justice is the best justice we can have and while I'm not entirely happy with it because achieving transitional justice won't bring back the dead; I aim to go beyond transitional justice with my art. Transitional justice, and art, can be overrated, expensive and very capitalist. And it's capitalism that produces so many wasted bodies. So, in my art, I am this wasted body—that I use for performances, including carving the Star of David on my arm—and I am the transition. I believe that both art and justice should be a transition out of oppression. They are not goals, but tools, and the combination can set us free.

---

[37] Olivera Simic and Kathleen Daly ''One Pair of Shoes, One Life': Steps towards Accountability for Genocide in Srebrenica' *The International Journal of Transitional Justice*, Vol. 5 (2011), 477–491.

In her narrative, it is clear that Jovana's exhibition, like Biliana's photographs, offers a space for reflection about the transitional justice process. Jovana's work is driven by the desire to present an alternative vision for how transitional justice can be achieved. For instance, carving the Star of David on her arm becomes a means of drawing attention to the predicament of homosexual people in Serbia, highlighting a connection between contemporary social oppression of homosexuality and resistance towards transitional justice processes. Likewise, displaying blood-red shoes to indicate the lives lost at Srebrenica in an exhibition about homosexual rights and transitional justice pushes us to consider and take seriously the connections between human rights abuses and oppression of homosexuals. Many activists—including Jovana—highlight that the nationalized social and political environment in Serbia which evades cooperation with the ICTY or violently rejects Serbian complicity in Srebrenica is an environment where homosexuality is considered to be anti-Serbian; hence, 'go back to Croatia'.[38] Noticing the connections between transitional justice processes and social attitudes towards homosexuality addresses the challenge put forward by Fionnula Ni Aolain that feminist scholars should 'address with more precision and imagination the experiences of harms done to women, finding new ways to acknowledge the complexity of harm for women in transitional contexts'.[39] These connections are not only important reminders of the contested nature of *what* and *how* to remember an atrocity, but also of the temporal complexity that is invoked when Jovana makes these connections in her artistic activism. For Jovana, transitional justice is not just about remembering the atrocity in Srebrenica, it is also about recognizing the broader social and political context in Serbia that enabled Srebrenica to happen. For Jovana, the very act of what we remember is critical to the future direction of Serbia: How can contemporary violence towards homosexuals be addressed if the Serbian state and society does not recognize connections to the violence of the broader social and political context that enabled the atrocity at Srebrenica?

Stressing the importance of the present and the future challenges the strictly chronological notion of time in transitional justice. This echoes the notion put forward by Berber Bevernage that alternative forms of justice offer an 'implicit rejection of the quasi-reversible time of justice' and as such 'all injustice is, fundamentally, irreversible'.[40] Nevertheless, 'it is precisely the emphasis on the endurance of historical injustice and on the presence of the past…[which] transforms remembrance and historical truth into forms of justice'.[41] As Jovana points out, 'transitional justice won't bring back the dead', but there is still a value in the process of transitional justice because it is possible to achieve meaningful justice

[38] See http://www.frontlinedefenders.org/Serbia for some discussion of the connections (accessed 10 September 2012).

[39] Fionnuala Ni Aolain, 'Advancing Feminist Positioning in the Field of Transitional Justice' *The International Journal of Transitional Justice*, Vol. 6, No. 3 (2012), 207.

[40] Berber Bevernage, 'Time, Presence, and Historical Injustice' *History and Theory* Vol. 47 (2008), 155.

[41] Bevernage, 'Time, Presence'.

offering a 'transition out of oppression', which, for her, includes a future where homosexuals are free. For Jovana, achieving deep and long-lasting justice requires disrupting the linear story of progress and the claim that facing the past will solve the problems of the present, highlighting that social violence in the present is connected both to how the past is dealt with and to how the future is hoped for. Through challenging the idea that transitional justice is merely a process of facing the past, Jovana makes connections to the present, highlighting, like Biliana, that the present is also a problem. For Jovana, contemporary social oppression towards homosexuality is simultaneously connected to how the Serbian role in the war crimes of the 1990s is configured and the future direction of Serbia.

Conclusions: Temporal Disruption and Working for a Better Future

Through their artistic engagement, both Biliana and Jovana offer an alternative to the liberal vision of transitional justice as meeting certain legal conditions. This is not a rejection of these important legal and institutional transformations necessary for transitional justice, but a call for a broader vision. For them, it is necessary for transitional justice processes to address social violence in contemporary Serbia: whether the violence is opposition to Women in Black, or opposition to homosexuality. There is some scepticism about the ability of liberal visions of transitional justice to be successful in addressing these social violences, in part because, as Jovana puts it, 'transitional justice is our ticket to the EU and bigger salaries… [meaning that] the concept is treated like merchandise'.[42] Jovana suggests here that the danger of liberal visions of transitional justice is that the process becomes instrumental, and does not deal with the deeper problems present in Serbian society. Art provides space for personal and public deliberation upon what transitional justice means, opening alternative ways of thinking about how to deal with past human rights abuses. In part, these spaces are created because the linear narratives about transitional justice are disrupted via artistic engagement, allowing us to tap into a broader vision of transitional justice with a greater degree of temporal complexity.

In urging for temporal complexity, both Biliana and Jovana are urging us to not 'make frontiers with our past', as 'the limitations of facing the past limit our present'.[43] Through their artistic engagement, both Biliana and Jovana are not merely offering a critique of the past or present but—critically—highlight how the past is remembered and the connections of these memories and perceptions of the past to our hopes for the future. The implication here is that linear narratives of

[42] Interview by Laura McLeod with Jovana Dimitrijević, Belgrade 19 September 2011. See Subotić *Hijacked Justice* for more discussion about the role of the EU in transitional justice in the Western Balkans.

[43] Email correspondence with Biliana Rakočević 25 March 2012.

transitional justice limit the possibility of radical social change. Disrupting the linear temporality of the narrative opens the possibility of escaping the (temporal) limitations of transitional justice. Biliana and Jovana disrupt the linear narrative of transitional justice through their artistic engagement in two ways: first, by revealing the politicized nature of transitional justice processes and second, by emphasizing hopes and dreams for the future.

The first way that both Biliana and Jovana disrupt the linear narrative about transitional justice is by revealing the politicized nature of transitional justice processes via their artistic engagement. Biliana's photographs serve to remind us that facing the past involves an element of choice 'about what is remembered and forgotten', although she argues that there are limitations about what we can remember and forget: that 'in Serbia it is more about the choice about what is given to us to remember and what is collectively wanted for us to forget'.[44] Additionally, Jovana highlights the politicized nature of art, even where artists claim that their work is not political, arguing that 'you can't have art that is not political. Because… [we all live] in this context and whatever you do, counts in a way. I think it's just a cop out, to say stuff like "oh, I'm not political".[45] Revealing the politicized nature of both artistic engagement and transitional justice disrupts our temporal understanding of transitional justice as a process dealing with past human right abuses in the present transitional moment.

Second, Biliana and Jovana also disrupt the linear narrative about transitional justice because they take the future as their starting point for their artistic engagement. In other words, they believe that facing the past is a future-centred notion that the very process of facing the past affects how the future looks. Understanding the importance of the future in public debates about transitional justice potentially opens alternative ways of framing the issue in a society marked by cultural resistance and denial of the war crimes committed. By pushing for a deeper consideration of transitional justice, the very process of transitional justice can address the social violences that exist in the present. Jovana believes that her work 'wouldn't make any sense if [she] just dealt with the past', as she is aiming to improve the future.[46] In this respect, recalling the past is about the direction of the future. It is Serbia's future that is at stake, not Serbia's past or the memory of Serbia's past: facing the past is a future-located notion, and so the future is thrust to the forefront in their artistic projects related to transitional justice.

Challenging the liberal linearity of transitional justice raises questions about what the achievement of transitional justice looks like. Transitional justice as a process striving to achieve closure is fraught with difficulties[47] and so the

---

[44] First quotation Porter, *Peacebuilding*, 126. Second quotation: email correspondence with Biliana Rakočević 27 March 2012.

[45] Interview by Laura McLeod with Jovana Dimitrijević, Belgrade 19 September 2011.

[46] Interview by Laura McLeod with Jovana Dimitrijević, Belgrade 19 September 2011.

[47] See Brandon Hamber and Richard A.Wilson 'Symbolic closure through memory, reparation and revenge in post-conflict societies' *Journal of Human Rights*, Vol. 1, No. 1 (2002), 35–53.

'achievement' of transitional justice is not an endpoint *per se*, but rather a set of processes enabling change. However, whether the changes effected are 'good', 'bad' or 'value-neutral' is open to debate.[48] Art has an important role to play in these debates in providing a space for reflection about the practice of transitional justice via exposing the temporal complexity of transitional justice. Specifically, we suggest that art stimulates exploration of alternatives. One such alternative is the women's courts currently being established by a coalition of women's organizations in the Western Balkans.[49] The women's courts challenge existing ways of dealing with gender justice and reconciliation by asking women to testify about their experiences of conflict and their visions for the post-conflict context, making recommendations which will be disseminated to the region's formal legal systems. Jovana is currently working on a film about the Women's Courts as a means of provoking deeper consideration about the project. Art serves to remind us that we have choices about how to pursue transitional justice and plays an important role in exposing the possibilities of alternative visions of transitional justice, via exposing the temporal complexity inherent in the process and practice of transitional justice.

How to continue the disruption of the linear narrative of (liberal) transitional justice? Both Biliana and Jovana believe that it is important to provoke reflection, and critical to this is the use of art that represents these alternative ideas in an accessible manner. Jovana believes it critical to develop innovative communication to increase the chances of a receptive audience of people who publically or privately resist acknowledgement of Serb responsibility for the war crimes committed.[50] She argues that utilizing recognizable popular culture and making 'unexpected combinations' (such as drawing on elements of Japanese horror in a documentary film about Women's Courts) is a more effective ways of reaching people who are 'outside' the circle of activists who already support a wide range of perceptions about transitional justice.[51] Biliana agrees that it is imperative to 'transmit information better' as 'knowledge is a must'.[52] The open nature of street performances offers a strong path towards artistic engagement in the future, as street performances push the casual stroller to stop, look and listen simulating reflection. Visual mediums, including photographs and film, are also means of provoking consideration upon the transitional justice process.

Finally, we believe that utilizing the notion of temporal complexity allows for a feminist vision of transitional justice which 'incorporates non-hegemonic practices' and is 'aware of the complexities and contradictions of its own dominant

---

[48] Bell. 'Transitional Justice, Interdisciplinarity', 6.

[49] Public proceedings will begin in 2013. See http://www.globalfundforwomen.org/impact/success-stories/top-10-wins-for-womens-movements and http://www.zenskisud.org/index.html (in Serbian/Croatian/Bosnian). Accessed 6 September 2012.

[50] Jovana Dimitrijević email correspondence 27 March 2012.

[51] Ibid.

[52] Biliana Rakočević email correspondence 27 March 2012.

discourses'.[53] Simply increasing the number of women involved in transitional justice processes 'does not equate in any simple way with a feminist reshaping' of the agenda.[54] It is therefore about challenging or critiquing the agenda. Using art to draw attention to the social resistance or violence towards those urging for political responsibility challenges the effectiveness of the legal liberalism of conventional approaches to transitional justice. Using art to disrupt the conventional temporality of the narrative about transitional justice can open up a greater understanding of the complexity of transitional justice.

Bibliography

1. Bell, Christine. 2009. Transitional justice, interdisciplinarity and the state of the 'field' or 'non-field'. *The International Journal of Transitional Justice* 3: 5–27.
2. Bell, Christine, and Caroline O'Rourke. 2007. Does feminism need a theory of transitional justice? An introductory essay. *International Journal of Transitional Justice* 1: 23–44.
3. Bell, Vicki. 2011. Contemporary art and transitional justice in northern ireland: The consolation of form. *Journal of Visual Culture* 10(3): 324–353.
4. Bevernage, Berber. 2008. Time, presence, and historical injustice. *History and Theory* 47: 149–167.
5. Buikema, Rosemarie. 2012. Performing dialogical truth and transitional justice: The role of art in the becoming post-apartheid of South Africa. *Memory Studies* 5(3): 282–292.
6. Dimitrijevic, Nenad. 2008. Serbia after the criminal past: What went wrong and what should be done. *The International Journal of Transitional Justice* 2(1): 2–22.
7. *Documents on Ron Haviv's Exhibition "Blood and Honey" in Novi Sad.* 2003. Novi Sad: Vojvodjanka-Regional Women's Initiative.
8. Duhaček, Daša. 2006. The making of political responsibility: Hannah arendt and/in the case of Serbia. In *Women and Citizenship in Central and Eastern Europe*, eds. Jasmina Lukić, Joanna Regulska and Darja Zaviršek Ashgate, 205–221. UK: Aldershot.
9. Edkins, Jenny. 2002. After the subject of international security. In *Politics and post-structuralism: an introduction*, eds. A. Finlayson and J. Valentine, 66–80. Edinburgh: Edinburgh University Press.
10. Gajicki, Marija. 2003. Case study. In *Documents on Ron Haviv's Exhibition "Blood and Honey" in Novi Sad.* Novi sad: Vojvodjanka-Regional Women's Initiative.
11. Grødeland, Åse Berit. 2006.Public perceptions of non-governmental organisations in Serbia, Bosnia & Herzegovina, and Macedonia. *Communist and Post-Communist Studies* 39:221–246.
12. Hamber, Brandon, Liz Ševčenko, and Ereshenee Naidu. 2010.Utopian dreams or practical possibilities? The challenges of evaluating the impact of memorialization in societies in transition. *The International Journal of Transitional Justice* 4(4):397–420.
13. Hamber, Brandon and Richard Wilson. 2002. Symbolic closure through memory, reparation and revenge in post-conflict societies. *Journal of Human Rights*1(1):35–53.
14. McLeod, Laura. 2011. Configurations of post-conflict: Impacts of representations of conflict and post-conflict upon the (political) translations of gender security within UNSCR 1325. *International Feminist Journal of Politics* 13(4): 605–622.

[53] Ni Aolain, 'Advancing Feminist Positioning', 207.

[54] Bell and O'Rourke 'Does Feminism need a Theory of Transitional Justice?', 34.

15. Aoláin, Ní. 2012. Fionnuala 'advancing feminist positioning in the field of transitional justice'. *The International Journal of Transitional Justice* 6(3): 205–228.
16. Obradovic-Wochnik, Jelena. 2009. Knowledge, acknowledgement and denial in Serbia's responses to the Srebrenica massacre. *Journal of Contemporary European Studies* 17(1): 61–74.
17. Obradovic-Wochnik, Jelena 'Serbian civil society as an exclusionary space: NGOs, the public and 'coming to terms with the past. In *Civil Society and Transition in the Western Balkans*, eds. V. Bojcic-Dzelilovic, J. Ker-Lindsay and D. Kostovicova. Basingstoke: Palgrave McMillan, forthcoming 2013.
18. Obradović-Wochnik, Jelena, and Alexander Wochnik. 2012. Europeanising the 'Kosovo question': Serbia's policies in the context of EU integration. *West European Politics* 35(5):1158–1181.
19. Porter, Elizabeth. 2007. *Peacebuilding: Women in international perspective.* London: Routledge.
20. Shepherd, Laura J. 2008. *Gender, violence and security: Discourse as practice.* London: Zed Books.
21. Simic, Olivera, and Kathleen Daly. 2011. One pair of shoes, one life: Steps towards accountability for genocide in Srebrenica. *The International Journal of Transitional Justice* 5:477–491.
22. Spoerri, Marlene and Annette Freyberg-Inan. 2008. From prosecution to persecution: Perceptions of the international criminal tribunal for the former Yugoslavia (ICTY) in Serbian domestic politics. *Journal of International Relations and Development* 11(4):350–384.
23. Subotić, Jelena. 2009. *Hijacked justice: Dealing with the past in the balkans* Ithaca: Cornell University Press.
24. Weaver, James, and Jeanne Colleran. 2011. 'Whose memory? Whose justice? Personal and political trauma in ariel dorfman's. *Death and the Maiden*' *Performance Research: A Journal of the Performing Arts* 16(1):31–42.
25. Zajović, Stašta. 2007. *Transitional justice: A feminist approach.* Belgrade: Women in Black.

Chapter 3
Education and Photography at Tuol Sleng Genocide Museum

Maria Elander

Introduction

How do photographs teach a past that is marked by atrocities? How are photographs invoked to teach and what are the limits of this teaching? These are questions that prompted this chapter. While the questions are relevant for all uses of photographs after an atrocity, they come to the fore in relation to the educational aspirations of the international(ized) Extraordinary Chambers in the Courts of Cambodia, the ECCC, and its usage of the exhibition of mugshots in the Tuol Sleng Genocide Museum.[1]

The Tuol Sleng Genocide Museum in the Cambodian capital of Phnom Penh is a museum, a memorial and an archive. Once a high school, after the Khmer Rouge took over in 1975, it became the site of the S-21 Security Centre, the main security centre in the Democratic Kampuchea. Headed by Kaing Guev Eak, alias Duch, some 14–17,000 persons were taken there to 'confess' their disloyalty to the regime and be punished. Only a handful survived. Shortly after the Vietnamese ousted the Khmer Rouge from the capital, the transformation of the site into a museum began. Tuol Sleng is what Patrizia Violi has called a trauma site: 'neither real museums nor cemeteries, nor places of worship, nor monuments—they are all of these together, and perhaps even more'.[2] For the new regime, the site became important evidence of the Khmer Rouge atrocities: foreign delegations were already in March 1979 guided through the museum so they would testify to the atrocities. But the site is also significant for Cambodians: the public was allowed

---

[1] This chapter is based on research I conducted in Phnom Penh in June and July 2011, enabled by funding through MATS and the Office of Research, Melbourne Law School, as well as by the generous support and help by staff at the ECCC and various NGOs in Phnom Penh.

[2] Patrizia Violi 'Trauma Site Museums and Politics of Memory: Tuol Sleng, Villa Grimaldi and the Bologna Ustica Museum', (2012) 29(1) *Theory, Culture & Society* 36–75, 42.

M. Elander (✉)
Melbourne Law School, University of Melbourne, Melbourne, Victoria 3010, Australia
e-mail: elanderm@unimelb.edu.au

P. D. Rush and O. Simić (eds.), *The Arts of Transitional Justice*,
Springer Series in Transitional Justice 6, DOI: 10.1007/978-1-4614-8385-4_3

access in July 1980, and since then, people have gone there *en masse* searching for relatives, hoping to find their lost loved ones.[3]

Tuol Sleng is distinguished by an almost obsessive conservation, where most has been left intact to stand as 'evidence'. Amongst its most well-known features is its collection of photographs. With meticulous organization, every prisoner was photographed upon entry and some 7,200 photographs have remained.[4] Today, many of these photographs are on display in the museum. Room after room, wall after wall, pictures of men, women and children staring into the camera, with disbelief, terror, surprise, sorrow or in spite.

The museum has come to play an important part in the outreach work of the ECCC. Set up in 2004, the Court has jurisdiction to try 'senior leaders' and 'those most responsible' for the atrocities during the Khmer Rouge regime. Located in proximity to the crimes committed, the Court sees the importance of engaging the larger public that was affected. Around the world, outreach has been increasingly recognized as a key aspect for successful international and hybrid courts,[5] as a channel of information, dialogue and feedback between the court and the affected communities. Outreach at the ECCC has been described to have as primary aims the dissemination of information about the court and about trauma, promoting and facilitating participation in the trials, and organizing public education on the history of the Khmer Rouge regime.[6] For this latter aim of education, the 'flag-ship'[7] is a study tour to Tuol Sleng.

In this chapter, I take a closer look at the usage of the Tuol Sleng Genocide Museum as an *educational* tool, used by an international(ized) legal institution that through its outreach program extends its mission beyond activities in the criminal courtroom—holding those most responsible to account—to a transitional justice project on educating the general public on history. I interrogate what the ECCC considers this educational element holds or is intended to hold; its use of the term suggests that it is something distinct, associated perhaps, but still distinct from

---

[3] David Chandler, *Voices from S-21, Terror and History in Pol Pot's Secret Prison* (Berkeley, Los Angeles, London: University of California Press, 1999) 4, 8.

[4] The Yale Cambodian Genocide Program has a collection of 5,000 photos, but has stated the correct number is uncertain. http://www.yale.edu/cgp/cimgdoc.html. In the MoMA exhibition and an accompanying book, the number is given as 6,000. In August 2012, a collection of 1,200 photographs supposedly from S-21 was given to the NGO DC Cam and these are currently being verified. See Phnom Penh Post 'Mystery Surrounds S-21 Faces', 21 August 2012, http://www.cambodiatribunal.org/sites/default/files/news/Phnom%20Penh%20Post%208-21-12.pdf.

[5] Peter Manning, 'Governing memory: Justice, reconciliation and outreach at the ECCC', *Memory Studies* 5(2) (2011): 167; Norman Henry Pentelovich, 'Seeing Justice Done, The Importance Prioritizing Outreach Efforts at International Criminal Tribunals', *Georgetown Journal of International Law* 39 (2008): 445–495; Janine Natalya Clark, *International War Crimes Tribunals and the Challenge of Outreach*, *International Criminal Law Review* 9 (2009): 99–116; Jaya Ramji-Nogales, 'Designing Bespoke Transitional Justice: Pluralist Process Approach' *Michigan Journal* of International Law 32 (2010): 1–72.

[6] Manning, supra note 6 at 3.

[7] ECCC, Court Report No 32 (January 2011): 1.

other potential aims such as memorialization or remembrance. It is thus the ECCC's own use of 'education' as an aim of its work that sparks this interest.[8]

While outreach at the ECCC is more encompassing than the study tour, and the study tour also includes visits to the Choeung Ek Killing Fields and the ECCC compound,[9] in this chapter, I am interested particularly in the role photographs, as a form of image-making, plays to disseminate a didactic message. The photographs here become a medium of communication between the ECCC and the general public, but they are also mediated by a distinct institution, that is the museum. The photographs held by the Tuol Sleng Genocide Museum cross a number of genres: they were produced as mugshots, meant to identify the criminal of the regime and as such associated with an institution of control; they are portraits, giving them a certain affective status for the surviving loved ones associated with an institution of remembrance; they hang and have elsewhere appeared as forms of art, associated with the institution of gallery; they function as documents or data in archive, holding information about the past; and they are credited with the status of evidence, showing the present what happened in the past, alluring to a legal status. In this chapter, I am particularly interested in the place, crossings and limits of these roles. Transitional justice, as a larger project, is about movement, transition from one place to another. How do photographs partake in this movement? This chapter then aims to tease out the meanings and implications of the reliance upon the Tuol Sleng photographs in a larger narrative of Khmer Rouge atrocities, supported or produced by the ECCC.

The chapter begins with background on Tuol Sleng and its role during the Khmer Rouge and since as a museum. This is followed by brief background on the ECCC in order to link and explain the relevance of a close reading of the pictures in a book on transitional justice. The subsequent sections are a close reading of the photographs at the Tuol Sleng, their genres and placements. The main question of this chapter is then, how do photographs teach—and specifically teach in the context of a legal and social response to a history scarred by atrocity?

S-21 and the Khmer Rouge

On 17 April 1975, the Khmer Rouge entered the Cambodian capital Phnom Penh. This was the start of the three-year and nine-month-long period under the rule of Pol Pot and the Khmer Rouge. As the Democratic Kampuchea, hereinafter DK, the

---

[8] Hence, this chapter does not engage in the debate on the didactic purposes of a trial. For an example of such work, see Lawrence Douglas *The Memory of Judgment, Making law and history in the trials of the Holocaust* (Yale University Press, 2001).

[9] For other works dealing with and analysing outreach at the ECCC, see Rachel Hughes, 'Legal Outreach and the Extraordinary Chambers in the Courts of Cambodia', paper presented at the Historical Justice and Memory Conference, Swinburne University, February 14–17 2012; Pentelovitch, supra note 6; and Manning, supra note 6.

country set itself on a path towards what was meant to be agricultural development but resulted in the death of some 2 million people or one quarter of the population: in purges and through famine and disease.[10]

Part of the Khmer Rouge infrastructure was a system of security centres, of which the most important was S-21. Located in a former high school in Phnom Penh, S-21 appears in the DK records from sometime in September 1975 but rose in significance after Duch took over the management in June 1976.[11] There are records of around 14,000 persons entering S-21, but since the logs from 1978 are incomplete, the total number may be closer to 17,000.[12] Less prison than interrogation and torture facility, S-21 was the place from where the country's counter-espionage and information gathering was run.[13] It was a centre of total control where extensive confessions by each and every 'traitor' were recorded with meticulous precision, producing a bulk of knowledge that was then used to find further 'traitorous elements'. The process of interrogation and production of confession made the process resemble a juridical one, but with the important difference that entering the site assumed guilt. While some died at the site, most were taken to be killed at nearby Choeung Ek, known today as 'the Killing Fields'. A handful survived; almost all due to having unique skills, such as painting images of Pol Pot or sculpturing. But apart from this handful, entering S-21 was a death sentence.

In this paranoid production of knowledge, the demand for meticulous information included identification of every prisoner. Upon entry, each individual had his/her picture taken and the resulting mugshot was then attached to the person's file. The mugshots were taken by a team of six photographers, of whom the best known is its team leader Nhem En.[14] In a way similar to other criminal legal institutions around the world, the mugshot was produced with the purpose of cataloguing and information gathering, inscribing the object with a certain criminality, drawing on perceptions of the camera and photograph to reflect 'truths'.[15]

The Khmer Rouge regime ended in Phnom Penh when Vietnamese forces entered the city on 6 January 1979. Amongst the Vietnamese were a couple of

---

[10] Tom Fawthorp and Helen Jarvis, *Getting Away with Genocide? Elusive Justice and the Khmer Rouge Tribunal* (Sydney: University of New South Wales Press, 2005): 3. For other work on the Khmer Rouge period and its aftermath, see *inter alia* David Chandler, supra note 4; Alexander Laban Hinton, *Why did they kill? Cambodia in the shadow of genocide* (Berkeley, Los Angeles, London: University of California Press, 2005).

[11] Chandler, supra note 4, at 4.

[12] Ibid at 6.

[13] Ibid at 15.

[14] Nhem Ein was identified as one of the six photographers at Tuol Sleng by the journalist Niven in the1990 s. Nhem has since given several interviews, and in 2007, he gave testimony before the ECCC. While Nhem was 'team leader', he only took mugshots and never pictures of diseased. Trial Transcript, Duch trial, 4 Aug 2008, p 107–108.

[15] See John Tagg *Burden of Representation: Essays on Photographies and Histories* (Macmillan Education, London, 1988) 74–76.

photojournalists who, when a couple of days later they were walking around the empty city, stumbled upon an anonymous-looking complex, reeking of decomposing bodies. S-21 had been left in a rush, and on the lower floors, the two men found the bodies of fourteen men recently killed, some still chained to their beds. The men photographed what they had found and notified the officials. During the following days, the Vietnamese along with Cambodian assistants found thousands of documents, mugshots, undeveloped films, notebooks and other DK publications.[16] And as a way to come to grips with what had occurred, the work of transforming the site into a museum began within a couple of months, under the leadership of Vietnamese curator Mai Lam.[17]

The Tuol Sleng Genocide Museum has always had a didactic aim. In its early days, it played an important part in proving to foreigners, in the face of ignorance and some disbelief, that atrocities had occurred. A report dated 1980 from the Ministry of Culture, Information, and Propaganda states that the museum was 'used to show the international guests the cruel torture committed by the traitors to the Khmer people'.[18] Foreign delegations were guided through the museum, and many noted in the museum guestbook that while they had been sceptical at first, they had now been convinced of the atrocities.[19] But the pedagogical aim was also intended for the local population. The Ministry report notes that the museum was an 'important element in educating the masses' as it was open for the public on Sundays.[20] That this educational tone was intentional is also made clear by the main curator Mai Lam, who later explained that 'For seven year I studied…to build up the Museum…for the Cambodian people to help them study the war and the many aspects of war crimes… For the regular people who cannot understand, the museum can help them'.[21]

The ECCC

Although the Khmer Rouge was ousted from Phnom Penh in 1979, fighting between the Vietnamese-supported government and the Khmer Rouge continued throughout the 1980s and early 1990s. In the UN-led peace negotiations in the early 1990s, emphasis was placed on peace, not on accountability, and the Peace

---

16 Chandler, supra note 4, at 1 2.

17 Mai Lam himself is unsure whether it was in February or March 1979. See Chandler, supra note 4 at 5.

18 Quoted in Judy Ledgerwood, 'The Cambodian Tuol Sleng Museum of Genocidal Crimes: National Narrative', *Museum Anthropology* 21(1) (1999): 88.

19 Ibid at 89.

20 Quoted in ibid at 88.

21 Interview by Sara Colm in 1995, quoted in Chandler, supra note 4, at 8.

Accord was left without any mention of responsibility.[22] In 1997, the Cambodian government wrote to the UN asking for assistance in bringing Khmer Rouge leaders to justice. The result was the ECCC. Set up through an agreement between the Cambodian government and the UN that came into effect in 2004, its jurisdiction is limited to 'senior leaders' and 'those most responsible' for the atrocities. The S-21 leader Duch was the first to stand trial, and in 2010, he was found guilty of crimes against humanity and grave breaches of the Geneva Conventions[23] and sentenced by the Supreme Chamber to life imprisonment.[24] The second trial against the three[25] most senior surviving leaders has been severed,[26] i.e. split into several smaller trials, and the first dealing with forced movement of the population and related crimes against humanity began in November 2011.[27]

Outreach

As in other international(ized) courts, the responsibility for ensuring public engagement with the trials is organized at the ECCC through its outreach. During its first year of operating, the ECCC had very little resources for outreach, and consequently, much of it was conducted by local NGOs with which the ECCC was affiliated. Local NGOs like DC Cam, CHRAC, KID, CSD and CDP[28] played key roles in spreading information about the Court to the public.[29] But outreach has

---

[22] With the Paris Peace Accord of 1991, the Khmer Rouge was legitimized and returned to Phnom Penh, but only to leave again before the UN supported elections of 1993. After the elections in 1993, the National Assembly in 1994 passed a law that outlawed the Khmer Rouge. In 1996, a Royal Decree granted high-ranking Ieng Sary pardon. See Suzannah Linton, 'Putting Cambodia's Extraordinary Chambers into Context', *Singapore Year Book of International Law and Contributors* 11 (2007): 200–201; and Jarvis & Fawthorp, supra note 11, for thorough discussions on the peace deal and its aftermath in terms of peace and/or justice.

[23] *Prosecutor v. Kaing Guek Eav alias Duch* (Judgment) (Extraordinary Chambers in the Courts of Cambodia (ECCC), Trial Chamber, Case No 001/18-07-2007/ECCC/TC 26 July 2010) 567.

[24] *Prosecutor v KAING Guek Eav* (Summary of Appeal Judgement) (Case File 001/18-07-2007/ECCC/SC) 3 February 2012.

[25] A fourth person, former social action minister Ieng Thirith, was indicted but in November 2011 found unfit for trial. She was finally released in September 2012.

[26] *Prosecutor v. Nuon Chea, Ieng Sary, Ieng Thirith, Khieu Samphan* (Severance Order Pursuant to Internal Rule 89ter) ECCC Trial Chamber, Case File/Dossier No. 002/19-09-2007-ECCCITC, 22 Sep 2011.

[27] In February 2013, the Supreme Court Chamber annulled the Trial Chamber's severance decision. At the moment of writing, the implications of this annulment are unclear. (*Decision on the Co-Prosecutors' Immediate Appeal of the Trial Chamber's Decision Concerning the Scope of Case 002/01* (Feb. 8, 2013).

[28] Documentation Center of Cambodia, Cambodian Human Rights Action Committee, Khmer Institute of Democracy, Center for Social Development, Cambodian Defenders Project.

[29] Christoph Sperfeldt, 'Cambodian Civil Society and the Khmer Rouge Tribunal', *International Journal of Transitional Justice* 6 (2012) 149–160; Pentelovich, supra note 6 at 470.

become increasingly important part of the ECCC's work as well. In its organizational structure, outreach falls under the mandate of the public affairs section (PAS) and its work includes publication of information material and stickers, a monthly Court Report, radio and television programmes, updating the ECCC Website and organizing public forums around Cambodia.[30] As mentioned in the introduction, while outreach has a general aim of ensuring that the public 'sees justice done', outreach at the ECCC also holds an outspoken didactic component of teaching about the Khmer Rouge and the history during DK.[31] While it is possible that the different sections of the Court (like the two chambers and PAS) disseminate different messages, it is this outspoken didactic component of the outreach program that is of interest here.

Before the ECCC began its outreach work, NGOs like DC Cam and CSD arranged study tours through which they bring villagers to learn more about the DK period and the ECCC. The tours have similar components: a visit to Tuol Sleng Genocide Museum, followed by the Choeung Ek Killing Fields and then finally the ECCC itself where villagers meet with court officials for information and Q and A.[32] In 2010, the ECCC launched its own study tour with the same three stops.[33] During the hectic years of 2010 and 2011, the ECCC brought every Tuesday and Thursday around 300 Cambodians from villages around the country on the tour. By the end of 2010, villagers from all of Cambodia's 24 districts had partaken in the tour, and a year later, the total number of participants reached some 26,000 Cambodians.[34]

For the PAS of the ECCC, the educational study tour can 'help improve understanding about what happened during Democratic Kampuchea, especially among the young people'.[35] The tour is meant to partake in a transitional justice project by both stimulating knowledge and creating the possibility of closure. In the words of the ECCC Court Report, the tour is 'educational for many participants as well as cathartic for some.... Many participants found their relatives and friends in the mugshots at Tuol Sleng'.[36] While the wording in a report can be examined in terms of self-representation and the need for a particular self-representation in a particular social climate, the repeated references to education only become more interesting. So how is this education achieved?

[30] ECCC website, Public Affairs Section, http://www.eccc.gov.kh/en/office-of-administration/public-affairs accessed 20 July 2012.

[31] See e.g. ECCC Court Report 31 (November 2010) 4.

[32] DC Cam journal *Searching for the truth*, 1st quarter 2006; on CSD see Manning, supra note 6.

[33] ECCC *Court Report* 33 (February 2011): 4; DC Cam director Youk Chhang in 2011 explained that they changed focus, from the masses to working closely with a smaller number of very active or local leaders, as well as students, all of whom then disseminate information. Personal communication, 5 July 2011.

[34] ECCC *Court Report* 46 (February 2012); contradictory data in ECCC *Court Report* 32 (January 2011).

[35] ECCC *Court Report* 31 (November 2010): 4.

[36] ECCC *Court Report* 32 (January 2011): 3.

The study tour starts already on the eve before travelling to the sites in Phnom Penh, when villagers are shown shorter documentaries in collaboration with Bophana Audiovisual Resource Centre[37] about the ECCC. This is followed by full-length documentaries such as *About my Father*, which follows the journey of a civil party, or *Red Weddings*, which focuses on forced marriage under the Khmer Rouge.[38] Since February 2012, screenings have also included a video of Duch's apologies made in Court, the dissemination of which was part of the reparations awarded in the judgment.[39] Villagers then get up before dawn to head towards Phnom Penh. There, they are taken to the Tuol Sleng Genocide Museum, the Choeung Ek Killing Fields and the ECCC compound on the outskirts of the city. If there are hearings on that day, the group will attend the trial during a session. While there is a guide accompanying the groups to Tuol Sleng and Choeung Ek to answer any questions by the participants, much of the time the participants are left to explore on their own.[40] Nonetheless, that the purpose of the tour is educational is without a doubt. As former chief of Public Affairs Reach Sambath explained, 'I hope this Study Tour helps them understand the history of their own country better so that they can help to prevent the regime reoccurring'.[41] So what then is it a visitor to Tuol Sleng encounters? How is visiting the museum and seeing the photographs a learning experience?

Learning from Photographs

The Tuol Sleng Genocide Museum consists of four main buildings standing in a semicircular formation with some smaller buildings in the middle. Immediately after entering the site, the visitor is faced with the graves of the 14 bodies found by the Vietnamese. Further away, a few trees offer some shade, and at the end of the courtyard, a small tourist shop and a mobile wagon store offer visitors cold drinks or one of the many academic and journalistic books on the Khmer Rouge. Much of the site has been left intact, in particular buildings A and C. In building A, visitors can enter the rooms where the Vietnamese journalists found bodies still shackled. The beds to which prisoners were chained are still there, the floor is still stained with blood (it is said the stench was horrifying for a long time),[42] while the walls hold the pictures the photojournalists took. Similarly intact, building C consists of a lower floor with tiny brick cells where individuals were kept and upper floors

[37] www.bophana.org.

[38] Both are Bophana film productions. See e.g. ECCC *Court Report* 31 (November 2010); Manning, supra note 6; Hughes, supra note 10.

[39] ECCC *Court Report* 47 (March 2012): 1.

[40] See Hughes, supra note 10; Manning supra note 6.

[41] Reach Sambath in ECCC *Court Report* 31 (November 2010) 4.

[42] Ledgerwood, supra note 19, at 90.

with large rooms where groups of individuals were shackled. Buildings B and D appear more curated, with additional exhibits. In building D, visitors find more equipment used for torture, a photograph of the dismantled (in 2006) map of skulls and paintings made by survivor Vann Nath, depicting daily life with its torture. Finally, building B, on which the rest of this chapter will primarily focus, exhibits most of the photographs, that is, the portraits or mugshots.

Archive

The photographs were produced as mugshots within a criminal institution as part of Angkar's process of producing knowledge about the population and its traitorous elements. The original photographs were of smaller size and attached to the person's file. In the last days of the regime, the photographs and files were for some reason separated, leaving most photographs unnamed and in disarray. The photographs were found by the Vietnamese when they entered the compound and its importance as data information was not missed. Tuol Sleng itself holds in its possession some six thousand photographs. As an archive, the collection was until the 1990s considered particularly precarious and scholars debated on how accessible it was. The archive, with its photographs and its documents, was thought to hold information not only about the Khmer Rouge period but also about individuals who were involved in political life during the 1980s.[43] In this way, the archive was understood as a reservoir of images that held revealing truths.

Today, the Tuol Sleng photography archive is held at a number of places. During the early 1980s, human rights activist David Hawk worked in the archive and made copies of the photograph negatives. In 1991, Cornell University was accorded the responsibility of cataloguing and preserving the documents, which by then had come under the jurisdiction of the Ministry of Culture. It also built a microfilm repository, of which one set was taken to Cornell, while one remained with the museum.[44] Shortly after, in 1994, Yale University together with DC Cam, then an affiliate of Yale but today an independent NGO, began a massive project of documenting and studying the atrocities, including the Tuol Sleng archives, under the Cambodian Genocide Project. As a result, today anyone with Internet can access some 5,000 of the photographs through Yale's depository, searching through the database under keys such as 'clothing', 'age' and 'gender'.[45] The archive continues to grow as more photographs are found. The Cornell project was

---

[43] See discussions between Shawcross, Becker and Vickery in Rachel Hughes, 'The abject artefacts of memory photographs from Cambodia's genocide' (2003) 25 *Media, Culture and Society* 23–44, 26–27.

[44] Ibid 26–27; Chandler, supra note 4 at 11; Cornell University, Division of Rare and Manuscript Collections, Tuol Sleng Prison Confessions and Photographs, #4883. http://rmc.library.cornell.edu/ead/htmldocs/RMM04883.html.

[45] See http://cgp.research.yale.edu/cgp/cts/ctssearch.jsp.

at the time thought to be complete, but in 1995, a collection was presented to DC Cam by the Cambodian Ministry of Interior, and since then, hundreds of documents have made their way to DC Cam.[46] Just recently, a former employee of the 1980s government donated 1,400 photographs.[47] As archival documents, the photographs continue to attract attention from scholars from Cambodia and internationally. Finding a photograph means a trace to someone who most likely simply disappeared and thus becomes *evidence of a crime*—of torture and killing and more generally the photographed's fate.

As portraits, many of the six thousand photographs are on display at Tuol Sleng Genocide Museum. Shortly after their discovery, the photographs and negatives were developed and enlarged by an East German team, and since 1980, a collection has been presented at the museum.[48] In this way, the photographs moved from being mugshots in a criminal institution, to data in an archive and to portraits in museum exhibits.

In this format, the photographs have since 1994 been on display at exhibits around the world. In 1997, New York Museum of Modern Art attracted much attention to its exhibition. Hundred photographs were selected for this exhibition, but were despite their existence at Tuol Sleng presented as having been 'discovered' by two American journalists in an attempt to 'rescue an endangered photographic archive'.[49] In this way, the collection became part of a narrative of Westerners rescuing precarious and problematic material. At the same time, the exhibition raised questions regarding the positioning of photographs produced as part of an atrocity within an institution of modern art. Is a gallery the most appropriate location or do they belong in a place more associated with politics or history? In this instance, the curators focused on their emotive qualities and did not contextualize their existence in relation to, for example, the US engagements with the region that immediately preceded the Khmer Rouge regime.[50]

Museum Exhibition

Back in Tuol Sleng, upon entry of building B, the visitor is soon surrounded by the photographs, on the walls as well as on free-standing boards in the room they appear as masses. Most depict a single individual in a typical mugshot manner: a man, woman or child sitting down being photographed from chest up facing the

---

[46] Chandler, supra note 4, at 12.

[47] Voice of America, 'Nearly 1,500 Khmer Rouge Prison Photographs Donated to Documentation Center', August 24, 2012.

[48] Chandler supra note 4 at 27.

[49] Niven and Riley's Photo Archive Group, 1993, in Hughes (2003), supra note 46, at 29.

[50] See Hughes (2003) supra note 46, at 36–37 and Rachel Hughes, *Fielding Genocide: Post 1979 Cambodia and the Geopolitics of* Memory (Doctoral Thesis, University of Melbourne, 2006), for thorough discussion on this exhibition.

photographer. In a few, the person is chained to a bystander, and in others, a mother is holding her infant child. Most photographs appear in larger collectives—in rows of six x twelve or more photographs—arranged by a common trait. At first, they appear indistinguishable: the men and women become a mass of faces or what Sontag called 'an aggregate of victims'.[51] As mass, the photographs remain what Barthes called *studium*, horrible 'scenes' that require the 'rational intermediary of an ethical and political culture'.[52]

The pictures initially become one, but looking closer, their individual traits appear. There is a board with young girls, one with young boys, and out of context, they could have been pictures for a school catalogue. I think of my own collection of photographs of classmates in primary school, thinking they look too much the same. It is, to continue with Barthes' terminology, the *punctum* that pulls the viewer closer. Something in the pictures that punctures you, compels you, draws the viewer in, forces you to look closer.[53] One person stares with disbelief, another terrified, a third smiles as if in contempt and a fourth smiles as if trying to soften or persuade the onlooker. They are old men and women, teenagers looking as if coming direct from battle, women and men thin in starvation, women carrying their babies, young girls and young boys–too young to be doing anything other than playing.

The mugshots of a few prominent persons are enlarged and a few are displayed together with harrowing pictures taken after their death. Not all were photographed post-mortem: only if they were prominent and as proof of their death, or if they had died 'by mistake', that is, if the interrogations had been too rough or in the case of only a few, they had managed to commit suicide.[54] But apart from these few photographs of corpses, it is the photographs of the living dead that dominate the museum.

The mugshots are horrifyingly striking in their simplicity. Appearing in a context that has been conserved almost entirely, where today's visitor enters what appears to be the very same room and seeing the very same things as those killed in the 1970s, the photographs are presented as remnants from the past. What appears to be a lack of manipulation—a grainy photograph, a black spot here and lack of light there—makes the pictures appear more real, adding to a perception of authenticity.[55] It is as if the poor quality of the photographs both strengthens their documentary status and intensifies the affective encounter with the photographs.[56]

---

[51] Susan Sontag, *Regarding the Pain of Others* (Picador 2003), 61.

[52] Roland Barthes *Camera Lucida* (Vintage 2000 (1980)) 26.

[53] Ibid, at 27.

[54] Duch Testimony Transcript of trial proceedings, 28 July 2009, 40; Chandler, supra note 4, at 27.

[55] On authenticity and art, see Sontag, supra note 54, at 26–27.

[56] Compare with the US Holocaust Memorial Museum, where 'curators found that they preferred so-called dirty photographs—those marred by scratches, dust, dirt, and generations of copying—that gave the photograph a badge of authenticity.' Barbie Zelizer *Remembering to Forget: Holocaust memory Through the Camera's Eye* (Chicago and London: University of Chicago Press, 1998) 195.

The encounter with the photographs prompts questions over being in one's position as visitor, a viewer. What does it mean to view photographs, produced as mugshots and under horrendous circumstances? Can you look at the photographs without being accused of voyeurism? Or is it only those who can 'do' something, like a doctor performing a surgery, who can avoid being accused of voyeurism?[57] The potential voyeurism is problematic at Tuol Sleng. Here, the visitor faces the prisoner, meets her or his eye and does so from the same position of the photographer. And just as the photographer Nhem En then knew, today's viewer holds the same superior knowledge—that of the imminent death. The visitor's gaze in this way not only witnesses the scene but does so from the position of the former perpetrator. As problematic as this is, viewing the photographs holds something else as well. To look at the photographs has an affective dimension as well that creates a relationship between the image and the viewer. This affective dimension of the photographs has a potential to open up a space for connections, connections between viewers[58] and as such creating communities. I will return again to this affective dimension as the productive limit of the educational and evidential role that the photographs are made to take on.

Evidence

But regardless of a potential of connecting viewers, the ECCC study tour has the more explicit aim of educating the public. So what is it one *learns* from viewing them? Curator Mai Lam envisioned the photographs as standing in as 'evidence' of the crimes of the Khmer Rouge'.[59] Meanwhile, the ECCC Court Report chooses to quote a visitor in one of the study tours, saying that the visit had provided the evidence needed to support stories previously heard.[60] How do the photographs perform as evidence?

Barthes envisioned that photographs hold a unique status as *medium*, as a transfer and transport of the past. While 'language is, by nature, fictional', the photograph 'is indifferent to all intermediaries: it does not invent; it is authentication itself… Photography never lies'.[61] For him, the photograph is a gate to the past. In this way, it is for him, 'at once the past and the real'.[62] Barthes suggests that the power of a photograph is formed in its holding onto, its cleaving to the

---

[57] Ibid at 42.

[58] For a discussion on image and affect, see Alison Young 'The Scene of the Crime: Is there such a thing as "just looking"?' in Keith J Haywar and Mike Presdee (eds.) *Framing Crime: Cultural Criminology and the Image* (New York: Routledge, a GlassHouse book, 2010) 83–97; 84–85.

[59] Ledgerwood, supra note 19 at 89.

[60] Quoted in Court Report No 32, January 2011, 3.

[61] Barthes, supra note 55, at 87.

[62] Ibid, at 82.

past. It is not that photographs reflect a 'real', but instead the eventuality of the photography takes place as the return of a past real. The past forcefully comes to the present, demanding attention.[63] Accordingly, Tuol Sleng seems to assume a self-evident power in the photographs that the evidentiary force is in the photographs themselves, disclosing the past to the viewer. In line with this rationale, information at the museum is remarkably scarce. That is, there are few *words* at Tuol Sleng; very few signs or posts explain or provide further information and context. Initially, guides accompanied all visitors through the museum, but this is far from the case for all contemporary visitors. The ECCC study tour usually consists of two or three hundred villagers, accompanied by a guide who alone simply cannot explain or guide all. Instead, picture upon picture, man, woman, child stare at the visitor, in what seems to be a gesture of giving self-explicatory evidence.

In line with this reliance upon the self-explanatory evidential force, most photographed appear anonymous to the viewer, with the exception of a handful of prominent people. This withholding of identity was a deliberate act by the curator and is even more noteworthy as it stands in contrast to many other atrocity memorials across the globe.[64] While the identity of some remains unknown, others are only anonymous for the museum visitor. During the first years, visitors who identified their loved one would write her or his name directly on the photograph. However, this was disallowed, 'as the photos were "evidence" and the cost of replacing damaged photos were high and at times not even possible'.[65] The ban suggests, as Hughes notes, that the authorities did not consider the museum an appropriate site for personal memorialization and mourning.[66] It also suggests that for the museum authorities, anonymity was not problematic but rather preferred.

But what in the Tuol Sleng photographs is self-evidential? Out of context, the photographs at Tuol Sleng are simple mugshots, depicting a man or a woman that through its format inscribes the subject with criminality. But it is not the criminality of those depicted that is displayed, and the force of the photographs does not lie so much in what they depict. It is rather in their existence. It is the fact that there are masses of mugshots produced in conjunction with the killings of masses of Cambodia's population that is meant to stand as the evidential link between a regime and the deaths. The Tuol Sleng photographs in this way appear as objects 'that have survived actual events as evidence, although they cannot directly "show" those events'.[67] The evidential force of the photographs is rather their production as the mugshots than each image and picture. It is the photograph—its organization and presentation—and not what is depicted that is the remnant of a past atrocity.

---

[63] Ibid, at 88–89.

[64] Violi, supra note 1, at 49.

[65] Hughes (2006), supra note 53 at 189.

[66] Ibid at 189.

[67] Hughes, (2003) supra note 46, 28.

Yet even so, it is necessary to interrogate their status as remnants. Photographs are not equivalent to memories and may just as well act as counter-memory in that it can block and replace what is remembered.[68] It is important to note that remnants like the photographs are always mediated 'not through recollection but through projection, investment, and creation'.[69] The same photograph may very well come to represent multiple and conflicting pasts. Barbie Zelizer in her study of Holocaust photographs found that photographs were republished and reprinted in later decades 'not necessarily because they supported a photo's original publication but because they helped launch new rhetorical arguments'.[70] In this way, photographs anchor arguments in a (represented) past and appear to the contemporary viewer mediated by both this representation and contemporary contexts.

What this points to is the way the space for interpretation opens when the photographs are assumed to 'speak for themselves' and not accompanied by information. Without prior knowledge of the Khmer Rouge regime, the visitor to Tuol Sleng gains little information. For someone like Sontag, this openness comes as no surprise as she argued that understanding can only come from narrations: 'whether the photograph is understood… its meaning—and the viewer's response—depends on how the picture is identified or misidentified; that is, on words'.[71] Her remark prompts us to interrogate the didactic potential in the photographs: if they cannot speak, how can they teach? Without texts accompanying the photographs at Tuol Sleng, they remain caught in a tension between their presentation as evidence and as remnants invoking memories and past. *They are presented as evidence, but lack the contextualizing narration; they stand as remnants but rely on memories created elsewhere.* This tension is also evident in the usage of the photographs by the ECCC. While the ECCC in its report refers to a visitor's encounter with the photographs as 'evidence', the Court itself does not employ the word in relation to the Tuol Sleng collection. In contrast to a museum curator, the meanings attributed to 'evidence' hold particular meanings in a court of law. In a legal context, before an image is accepted as 'evidence', it must be scrutinized, examined and cross-examined. In other words, it relies on context provided through language for its status. Nonetheless, the ECCC uses the photographs in an outreach context as 'historical data', but with the same belief in their self-explanatory force.

---

68 Barthes, supra note 55, at 89.

69 Marianne Hirsch 'Projected Memory: Holocaust photographs in Personal and Public Fantasy' in Mieke Bal, Jonathan Crewe & Leo Spitzer (eds) *Acts of Memory: Cultural Recall in the Present* (Dartmouth College, University press of New England, Hanover, 1999) 2–23, 8.

70 Zelizer, supra note 59, at 187.

71 Sontag, supra note 54, at 29 and 89.

Narration

The presentation of the photographs as self-explicatory and self-evidential leaves the visitor relying on exterior context for their interpretation. By themselves, the collection of photographs does not provide any context, past or current. Concerned about this relation between photographs as evidence and their context, Tagg argued that the evidential force is not so much *in* the photograph as it is 'a complex historical outcome and is exercised by photographs only within certain institutional practices and within particular historical relations'.[72] Put differently, photographs are, like all objects, dependent on their particular history and context, as well as that of the present. Like any other medium or object, the photograph must be interpreted. Alone, a photograph can be read in several ways. The danger is, as Sontag points out, that 'eventually, one reads into photograph what it *should* be saying'.[73] Just as Zelizer noted above how photographs can be used in multiple and contradictory settings, the Tuol Sleng photographs have been used in a number of narratives.

In the West, the Tuol Sleng portraits have come to represent all victims of the Khmer Rouge. Popular media often display the mugshots as illustration of the atrocities, at times accompanied by explanations on how the Khmer Rouge killed all intellectuals and oppositional voices.[74] Visiting Tuol Sleng is thus rarely a first encounter with the photographs.[75] For a Western audience, the site and its photographs have also been presented with reference to the Holocaust, such as in the 1979 documentary, where John Pilger compared the site to a Cambodian Auschwitz.[76] And it remains controversial whether and the extent to which the museum itself was crafted in reference to Holocaust sites and museums. Thion has argued that the museum was constructed with deliberate parallels to Nazi camps 'in an effort to attract part of the sinister charisma of Auschwitz'.[77] Even if the museum is not a direct copy of Western Holocaust museums, in his research on curating atrocity museums, Mai Lam visited Germany, Russia, France and Czechoslovakia. Additionally, East German specialists with expertise in Holocaust memorials assisted in building Tuol Sleng.[78] Inexplicit, or at times explicit, Nazi references in

[72] John Tagg *The Burden of Representation, Essays on Photographies and Histories* (Macmillan Education, London, 1988) 4.

[73] Sontag, supra note 54 at 29.

[74] e.g the CNN documentary Scream Bloody Murder. Also see Sontag supra note 54 at 60. I have discussed this further in Maria Elander 'The Victim's Address: Expressivism and the Victim at the Extraordinary Chambers in the Courts of Cambodia', *International Journal of Transitional Justice* 7 (2013) 95–115.

[75] See Edkins discussing the implications of the attributes in Jenny Edkins, 'Exposed Singularity' (2005) 9(4) *Journal for Cultural Research* 359–386, 367.

[76] *Year Zero: the Silent Death of Cambodia* (1979).

[77] Thion 1993 in Ledgerwood, supra note 19, at 89.

[78] For a discussion see Ledgerwood, supra note 19 at 89.

this way inevitably fill in for that which is left to speak for itself at the museum with pre-conceived understandings of who is killed in mass purges.

In Cambodia, the references to Nazism along with the institutional connections to Vietnam have prompted long-standing debate over 'authenticity'.[79] But here, the mugshots also take part in another narrative. Ledgerwood has argued that Tuol Sleng plays an important part in the state narrative established during the 1980s on the Khmer Rouge period. In this narrative, a 'glorious revolution' was 'hijacked' by a 'handful of sadistic, genocidal traitors'—the 'Pol Pot-Ieng Sary clique'.[80] At the museum, this narrative of a responsibility that lies only with a few collapses time and space, and effectively silences any differences during the period and amongst areas or groups.[81] In this vein, a few of the enlarged photographs are accompanied by signs in Khmer, and the English and French translations attribute guilt over the atrocities to the Pol Pot-Ieng Sary clique. This identification of a few 'prominent' victims—and only these—who became 'martyrs' for the (future) regime, also meant that the public could safely identify a relative as having been purged at S-21, without questions or suspicions about loyalties during the DK period.[82]

In addition to these narratives, the recent usage of the Tuol Sleng photographs in educational tours by an international(ized) court places the photographs in yet another narrative with its own logic and rationale. Here, it is a criminal law context where there is only room for perpetrators and victims (and potential witnesses), creating a dichotomy of subjects. An early report by DC Cam on its study tour points to both the representational aspect and the linkage between memory and the ECCC in that 'This tour… not only allow permits villagers to see with their own eyes how the Cambodian genocide is remembered by others across the country, but also because it incorporates the role of the victim in the tribunal'.[83] By using the photographs and the museum in its outreach work, the ECCC picks up the pre-established narrative but authorizes and further enforces it.

The Perpetrator and the Victims

The way that the photographs are presented as self-evidential currently relies upon their anonymous appearance. This anonymity has meant that fewer questions are asked about the people who were killed at S-21. Consequently, it has also meant fewer questions about why a regime killed so many of its own—its own people but also people who were more or less devoted Khmer Rouge. It serves to repeat that the

---

[79] Ibid.

[80] Ibid. at 82 and 91.

[81] Ibid at 82 and 83, building on Vickery's Standard Total View.

[82] Hughes, supra note 53 at 141.

[83] DC Cam *Searching for the Truth* (2006, 3rd quarter) 18.

vast majority of those smashed at S-21 were lower and middle range Khmer Rouge cadres. The anonymous mugshot does not reveal that the boy was a soldier fighting for the Khmer Rouge but accused of treason, that the man suddenly named in a 'string' as a CIA/KGB informer was a local leader or that the woman allegedly 'destroying the revolution' by stealing some fallen fruit in the forest was a hard-working farmer, believing in the cause.[84] Additionally, 151 of those killed were former staff at S-21.[85] Smashed, having fallen victim to the paranoia of the regime, but at one time also its supporter. This aspect of the victims of the S-21 is mostly silenced or brushed over. For some, this 'masking' of the background of those killed is even what ensures the site is an 'authentic marker of the genocide'.[86] In this logic, there are only perpetrators and victims, no one in between and no one both.

This silencing of the complexity of the victim–perpetrator dynamic is enforced by the ECCC. As a criminal law institution, it is based on the finding and allocation of responsibility. But as an international(ized) institution, its jurisdiction is strictly limited. ECCC's jurisdiction only covers *senior leaders* and *those most responsible*. This focus only on a few is repeated in one of the most persistent messages by the ECCC, repeated particularly in its outreach work: 'ordinary Khmer Rouge have nothing to fear;'[87] responsibility lies only with a handful of men and no one else needs to worry. In this vein, people in former Khmer Rouge strongholds like Pailin have been encouraged by ECCC representatives during the study tour to file complaints or become civil parties, emphasizing that also former Khmer Rouge cadre can be victims.[88] In this rush to victimhood, it is not that previous participation as Khmer Rouge is repressed, but that it cannot be narrated by the ECCC as responsibility and therefore must be disavowed. As form of disavowal, the reliance upon the anonymous photographs at Tuol Sleng then is not surprising: rather than to complicate, to encourage questions on how and why people not only fall victim to but also participate in atrocities, the ECCC reinforces a narrative where responsibility and guilt lie only with a few of the leaders, architects or 'masterminds' and everyone else is a victim. This articulation of mass victimization is close to the state narratives produced during the 1980s, where the responsibility of a few 'traitors' caused the victimization of all.

---

[84] All common reasons for perceived 'treason'. CIA/KGB came to mean any foreign agency and often had nothing to do with the US or Soviet.

[85] Duch judgment, supra note 24, at 141.

[86] For example, Lisa M. Moore, '(Re) Covering The Past, Remembering Trauma: The Politics Of Commemoration At Sites Of Atrocity', *Journal of Public and International Affairs* Spring (2009) 53.

[87] Manning supra note 6, at 2.

[88] Ibid at 10.

Conclusion

Outreach has become an increasingly important aspect of the work by international(ized) courts and tribunals. In working for a thicker transitional justice,[89] outreach is presented as a useful forum for involving more people and posing more difficult questions. But with an outspoken aim of education, such as that of the ECCC outreach program, also comes the responsibility of narrating history for now and future generations.

With its limited resources, the educational outreach at the ECCC relies upon pre-existing places such as Tuol Sleng. In Tuol Sleng, the ECCC finds an institution where images traverse genres, holding different narratives directed to internationals and locals in place while illustrating the mass at the same time as the individual victim. But by using Tuol Sleng, the ECCC is left with an already established narrative, which it then further reinforces with its authority. Thus, rather than complicating the story, the ECCC with its already strictly limited jurisdiction strengthens a narrative that the atrocities were caused by only a handful and left thousands, millions of victims silenced.

This is made possible by the multiplicity of possible readings of the photographs at Tuol Sleng. They appear as mugshots, portraits in art galleries and archival documents. Inside the museum, the photographs hang without comments. Their presentation relies upon an assumed self-evidential force. While viewing them is without doubt disturbing, does this help to 'prevent the regime reoccurring', as hoped by the ECCC outreach? Would not narrating the multiple stories of the victims serve to complicate our image of the victim, force us to learn more, understand more?

As I have argued, images have a capacity to create relationships with and amongst the viewers. Perhaps it is this potential that needs more interrogation and emphasis, rather than a belief in a self-evidential status in providing knowledge or information. Sontag dismissed the possibility that photographs can make us understand. 'Photographs', she said, 'do something else: they haunt us'.[90] Photographs haunt us in the way that they pull us closer, capture us and rupture the flow of our common sense. They can place us both 'before something' and outside, in ecstasis. This haunting, or perhaps rhythmic,[91] character of photographs then suggests a different role than as evidence in a transitional justice project. Photographs may create relationships, connections in a community, but at the same time also make us stop and reflect upon these relationships.

---

89 See e.g. Kieran McEvoy, 'Beyond Legalism: Towards a Thicker Understanding of Transitional Justice' (2007) 34(4) *Journal Of Law And Society* 411–440.

90 Sontag, supra note 54, at 89.

91 On art and rhythm, see Giorgio Agamben, *The Man Without Content* (trans Georgia Albert, Stanford University Press, 1999): 59–63.

Acknowledgments Thanks to Peter Rush for his generous help with this chapter, Rachel Hughes for useful comments on earlier drafts, as well as to Dianne Otto.

Bibliography

1. Agamben, Giorgio. 1999. *The man without content.* (trans Georgia Albert) Stanford University Press.
2. Barthes, Roland. 1980. *Camera lucida* (Vintage 2000).
3. Chandler, David. 1999. *Voices from S-21, terror and history in Pol Pot's secret prison.* Los Angeles: University of California Press.
4. Clark, Janine Natalya. 2009. International war crimes tribunals and the challenge of outreach. *International Criminal Law Review* 9: 99–116.
5. Cornell University, Division of Rare and Manuscript Collections, Tuol Sleng Prison Confessions and Photographs, #4883 http://rmc.library.cornell.edu/ead/htmldocs/RMM04 883.html.
6. DC Cam journal *Searching for the truth,* 1st quarter 2006.
7. Douglas, Lawrence. 2001. *The memory of judgment, making law and history in the trials of the Holocaust.* Yale University Press.
8. ECCC Court Report 31 (November 2010).
9. ECCC Court Report No 32 (January 2011).
10. ECCC Court Report 33 (February 2011).
11. ECCC Court Report 46 (February 2012).
12. ECCC Court Report 47 (March 2012).
13. ECCC website, Public Affairs Section. http://www.eccc.gov.kh/en/office-of-administration/public-affairs.
14. Edkins, Jenny. 2005. Exposed singularity. *Journal for Cultural Research* 9(4): 359–386.
15. Elander, Maria. 2013. The victim's address: Expressivism and the victim at the extraordinary chambers in the courts of Cambodia. *International Journal of Transitional Justice* 7: 95–115.
16. Fawthorp, Tom, and Helen Jarvis. 2005. *Getting away with genocide? Elusive justice and the Khmer Rouge tribunal.* Sydney: University of New South Wales Press.
17. Hinton, Alexander. 2005. *Laban why did they kill? Cambodia in the shadow of genocide.* Berkeley, Los Angeles, London: University of California Press.
18. Hirsch, Marianne. 1999. Projected memory: Holocaust photographs in personal and public fantasy. In *Acts of memory: cultural recall in the present,* eds. Mieke Bal, Jonathan Crewe, and Leo Spitzer, Hanover: Dartmouth College, University press of New England.
19. Hughes, Rachel. 2003. The abject artefacts of memory photographs from Cambodia's genocide. *Media, Culture and Society* 25: 23–44.
20. Hughes, Rachel. 2006. Fielding genocide: Post 1979 Cambodia and the geopolitics of memory. Doctoral Thesis, University of Melbourne.
21. Hughes, Rachel. 2012. Legal Outreach and the extraordinary chambers in the courts of Cambodia. Paper presented at the historical justice and memory conference, Swinburne University, 14–17 Feb.
22. Linton, Suzannah. 2007 Putting Cambodia's extraordinary chambers into context. Singapore Year Book of International Law and Contributors 11.
23. Ledgerwood, Judy. 1999. The Cambodian Tuol Sleng museum of genocidal crimes: National narrative. *Museum Anthropology* 21(1).
24. Manning, Peter. 2011. Governing memory: Justice, reconciliation and outreach at the ECCC. *Memory Studies* 5(2).
25. McEvoy, Kieran. 2007. Beyond legalism: Towards a thicker understanding of transitional justice. *Journal of Law and Society* 34(4): 411–440.

26. Moore, Lisa M. 2009. (Re) Covering the past, remembering trauma: The politics of commemoration at sites of atrocity. *Journal of Public and International Affairs* Spring 53.
27. Pentelovich, Norman Henry. 2008. Seeing justice done, the importance prioritizing outreach efforts at international criminal tribunals. *Georgetown Journal of International Law* 39: 445–495.
28. *Phnom Penh Post* 'Mystery Surrounds S-21 Faces', 21 August 2012 http://www.cambodiatribunal.org/sites/default/files/news/Phnom%20Penh%20Post%208-21-12.pdf.
29. Ramji-Nogales, Jaya. 2010. Designing bespoke transitional justice: Pluralist process approach. *Michigan Journal of International Law* 32: 1–72.
30. Sperfeldt, Christoph. 2012. Cambodian civil society and the Khmer Rouge tribunal. *International Journal of Transitional Justice* 6: 149–160.
31. Sontag, Susan. 2003. *Regarding the pain of others*. Picador.
32. Tagg, John. 1988. *Burden of representation: Essays on photographies and histories*. London: Macmillan Education.
33. Violi, Patrizia. 2012. Trauma site museums and politics of memory: Tuol Sleng, Villa Grimaldi and the Bologna Ustica Museum. *Theory, Culture and Society* 29(1): 36–75.
34. Voice of America. 2012. Nearly 1,500 Khmer Rouge Prison Photographs Donated to Documentation Center. 24 Aug 2012.
35. Yale Cambodian Genocide Program http://www.yale.edu/cgp/cimgdoc.html.
36. Young, Alison. 2010. The scene of the crime: Is there such a thing as "just looking"?. In *Framing crime: Cultural criminology and the image*, eds. Keith J Haywar and Mike Presdee, New York: Routledge, a GlassHouse book.
37. Zelizer, Barbie. 1998. *Remembering to forget: Holocaust memory through the camera's eye*. Chicago and London: University of Chicago Press.

Cases

38. *Decision on the Co-Prosecutors' Immediate Appeal of the Trial Chamber's Decision Concerning the Scope of Case 002/01 (Feb. 8, 2013).*
39. Duch trial, Transcript of trial proceedings, 4 Aug 2008.
40. Duch Testimony, Transcript of trial proceedings, 28 July 2009.
41. *Prosecutor v. Kaing Guek Eav alias Duch* (Judgment) (Extraordinary Chambers in the Courts of Cambodia (ECCC), Trial Chamber, Case No 001/18-07-2007/ECCC/TC 26 July 2010).
42. *Prosecutor v KAING Guek Eav* (Summary of Appeal Judgement) (Case File 001/18-07-2007/ECCC/SC) 3 Feb 2012.
43. *Prosecutor v. Nuon Chea, Ieng Sary, Ieng Thirith, Khieu Samphan* (Severance Order Pursuant to Internal Rule 89ter) ECCC Trial Chamber, Case File/Dossier No. 002/19-09-2007-ECCCITC, 22 Sep 2011.

Chapter 4
Dispersed Truths and Displaced Memories: Extraterritorial Witnessing and Memorializing by Diaspora Through Public Art

Fayen d'Evie

Introduction

Shortly after 6 p.m. on 2 October 2010, in a Toronto stadium usually reserved for soccer matches and the annual Caribbean Carnival, artists Diane Misaljevic and Allan Kosmajac opened their installation *Fragments* to the viewing public. *Fragments* was one programmed element of *Nuit Blanche*, a highly patronized, sunset-to-sunrise contemporary art event. From dusk until dawn, over a cold autumn night, a fluctuating stream of visitors walked around and amongst a grid of over four hundred wooden boxes, spread across the playing field. Each box contained artefacts lent or donated by a person who self-identified as a survivor of genocide, torture, war crimes or other international human rights violations. The Canadian Centre for International Justice (CCIJ), which works with survivors of human rights atrocities to seek legal remedy and bring alleged perpetrators to justice, publicly endorsed and funded Misaljevic and Kosmajac's project and also collaborated in the call for artefacts. The CCIJ stated that their support for *Fragments* was an attempt 'to raise public awareness of a significant issue that is largely invisible in Canada, despite its impacts on the lives of Canadians' and 'to generate understanding of the need to support efforts by survivors to seek justice'.[1]

---

[1] "The Installations: Sightings and Fragments", accessed February 16, 2012, http://www.ccji.ca/nuit-blanche/index.php#ccij.

F. d'Evie (✉)
PO Box 1164 Castlemaine, VIC 3450, Australia
e-mail: fayendevie@gmail.com

P. D. Rush and O. Simić (eds.), *The Arts of Transitional Justice*,
Springer Series in Transitional Justice 6, DOI: 10.1007/978-1-4614-8385-4_4,

Misaljevic and Kosmajac's project thus coalesces two parallel trends in transitional justice: increased concern for engaging diaspora in post-conflict peacebuilding, particularly restorative justice[2]; and a proliferation in initiatives that mobilize post-conflict communities to participate in art-based healing.[3]

Drawing on the experience of the Liberian Truth and Reconciliation Commission, Young and Park have reinforced the significance of systematic programmes to engage diaspora in transitional justice processes, particularly given the following: the numbers of witnesses and alleged perpetrators known to be residing abroad; the economic and political influence of diaspora on conflict dynamics; and the right of refugees to contribute to collective truth narratives concerning gross violations of their human rights.[4] However, as Young and Park also note, financial and practical barriers severely compromise the extent to which diaspora have been able to access formal in-country transitional justice processes. Meanwhile Simić and Daly, have positioned informal, non-state memorializing projects as valuable components of a holistic transitional justice approach, arguing that such projects are uniquely placed to rebuild trust, cultivate solidarity and promote reconciliation, and crucially have the capacity to catalyse interaction beyond ethnic borders.[5] Misaljevic and Kosmajac's *Fragments* project offers fertile space for considering how an extraterritorial art intervention might expand opportunities for diaspora to participate in transitional justice processes. A critical feature of the *Fragments* project is that it was not conceived and implemented by an affected community group or non-profit organization, but rather was conceptualized and driven by Misaljevic and Kosmajac. This paper will therefore examine how certain decisions (explicit and implicit) taken by the artists during the design, development and production of *Fragments* structured the participation of diaspora and explore the implications from a transitional justice perspective.

The Collaborative Art Practice of Misaljevic and Kosmajac

An Enquiry into Personal and Collective Memory, Conflict and Trauma

Since the early 1990s, Misaljevic and Kosmajac have been creating public installations that explore cultural memory and reconciliation and bring attention to

---

[2] See, for example, Laura Young and Rosalyn Park, "Engaging Diasporas in Truth Commissions: Lessons from the Liberia Truth and Reconciliation Commission Diaspora Project," *The International Journal of Transitional Justice* Vol. 3 (2009): 344.

[3] See, for example, Olivera Simić and Kathleen Daly, "One Pair of Shoes, One Life': Steps Towards Accountability for Genocide in Srebrenica," *The International Journal of Transitional Justice* Vol. 5 (3) (2011): 489.

[4] Young and Park, 344.

[5] Simić and Daly, 489.

the experiences of survivors of conflict and human rights abuse. Their earlier collaborative works concentrated on the war in the former Yugoslavia and its aftermath. Kosmajac was born in Canada, but moved to Sarajevo as a child. He returned to Canada the summer of his eighteenth birthday, one year before the war broke out in the former Yugoslavia. He describes his compulsion to interrogate individual and collective memories of the war in terms of a sense of a responsibility as diaspora: ‘I felt a duty, because I wasn’t there, to accentuate it and not let it slip away.’[6] Misaljevic is of Bosnian/Croatian descent and was born and raised in Canada. She has discussed her interest in the Balkan conflict as the prerogative of second-generation survivors, akin to French artist Christian Boltanski’s preoccupation with holocaust post-memory.[7]

In 2004, Misaljevic and Kosmajac presented *Memento Mori*, an immersive video and sound installation, in the Church of the Holy Trinity in Toronto.[8] *Memento Mori* critiqued the media’s exploitation of the war in Sarajevo and underscored the media’s reliance on sweeping explanatory narratives. In 2005, Misaljevic and Kosmajac deepened their inquiry into individual and collective memory through a mixed media installation, *Faith in Facts* (2005). Providing a poetic mimicry of the destruction of cultural memory, the artists projected a slide of books that had been damaged during the bombing of the National Library in Sarajevo. At the outset of the exhibition, the artists stained the slide with a fungal mould, cultivated from a soil sample from Sarajevo. During the course of the exhibition, the mould gradually disintegrated the photographic image, acting as a metaphor for the decay of civility and the temporal sullying of individual memory.[9]

In early 2010, Julie Stewart, a school friend of Misaljevic who worked for the CCIJ and had followed the artists’ successive projects, approached them about developing a work that dealt with victims of atrocity and indicated that funding could be made available from the CCIJ.[10] Misaljevic and Kosmajac had periodically discussed expanding their work beyond a focus on the conflict in the former Yugoslavia, and therefore responded positively to Stewart’s suggestion. Inspired by the post-memory installations of Boltanski and also Colombian artist Doris Salcedo, Misaljevic and Kosmajac conceptualized an ambitious series of interconnected artworks. The Canadian artists conceived of the *Fragments* installation as a temporary memorial site for grieving and the public acknowledgement of suffering and also proposed a companion *Sightings* project (in which billboard-sized images of *Fragments* participants would be mounted on public transit

---

6 Allan Kosmajac, email message to author, February 28, 2012.

7 Ralf Beil, *Boltanski.Time*. Ostfildern: Hatje Cantz Verlag, 2006.

8 “Memento Mori”, accessed November 8, 2012, http://www.44art.ca/Site_11/Memento_Mori.html.

9 “Faith in Facts”, accessed November 8, 2012, http://www.44art.ca/Site_11/Faith_in_Facts.html.

10 For her role in catalysing the project, facilitating funding and assisting implementation, Julie Stewart is credited on certain project documentation as a collaborating artist.

platforms) to act as a counterpoint to the normal invisibility of survivors' experiences in the public sphere. Misaljevic and Kosmajac also planned a website that would integrate and augment the two projects and act as a longer term virtual space, allowing participants and the broader public to engage with the works beyond the time frame of the physical installations.

Meta-structures and Micro-truths

In early 2010, Misaljevic and Kosmajac produced and distributed invitations to participate in *Fragments* in both physical formats (flyers and posters) and electronic formats (email, Facebook and website announcements). They invited survivors of genocide, torture, war crimes and other international human rights violations, as well as families of murdered or disappeared persons, to donate or loan up to five personal artefacts that could either 'represent their past experiences, or their experiences of living with these memories even now they have found refuge in Canada.'[11] The artists provided examples of suitable artefacts (such as clothing, documents and photographs) but also welcomed 'any object of personal relevance.'[12] The invitations explicitly stated that the artefacts would be displayed at Lamport Stadium as part of a 'collective art installation.'[13] The artists committed to return the artefacts after the exhibition had finished. Misaljevic and Kosmajac also offered to photograph any items that survivors felt were of too much sentimental value to lend or donate and include these photographs in the installation in place of the physical artefacts.

Stewart and a colleague from the CCIJ, Johanna MacDonald, volunteered to mobilize survivors and their communities to donate artefacts. In total, 418 individuals lent or donated artefacts to the *Fragments* installation including the following: a family passport photo used by a refugee to escape Chile's Pinochet dictatorship; a train ticket to Auschwitz (see Fig. 4.1); a necklace that a Mexican man was wearing the day he and his wife were kidnapped and tortured by Los Zetas cartel; a stone commemorating the murder of a family member in Colombia; a book that a Tamil man read repetitively while in a Sri Lankan prison; and a letter written by a concentration camp survivor from Bosnia-Herzegovina, delivered by the Red Cross to inform his family he was alive (see Fig. 4.2). Although Misaljevic and Kosmajac initially welcomed any artefacts of relevance, during the process of collecting the artefacts they imposed two strict constraints: the objects should fit within a box of $14 \times 14 \times 3$ inches; and they should not contain explicit imagery of torture or violence, in order to avoid re-victimizing participants.

[11] Diane Misaljevic and Allan Kosmajac, "Fragments" (unpublished poster, 2010).

[12] Misaljevic and Kosmajac, "Fragments."

[13] Misaljevic and Kosmajac, "Fragments."

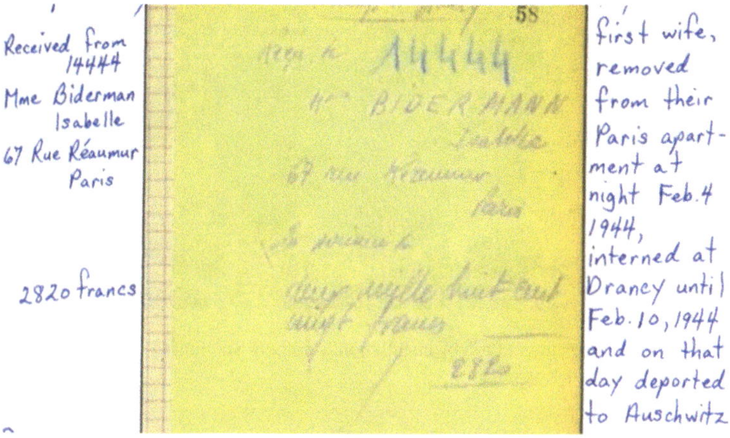

Fig. 4.1 Box 612: Train ticket to Auschwitz. Image courtesy of Allan Kosmajac

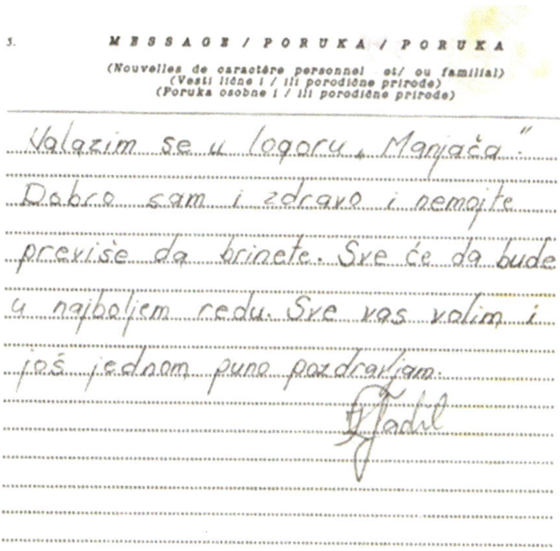

5.

MESSAGE / PORUKA / PORUKA

(Nouvelles de caractère personnel et/ ou familial)
(Vesti lične i / ili porodične prirode)
(Poruka osobne i / ili porodične prirode)

Nalazim se u logoru „Manjača".
Dobro sam i zdravo i nemojte
previše da brinete. Sve će da bude
u najboljem redu. Sve vas volim i
još jednom puno pozdravljam.
Fadil

Fig. 4.2 Box 492: 'I am in the Manjaca camp. I am good and healthy and don't worry too much. Everything will be OK. I love you all and send greetings once more, Fadil'. Image courtesy of Allan Kosmajac

In essence, through their invitation and subsequent instructions, Misaljevic and Kosmajac had presented a conceptual mechanism to place individual memory narratives, associated with specific traumatic events, within a collective framework. By inviting the submission of artefacts (rather than performative witnessing or audio–video recordings of testimony), the artists structured these micro-narratives as primarily object-based. Misaljevic and Kosmajac also asserted an egalitarian treatment of the object-narratives, by limiting the artefacts submitted by a participant to those that would fit within a single wooden box of a specified size,

Fig. 4.3 *Fragments*, documentation of installation, Lamport Stadium, Toronto, October 2, 2010. Image courtesy of Allan Kosmajac

inferring that each participant's narrative would be accorded equal visual weighting.

Misaljevic and Kosmajac did not attempt to filter the submitted artefacts in terms of validity or merit, nor did they seek to confirm whether every participant had legitimate claim to identify as a victim of human rights abuse. Consequently, and in spite of the involvement of the CCIJ and organization's focus on the legal accountability of perpetrators of human rights abuse, the *Fragments* project cannot be considered as a mechanism for forensic truth recovery. However, Misaljevic and Kosmajac's project could certainly be regarded as part of a more holistic approach to truth recovery and reconciliation. Fischer has argued that due to the practical limitations to prosecution in instances where large-scale human rights violations have occurred, reconciliation and conflict transformation can only emanate from a holistic approach to truth recovery, in which forensic truth recovery is complemented by the following: narrative truth (storytelling by victims and perpetrators, in which personal truths are communicated to a wide public); dialogical truth (truth of experience is established by interaction, discussion and debate); and healing or restorative truth (documentation of truth and acknowledgement which accords dignity to victims and survivors).[14] As conceived by Misaljevic and Kosmajac, the *Fragments* project combined elements of each of these processes: the call for artefacts invited object-based storytelling of personal micro-truths; the exhibition context offered a concrete opportunity for interaction, discussion and debate; and the project meta-structure was explicitly intended to produce a temporary memorial site for grieving and the public acknowledgement of the experiences (and losses) of survivors (Fig. 4.3).

[14] Martina Fischer, "Transitional Justice and Reconciliation: Theory and Practice," in *Advancing Conflict Transformation: The Berghof Handbook II*, ed. B. Austin et al. (Opladen/Framington Hills: Barbara Budrich Publishers, 2011), 411.

Materializing Memory

Narrative accounts of identity argue that a coherent self-narrative enables a person to order experiences, create meaning and exercise agency, and that trauma can shatter this self-narrative, leading to a feeling of estrangement and impeding one's capacity for effective agency.[15] French writer and Auschwitz survivor Charlotte Delbo described this estrangement with eloquence: 'Auschwitz is so deeply etched in my memory that I cannot forget one minute of it… I live next to it. Auschwitz is there, unalterable, precise, but enveloped in the skin of memory, an impermeable skin that isolates it from my present self… The skin enfolding the memory of Auschwitz is tough. Even so it gives way at times, revealing all it contains… the suffering I feel is so unbearable, so identical to the pain I endured… and I feel death fasten onto me.'[16] Psychoanalyst Dori Laub, also a survivor of the Holocaust, contends that a person who has experienced the trauma of a concentration camp is not naturally capable of extricating himself or herself from the event in order to describe it from the perspective of an external observer.[17] Following Laub's argument, witnessing is necessary not only so that others come to know what took place, but also more fundamentally, so that the witness can come to know and process the experience.

Extending Deleuze's theory of encountered signs, Bennett suggests that witnessing functions as an interface: 'a process of coming into view… bound up in a dynamic encounter with a structure of representation'.[18] Since diaspora by definition live in cross-cultural settings, one of the critical structural challenges of extraterritorial witnessing is that participating diaspora will tend to be operating within unfamiliar social and linguistic codes. As diasporic author Vikram Seth noted, 'this can heighten the sense of a derivative existence, in which one's tongue is perpetually "warped"'.[19]

In relation to the experiences of diaspora visiting Western museums, Lynch has observed that handling objects from a museum collection can enable diaspora to overcome the initial feelings of intimidation, to work through anxieties and alienation, to exercise remembrance, to process emotions stirred by the events remembered and to negotiate new narratives of self. In her analysis, Lynch recounts Klein's theory of internal object relations, which established the significance of the internalization of early relationships in the formation of the self, and

[15] Jacqui Poltera, "Self-narratives, Story-telling, and Empathetic Listeners", *Practical Philosophy* 10:1 (2010): 65.

[16] Charlotte Delbo, *Days and Memory* (Evanston: The Marlboro Press: Evanston, 2001), 2.

[17] Dori Laub, "Bearing Witness or the Vicissitudes of Listening," in *Testimony: Crises of Witnessing in Literature, Psychoanalysis and History,* ed. S. Felman and D. Laub, (New York: Routledge, 1992), 57–74.

[18] Jill Bennett. *Empathic Vision: Affect, Trauma and Contemporary Art* (Stanford: Stanford University Press, 2005), 31.

[19] Vikram Seth, *A Suitable Boy* (New York: Harper Collins, 1993), 68.

traces the expansion of Klein's theory to external objects.[20] In particular, she highlights Winnicott's investigation into the importance of manipulating external objects for symbol formation in children and Winnicott's determination that adults 'continue throughout life to use objects to develop, review, and redevelop a sense of self'.[21] Lynch's research was motivated by a concern that traditional museum norms may amplify the innate disconnection felt by diaspora, and also by a conviction that museums have a responsibility to use their collections to build ethical and social relationships. She urges museums to adopt constructivist approaches to learning and to develop opportunities for diaspora 'to 'do' things with objects… to use what is available to us in exploring the world—to 'play', in much the same way as an artist does.'[22] In this context, Lynch quotes Ybarra-Frausto's (1994) observation (based on the strategies of so-called Rasquachismo or Chicano diaspora artists) that sorting through objects allows 'syncretism, juxtaposition and integration… self-conscious manipulation of materials or iconography… the manipulation of… artefacts, codes and sensibilities.'[23]

Adapting Lynch's analysis, it could be argued that by emphasizing object-narratives and privileging a visual lexicon, Misaljevic and Kosmajac lessened some of the structural impediments associated with cross-cultural verbal witnessing. The artists provided a framework that allowed diaspora to review their sense of self and their feelings and recollections related to trauma and survival through the handling and manipulation of objects; significantly, this process was carried out in private, prior to the submission of the artefacts. Echoing Lynch's treatment of Ybarra-Frausto, Misaljevic and Kosmajac could be considered as artist–curators (and as artist–archivists, as will be discussed presently). Although Misaljevic and Kosmajac maintained artistic proprietary over the project, their conceptual framework delegated certain artistic decisions to the participating diaspora, who sorted through objects, sifting and handling, processing juxtapositions, and isolating materials and iconography to convey, through a visual lexicon, a selected self-narrative to a public audience.

In their invitation text, Misaljevic and Kosmajac had urged survivors to submit artefacts that represented either past experiences or contemporary experiences of living with memories of the past. In this way, diaspora were directed to select objects that could serve as mnemonic devices; artefacts that would materialize memory, providing a connection both physical and existential to a remembered past. Some participants submitted objects that they had brought to Canada as mementos of their past, such as a raincoat with distress marks from shrapnel, a

---

[20] Bernadette Lynch, "The Amenable Object: Working with Diaspora Communities through a Psychoanalysis of Touch", in *Touch in Museums: Policy and Practice in Object Handling*, ed. Helen Chatterjee (London: Berg, 2008), 266.

[21] Lynch, "The Amenable Object," 266.

[22] Lynch, "The Amenable Object," 268–269.

[23] Lynch, "The Amenable Object," 269.

school report card, teaching medals, or a child's book covered in scribbles.[24] Others submitted objects that acted as signifiers of a commitment to a present identity and agency that had evolved beyond victimhood. For example, a survivor of the Rwandan genocide submitted a pamphlet for Shelter Them, a charitable organization for Rwandan orphans that she had founded with her sister after arriving in Canada.[25] Thus, through the initial instructions guiding participation, diaspora were encouraged not only to frame their object-narratives in terms of the trauma endured, but also to contextualize their pasts, thereby integrating their traumatic past 'into a life with a before and after.'[26]

Archiving Trauma and Indexing Survival

Around fifty of the participating diaspora volunteered to assist in receiving, cataloguing, transporting and installing the submitted artefacts in Lamport Stadium. Misaljevic and Kosmajac had initially considered more intimate venues for the installation and originally favoured a church setting for its resonance with contemplation and memorializing.[27] However, the artists ultimately determined that a more expansive site would allow for wider participation and potentially provide greater impact. Misaljevic and Kosmajac realized that locating their installation in a stadium would evoke references to the adaption of stadiums in varied civil conflicts as structures for detention, torture and execution. Given the artists' cultural backgrounds, they were also aware that their plan to install white pine boxes (containing the artefacts) en masse in a grid across the stadium floor would introduce a reference to grave markers and heighten a connection to the conversion of Sarajevo's Olympic stadium into a cemetery during the wartime siege.

When the *Fragments* installation opened to the public at dusk on 2 October 2010, volunteers were still placing the final rows of boxes of artefacts. Once complete, a visitor could enter the stadium from the level of the bleachers and look down upon a spatial drawing of white grid points contained within the perimeter markings of the football field.

As the visitor descended to the stadium floor, the functionality of the grid points as receptacles emerged, but it was not until the visitor stooped or kneeled beside a

---

[24] "Fragments Box Index", accessed 17 September 2012, http://www.fragments.ca/Site_16/Box_Index.html.

[25] "Josephine Murphy", accessed 17 September 2012, http://www.fragmentsandsightings.ca/Site_14/Josephine.html. Also see "Shelter Them", accessed 26 January 2012, http://www.shelterthem.com.

[26] Susan Brison. "Outliving Oneself: Trauma, Memory and Personal Identity," in *Feminists Rethink the Self*, ed. D. Meyers (Colorado:Westview Press, 1997), 23.

[27] Descriptive details of the installation and artists' recollections of audience response are drawn from electronic communications with Diane Misaljevic and Allan Kosmajac on 28 February, 2012, and 17 September, 2012.

specific box that the artefacts inside came into clear view.[28] Through their choice of site, their consideration of spatial relationships and their use of artefacts and receptacles, Misaljevic and Kosmajac structured an encounter with an architectural archive. While individually, each box suggested a personal visual narrative, collectively, they offered an index of trauma and survival. In this sense, Misaljevic and Kosmajac manifested an archival impulse prevalent in post-war contemporary art, as varied artists have appropriated the archive to critique its status as the official repository of historical memory and its role in entrenching dominant narratives of state power.[29]

By inviting survivors to submit personal artefacts, by choosing not to filter the artefacts other than in terms of size and explicit imagery, and by electing not to verify identities, Misaljevic and Kosmajac allowed an archive to form with a decentred subjectivity. En masse, the boxes reinforced an account of society as constructed of multiple rationalities and context-dependent identities. If as Foucault and Derrida argued, control of the archive is the manifestation of power through the control of memory, then fragmentation of the archive assists in the structural breakdown of assertions of power.[30] From a transitional justice perspective, this splintering opens space for reconsidering the recorded histories and social memories—and indeed, the preserved mnemonic objects—pertaining to a conflict and its aftermath.

However, and crucially, rather than collating plural memories of a singular territorial conflict, the structure of representation of the *Fragments* archive was fundamentally deterritorialized. Wary of politicizing the installation, Misaljevic and Kosmajac had insisted on randomizing the placement of the boxes and took care to avoid ethnic or geo-political segregation. By employing this randomizing strategy and involving diaspora from diverse backgrounds (and also aboriginal survivors of abuse), Misaljevic and Kosmajac encouraged a decoupling of collective memorymaking from national geographies. As the *Fragments* meta-structure prompted participating diaspora to situate their object-narratives alongside those of exiles who had experienced similar traumas, but who came from other conflict settings, the archive provided an index at once sub-national (personal self-narratives) and supra-national (human solidarity).

Levy and Sznaider have proposed the concept of 'cosmopolitan memory' to understand collective memory within the context of a de-territorializing of politics and culture.[31] They suggest that when issues of global concern (such as ethnic cleansing) become part of extraterritorial local experiences (for example, through media representations), new memoryscapes emerge that transcend national

[28] Telephone interview by the author with Dr. Christine Conley, 25 January, 2012.

[29] Hal Foster, "An Archival Impulse," *October,* 110 (Fall) (2004): 3–22.

[30] Michel Foucault, *Archaeology of Knowledge* [Oxon: Routledge, 2002 (1969)]. Jacques Derrida, *Archive Fever: A Freudian Impression* (Chicago and London: University of Chicago Press, 1996).

[31] Daniel Levy and Natan Sznaider, "Memory Unbound: The Holocaust and the Formation of Cosmopolitan Memory," *European Journal of Social Theory* 5(1) (2009): 88–89,100–102.

boundaries and appeal to shared morality, common responsibility and universal human rights. Of course, cosmopolitan appeals of this sort counteract the decentring strategies discussed previously; fragmentation of the archive is displaced by reintegration. By grounding the *Fragments* project within an international human rights discourse, Misaljevic and Kosmajac shepherded the plurality of participants towards mutual identification through survivorhood, and in so doing, asserted their overarching control of the archive.

The Audience and the Spectacle

As discussed previously, Delbo and others have observed that in the aftermath of trauma, a survivor may feel estranged from their own self. Brison proposes that this estrangement can be understood in terms of a breakdown of the survivor's subjectivity in relation to others: 'Victims of human-inflicted trauma are reduced to mere objects by their tormentors: their subjectivity is rendered useless and viewed as worthless.' Accordingly, Herman suggests, 'the traumatic event… destroys the belief that one can be *oneself* even to oneself, in relation to others.' If the self is seen as fundamentally relational, there are important implications not only for understanding the repercussions of trauma but also for considering the role of an audience, which is of particular relevance to a discussion of public art projects such as *Fragments*.

In order to regain subjectivity in the wake of trauma, Brison maintains that survivors need 'an audience able and willing to hear us… Fortunately, just as one can be reduced to an object through torture, onc can become a human subject again through telling one's narrative to caring others… It is not sufficient for mastering the trauma to construct a narrative of it. One must (physically, publicly) say or write (or paint or film) the narrative, and others must see or hear it, in order for one's survival as an autonomous self to be complete.'[32] Psychiatrist Jonathan Shay, drawing on observations from his clinical work with Vietnam veterans suffering PTSD, similarly finds that although a new self-narrative can rebuild the fragmentation of consciousness caused by severe trauma, 'narrative heals… only if the survivor finds or create a trustworthy community of listeners.'[33]

Laub argues that because trauma disrupts conscious remembering, an empathic listener is a pre-condition for the survivor to come to know the traumatic event: 'While the trauma uncannily returns in actual life, its reality continues to elude the subject… [A] process of constructing a narrative, of reconstructing a history and essentially, of *re-externalizating the event…* has to be set in motion. This… can occur and take effect only when one can articulate and *transmit* the story, literally

[32] Brison, "Outliving Oneself," 23, 25, 29.

[33] Jonathan Shay, *Achilles in Vietnam: Combat Trauma and the Undoing of Character* (New York: Atheneum, 1994), 188.

transfer it to another outside oneself and then take it back again'.[34] While Brison and Shay frame an audience as necessary for effective healing, Laub more radically casts the listener as a participant in, and co-owner of, the witnessing process: 'Testimonies are not monologues; they cannot take place in solitude. The witnesses are talking to *somebody*.'[35] Laub also cautions that 'the absence of an empathic listener or… the absence of an addressable other, an other who can hear the anguish of one's memories and thus affirm and recognize their realness, annihilates the story… Moreover, if one talks about the trauma without being truly heard or truly listened to, the telling might itself be lived as a return of the trauma.'[36]

A critical question that emerges from these accounts is how the structural framework of the *Fragments* exhibition may have affected the empathic character of the audience, thereby facilitating or hindering the effectiveness of witnessing and memorializing processes.[37] Although audience numbers were not tracked, Misaljevic and Kosmajac estimate that a few thousand people visited the installation during its twelve-hour life.[38] Misaljevic and Kosmajac recall people entering and exiting the stadium and wandering amongst the boxes of artefacts, some hugging and crying.[39] The artists recognized many participants amongst the visitors, standing beside their own object-narratives in the field of boxes, or watching the reactions of other visitors, or examining the object-narratives of other diaspora. A number of visitors (participants or family/friends/acquaintances of participants) therefore had prior awareness of the conceptual premise of the exhibition and appreciated that the displayed artefacts had been donated by survivors of genocide, torture, war crimes and other human rights violations. However, many visitors had no such contextual knowledge and simply happened across the installation while touring the smorgasbord of exhibitions on offer during *Nuit Blanche*.

Nuit Blanche is a key feature of the City of Toronto's annual programme of events, marketed as a fun, engaging and accessible contemporary art experience:

---

34 Laub, "Bearing Witness," 69.

35 Laub, "Bearing Witness," 70, 71.

36 Laub, "Bearing Witness," 57, 68.

37 In-depth interviews with a comprehensive sampling of participants/audience would be useful to gain insight into this question, but are beyond the scope of this chapter. The present discussion focuses on a theoretical consideration of specific structural conditions in relation to audience empathy. With the assistance of Misaljevic and Kosmajac, the author attempted to interview a range of participants/viewers (non-exclusive categories), but as detailed records of participants and viewers were not kept, only six diaspora (four of whom were from the former Yugoslavia) and one non-diaspora viewer were located who agreed to be interviewed. The author would like to acknowledge and thank Patricio Bascunan, Irfan Cehajic, Midhat Cehajic, Dr. Christine Conley Josephine Murphy, Aldina Muslija and Fadil Kulasic for their willingness to share their recollections of the event.

38 Diane Misaljevic and Allan Kosmajac, electronic communication with the author, 28 February 2012.

39 Allan Kosmajac, telephone interview with the author, 28 February 2012.

'a playful sunset-to-sunrise celebration'.[40] The total economic impact of the 2010 festival is estimated at $34.7 million.[41] Being accepted as part of this high-profile public event enabled Misaljevic and Kosmajac to access the stadium for their installation, but also resulted in *Fragments* being integrated into the *Nuit Blanche* publicity campaign. While this expanded the potential public audience for the installation, it also enmeshed *Fragments* as part of a mass public spectacle, introducing several perils to the cultivation of an empathic audience. Firstly, there is the risk that a visitor touring the *Nuit Blanche* offerings in the spirit of revelry, and unaware of the premise of the exhibition, might have been disinterested or been dismissive or recoiled from the subject matter.[42] If participating diaspora observed such a reaction to their own object-narrative (or even other object-narratives resembling their own), then following Laub, there is a risk that they might have experienced a denial of their subjectivity, and potentially, retraumatization.

Secondly, there is the risk that a visitor who contextualizes *Fragments* as public entertainment might immerse in the aestheticization of trauma, trivializing the witnessing and memorializing processes.[43] It is certainly conceivable that, for some viewers, the theatricality of the *Fragments* installation might have been heightened by the dusk-to-dawn setting, the stadium location and its political references, and also the resemblance of the rows of artefact boxes to an abstracted cemetery. In his analysis of spectator responses to distant suffering, Luc Boltanski proposes that a spectacle of suffering is distinguished by a politics not of action but of 'observation of the unfortunate by those who do not share their suffering, who do not experience it directly and who, as such, may be regarded as fortunate or lucky people.'[44] He also argues that an enthusiasm of sentiment from a spectator may entrench identification of the perceived sufferer as a victim, and may also distract: 'The affected spectator is in danger of swamping the statement, of being too prominent… We no longer know anything about the unfortunate who takes second place as it were, but we know all the feelings he provokes in the spectator.'[45]

While it is possible that some visitors may have responded to the *Fragments* installation with the extremes of emotion described earlier (on the one hand, dismissal or revulsion; on the other, a perverse fascination or exploitative fetishism), it should be emphasized that nearly five hundred diaspora participated in the project. Consequently, and as reported by the artists, a significant proportion of the visitors were either participants or friends/relatives of participants, which provided a pool

[40] "Nuit Blanche," http://www.scotiabanknuitblanche.ca/about/event-history.html, accessed 4 September 2012.

[41] "Nuit Blanche."

[42] Luc Boltanski, *Distant Suffering: Morality, Media and Politics* (Cambridge: Cambridge University Press, 1993), 12.

[43] Boltanski, *Distant Suffering*, 12.

[44] Boltanski, *Distant Suffering*, 3.

[45] Boltanski, *Distant Suffering*, 98.

of viewers more likely to be caring and empathic. As a result, there was considerable scope for interaction amongst diaspora during the exhibition, acknowledging one another's object-narratives and sharing in in situ reflection on memories and experiences (manifesting Fischer's notions of dialogical truth and restorative truth[46]). However, in this context, a separate risk arises if, following Laub, an empathic person acting as a witness-to-witnessing becomes a co-owner of the traumatic event: 'through his very listening he comes to partially experience trauma in himself.[47]' Laub cautions that a conscientious listener can be subject to a flood of affect, which can stimulate defensive reactions such as a sense of paralysis, outrage, anger, withdrawal, numbness, awe, fear and/or hyperemotionality.[48] In situations where the witnesses-to-witnessing have experienced past trauma, as with the inter-diaspora audience interaction in *Fragments,* there thus exists real potential for the witnessing process itself to re-traumatize. This introduces a key limitation of public art projects as witnessing processes, since in most cases, due to pressures of time and finance, coupled with inadequate human resources (and principal actors proficient in art practice rather than psycho-social services), such projects are ill suited to precautionary and/or reflexive management of participant retraumatization.

Against Closure

After Auschwitz, Adorno decried the making of art as barbaric: 'too metaphorical… and too beautiful to confront history'.[49] Adorno's position was challenged by Joseph Beuys, who utilized abstraction and performative propositions to process a personal critique of trauma and to challenge the conventions of monumental memorialization.[50] Successive generations of artists have expanded the counter-monument discourse, arguing in favour of the absent memorial, the disembodied memorial and the unrealizable memorial. Underpinning such proposals have been concerns that traditional monuments, in attempting to provide a locus for public memory, bury events beneath layers of national myth and iconography, and perversely, divest the public of the obligation to remember: 'rather than preserving public memory, the monument displaces it altogether, supplanting a community's memory-work with its own material form.'[51]

---

[46] Fischer, "Transitional Justice and Reconciliation: Theory and Practice," 411.

[47] Laub, "Bearing Witness," 57.

[48] Laub, "Bearing Witness," 72–73.

[49] Eric Kilgerman, "Reframing Celan in the Painting of Anselm Kiefer," in *Visual Culture in Twentieth Century Germany: Text as a Spectacle*, ed. Gail Finney (Bloomington: Indiana University Press, 2006), 269.

[50] Gene Ray, "Joseph Beuys and the After-Auschwitz Sublime," in *Joseph Beuys: Mapping the Legacy*, ed. Gene Ray, (New York: D.A.P., 2001), 60.

[51] James Young, *At Memory's Edge: After-Images of the Holocaust in Contemporary Art and Architecture* (New Haven: Yale University Press, 2000), 94.

James Young, a member of the German commission guiding the design of a Memorial for the Murdered Jews of Europe, has traced the charged debate over the selection process, including accusations that the government's support for the citizen-driven initiative stemmed from a desire to 'unshoulder their memorial burden… A finished monument would, in effect, finish memory itself.' The design ultimately selected, and approved by the Bundestag, was a modification of a proposal by architect Peter Eisenmann and artist Richard Serra that shares certain aesthetic features with Misaljevic and Kosmajac's *Fragments*. In its original form, Eisenmann and Serra's design comprised a field of four thousand pillars, sized from ground level to sixteen feet high. Young notes that the proposal 'at once echoed a cemetery, even as it implied that such emblems if individual mourning were inadequate to the task of remembering mass murder.'[52] Eisenmann and Serra's design was particularly praised for its response to the closure dilemma, as it 'proposed multiple, collected forms arranged so that visitors have to find their own path… not an answer to memory but an ongoing process, a continuing question without a certain solution.'[53] However, the commission also expressed concerns that the taller pillars would dwarf visitors, enveloping them in a 'labyrinth maze' and thus would be unsuited to contemplation. As Young relates, Eisenmann[54] responded to this feedback by downscaling the size of the pillars to human-proportioned forms, such that '[v]isitors and the role they play as they wade knee-, or chest- or shoulder-deep into this waving field of stones will not be diminished by the monumental but will be made integral parts of the memorial, now invited into a memorial dialogue of equals.'[55]

Similar to Eisenmann's design, Misaljevic and Kosmajac presented visitors with a field of individual, geometric markers, collated within a mass grid through which a visitor could weave their own path. In this sense, *Fragments* echoed the functionality of Eisenmann's proposal; structuring decentred, personal memorializing processes that counter closure. Indeed, it is arguable that *Fragments* went further than Eisenmann's design by offering a memorializing format that privileged fluidity, multiplicity and subjectivity. First, rather than permanently fixed concrete forms, Misaljevic and Kosmajac supplied wooden boxes that were placed by hand and removed at dawn. Second, not only were visitors able to enter the installation from any side of the grid, but they also had expanded vertical/horizontal lines of approach, such that they could enter or exit the arena from either the height of the stadium bleachers or from the stadium floor. Third, the *Fragments* boxes were sited at ground level, and in contrast to Eisenmann's blank stone pillars, each box contained an individual's object-narrative. To inspect the contents of a box, a visitor was therefore required to bend or kneel, effectively assuming a

[52] Young, *At Memory's Edge*, 206.

[53] Young, *At Memory's Edge*, 206.

[54] Richard Serra withdrew from the process once modifications were requested, citing a threat to his artistic integrity.

[55] Young, *At Memory's Edge*, 210.

contemplative stance in relation to the subjective narrative, which provided for a dialogic encounter between the visitor (with their own historical memories or perceptions) and that particular object testimony.

Of course, the temporary nature of *Fragments* proscribed a discrete memorializing event, and as such, the structure precluded the on-going access to revisit and re-engage that Eisenmann's permanent memorial allowed. However, extending from Young's argument that the meanings ascribed to a monument are mutable ('contingent on the political, historic and aesthetic realities of the moment'), perhaps an opportunity exists for a recursive restaging of *Fragments*. In this way, at certain temporal intervals, participating diaspora might have an opportunity to rearticulate their shifting self-narratives, so that they and the broader public could reconsider the individual and collective narratives of conflict, trauma, survival, exile and social integration, as these evolve over time.

Most initiatives directed at expanding the participation of diaspora in transitional justice processes focus on integrating specific diaspora communities within national or regional frameworks. This norm of engagement structurally excludes diaspora who lack financial resources, political will or the personal capacity to take part in activities outside of their host settlement country and effectively imposes a territorial boundary on memory work. Through their *Fragments* public art project, Misaljevic and Kosmajac have provided a de-territorialized alternative: a mechanism for contextualizing micro-truths within a meta-structure, reinforcing participants' simultaneous identification as survivors, as diaspora and as members of a cosmopolitan social and cultural community. In so doing, Misaljevic and Kosmajac have presented a challenge to the field of transitional justice, opening space for critical reconsideration of prevailing delimitations, in favour of an expanded concept, which better accommodates the fragmentation and dispersal of communities that ensues in situations of mass conflict and violence.

Bibliography

1. Bennett, Jill. 2005. *Empathic vision: Affect, trauma and contemporary art*. Stanford: Stanford University Press.
2. Beil, Ralf. 2006. *Boltanski time*. Ostfildern: Hatje Cantz.
3. Bhabha, Homi K. 1994. *The location of culture*. London: Routledge.
4. Boltanski, Luc. 1993. *Distant suffering: Morality, media and politics*. Cambridge: Cambridge University Press.
5. Brison, Susan. 1997. Outliving oneself: Trauma, memory and personal identity. In *Feminists rethink the self*, ed. Diana Meyers, Alison Jaggar, and Virginia Held, 12–39. Boulder: Westview Press.
6. Canadian Centre for International Justice. 2012 The installations: Sightings and fragments. http://www.ccji.ca/nuit-blanche/index.php#ccij. Accessed 16 Feb 2012.
7. Delbo, Charlotte.1990. Days and Memory. Trans. Rosette Lamont. Marlboro: Marlboro Press.
8. Deleuze, Gilles. 1989. Cinema two: the time image. Trans. Hugh Tomlinson and Robert Galeta. London: Athlone Press.

9. Derrida, Jacques. 1996. *Archive fever: A Freudian impression*. Chicago and London: University of Chicago Press.
10. Felman, Shoshana, and Dori Laub (eds.). 1992. *Testimony: Crises of witnessing in literature, psychoanalysis and history*. New York: Routledge.
11. Fischer, Martina. 2011. Transitional justice and reconciliation: Theory and practice. In *Advancing conflict transformation: The Berghof handbook II*, ed. B. Austin, M. Fischer, and H.J. Giessmann, 405–430. Opladen/Framington Hills: Barbara Budrich.
12. Foster, Hal. 2004. An archival impulse. October 110(Fall):3–22.
13. Foucault, Michel. 2002. *Archaeology of knowledge*. Oxon: Routledge. (1969).
14. Kilgerman, Eric. 2006. Reframing Celan in the painting of Anselm Kiefer. In *Visual culture in twentieth century Germany: Text as a spectacle*, ed. Gail Finney, 266–284. Bloomington: Indiana University Press.
15. Klein, M. 1984 (1932). *The Psycho-Analysis of Children* (The Writings of Melanie Klein, Vol 2.), ed R. Money-Kyrle. New York: Free Press.
16. Laub, Dori. 1992. Bearing witness or the vicissitudes of listening. In *Testimony: Crises of witnessing in literature, psychoanalysis and history*, ed. Shoshana Felman, and Dori Laub, 57–74. New York: Routledge.
17. Levy, Daniel, and Natan Sznaider. 2009. Memory unbound: The holocaust and the formation of cosmopolitan memory. *European Journal of Social Theory* 5(1): 87–110.
18. Lynch, Bernadette. 2008. The amenable object: Working with diaspora communities through a psychoanalysis of touch. In *Touch in museums: Policy and practice in object handling*, ed. Helen Chatterjee, 261–272. London: Berg.
19. Poltera, Jacqui. 2010. Self-narratives, story-telling, and empathetic listeners. *Practical Philosophy* 10(1): 65–79.
20. Ray, Gene. 2001. Joseph Beuys and the After-Auschwitz Sublime. In *Joseph Beuys: Mapping the legacy*, ed Gene Ray, 55–74. D.A.P.: New York.
21. Scarry, Elaine. 1985. *The body in pain: The making and unmaking of the world*. New York: Oxford University Press.
22. Seth, Vikram. 1993. *A suitable boy*. New York: Harper Collins.
23. Shay, Jonathan. 1994. *Achilles in Vietnam: Combat Trauma and the undoing of character*. New York: Atheneum.
24. Simić, Olivera, and Kathleen Daly. 2011. 'One Pair of Shoes, One Life': Steps towards accountability for genocide in Srebrenica. *The International Journal of Transitional Justice* 5(3): 477–491.
25. Winnicott, D.W. 1971. *Playing and reality*. London: Tavistock.
26. Young, James. 2000. *At memory's edge: After-images of the holocaust in contemporary art and architecture*. New Haven: Yale University Press.
27. Young, Laura, and Rosalyn Park. 2009. Engaging diasporas in truth commissions: Lessons from the liberia truth and reconciliation commission diaspora project. *The International Journal of Transitional Justice* 3: 341–361.

Chapter 5
Ariel Dorfman's *Death and the Maiden* as a Mirror Reflecting the Dilemmas of Transitional Justice Policy

Padraig McAuliffe

Introduction

Ariel Dorfman's play *Death and the Maiden* (*La Muerte y la Doncella*) interacts with transitional justice discourse in two ways.[1] Firstly, it reflects what at the time where inchoate debates about how liberalizing polities should deal with human rights abusers from the *ancien regimes* and foreshadowed debates that would later concern the field. Secondly, staging the play constituted a form of transitional memorialization in itself. Set in 1991 in a country that bears the hallmarks of Dorfman's native Chile emerging into an uncertain democracy after Pinochet's long dictatorship, *Death and the Maiden*'s plot is essentially simple. The traumatized Paulina, who has survived torture and rape at the hands of the dictatorship, is married to Gerardo, a lawyer who has just agreed to serve on a truth and reconciliation commission. Its sole remit after a military self-amnesty is to investigate disappearances and deaths that occurred during the Dirty War. After suffering a blown-out tyre, Gerardo brings home Dr Roberto Miranda, a man whose voice, smell and mannerisms Paulina recognizes as those of a doctor who raped her to the music of the titular Schubert quartet during her incarceration. Because torture lies outside the terms of reference of her husband's commission, Paulina decides to bind the doctor to a chair and try him at gunpoint in the kitchen, coercing Gerardo into participation as Roberto's defence counsel. Roberto is forced to make a confession. The audience is never as certain as Paulina is of Roberto's guilt, even if his vocal tics, references to Nietzsche, possession of Schubert records in his car and inconsistencies in his testimony hint at his culpability.

The play's dramatic tension arises from the interaction of the urgent voice of Paulina as individual who embodies 'the suppressed rage, self doubt and isolation'

---

[1] Ariel Dorfman, *Death and the Maiden* (London: Nick Hern Books, 1991).

P. McAuliffe (✉)
School of Law, University of Dundee, Dundee, Scotland
e-mail: p.g.mcauliffe@dundee.ac.uk

P. D. Rush and O. Simić (eds.), *The Arts of Transitional Justice*,
Springer Series in Transitional Justice 6, DOI: 10.1007/978-1-4614-8385-4_5,

victims feel,[2] the moderation of Gerardo as national mediator of a palpably reversible transition and the resentment of Dr Miranda as reluctant participant. Transition in Chile, as in many Latin American states at the time, was based on a tripartite division between liberalizing groups who pressed for truth and justice to counter decades of authoritarian abuse and denial, those reluctantly ceding power who wished to limit accountability as far as possible, and separating the two camps those moderates who recognize the justice of the former's claim but who were unwilling to jeopardize the transition by pushing too far to achieve it. As a rare example of a play that is both overtly didactic and artistically successful, it is possible to read Paulina, Roberto and Gerardo, respectively, as proxies for these positions in a melodrama as staged, fraught and intricate as the national transition that forms its background. The questions asked are those that have obsessed dramatists since the days of Sophocles and Aristophanes. Is justice the same as revenge? Are there certain harms that are irreparable? Can a society be built on impunity? What happens to the powerless when they achieve power? However, in the context of post-Pinochet Chile, these questions gained an extra resonance. The play not only reflected a global scholarly and political debate that had yet to be fully delineated at the time—it in itself attempted to become part of the national process of reckoning with the past.

Written in three weeks at the start of 1991, the play's significance arises from the fact that it originates from a time when the field of transition justice as a self-conscious policy-making process was in its infancy. Indeed, the phrase 'transitional justice' was coined only later that same year.[3] Transitional justice is a fairly polysemic term but generally refers to a range of approaches that states and non-state actors may use to address systematic human rights violations from the past, including both judicial and non-judicial approaches. As the phrase 'transitional' would suggest, these mechanisms are generally (though not invariably) enacted at a point of political transition from repression or violent conflict to a more liberal, rights-respecting political order. Transitional justice is motivated by this polity's desire to account legally and historically for past abuses and rebuild the shattered social trust the abuses occasioned in the context of a reforming, democratizing system of governance. The core value of transitional justice is the notion of justice, but this remains conditioned by two key variables: how much justice the transitional security balances between the ancient and nouveau regimes will permit, and the priorities and values the resultant transitional justice mechanism(s) emphasize (or are allowed to emphasize). Both variables, namely the security dilemma of a fraught transition and the tension between prosecution and non-judicial mechanisms, provide the discursive and political context of Dorfman's play.

---

[2] James Weaver and Jeanne Colleran. "Whose Memory? Whose Justice?: Personal and Political Trauma in Ariel Dorfman's *Death and the Maiden*," *Performance Research: A Journal of the Performing Arts* 16 (2011):31, 33.

[3] Teitel claims that she coined the phrase "transitional justice" in this year (Ruti Teitel, "Editorial Note – Transitional Justice Globalized," *International Journal of Transitional Justice* 2 (2008): 1, 1.

The Play as a Reflection of Transitional Security Dilemmas

At the time this play was written, the field was still struggling towards even the relatively nebulous degree of self-definition outlined above. The appropriate parameters of accountability, legal retroactivity and due process standards, as well as the normative direction of such processes in the rush of political transitions in Latin America and the Eastern Bloc with the thawing of the Cold War were being explored tentatively at international conferences and in the academy.[4] This was a period when academics and policy-makers were only slowly awakening to the potential for international human rights obligations to override retroactivity concerns and self-amnesty that stymied earlier accountability processes. Indeed, it was only in that year that Orentlicher wrote her seminal article on the necessity of prosecution under international law as a conscious attempt to clarify the issue.[5] While a glut of novels dealing with the South African TRC some years later are valuable in demonstrating the evolving imaginary constructions of transitional justice, *Death and the Maiden* might be considered a 'pre-text' of transitional justice, foreshadowing some of the issues that would later become central to theoretical understandings of the field. The play is frequently name-checked in the literature.[6]

Above all, the play anticipates debates that scholarship and practice would only fully engage with in subsequent years. In particular, it reflects what became widely known as the peace versus justice debate in societies emerging from the shadow of repression or war, where even committed democrats and human rights activists acquiesced to limited criminal sanctions, amnesty and impunity. As Aryeh Neier, one-time Director of Human Rights Watch put it:

> Permitting the armed forces to make themselves immune to prosecution for terrible crimes seems intolerable; yet it also seems irrational to insist that an elected civilian government should commit suicide by provoking its armed forces.[7]

This arose from what Elster calls 'hard constraints' produced by negotiated transitions where accountability is a bargaining chip, with impunity traded for

---

[4] Paige Arthur, "How 'Transitions' Reshaped Human Rights: A Conceptual History of Transitional Justice", *Human Rights Quarterly* 31 (2009): 321, 329.

[5] Diane F. Orentlicher, "Settling Accounts: The Duty to Prosecute Human Rights Violations of a Prior Legal Regime" *Yale Law Journal* 100 (1991): 2537.

[6] For example Alexandra Barahona de Brito, "Truth, Justice, Memory and Democratization in the Southern Cone" in *The Politics of Memory: Transitional Justice in Democratizing Societies, ed.* Alexandra Barahona De Brito, Carmen González-Enríquez and Paloma Aguilar (New York: Oxford University Press, 2001), 119 at 156, Bronwyn Leebaw, "Human Rights Investigation and Dialogue," *Human Rights and Human Welfare* 5 (2005): 71, 78, Vasuki Nesiah, "Resistance in the Age of Empire: Occupied Discourse Pending Investigation," *Third World Quarterly* 27 (2006): 903, 905.

[7] Aryeh Neier, "What Should be Done About the Guilty?", *New York Review of Books*, February 1, 2000, 34 at 34.

justice. It was recognized that insistence on criminal justice could delay a peace that otherwise looked inevitable by 'stiffening the will to resist' of authority figures in negotiations.[8]

Chile, where the play is set, is the example *nonpareil* of this debate. In 1973, a military coup led by the commander-in-chief of the Chilean army, Augusto Pinochet, overthrew the democratically elected leftist government of Salvador Allende. The nature of the crimes committed by this *junta militar* changed over time from massacres in the early years to death squads mid-regime and garden-variety police brutality in the later years, but the most salient feature was the clandestine nature of the resultant human rights violations, which were illegal even under the laws of the junta.[9] Impunity, buttressed by official denial and the acquiescence of rule of law institutions, was the order of the day. The regime change, when it came, was probably the most restrictive of the Latin American transitions to democracy[10]—Pinochet lost at the ballot box by a narrow swing of 4 % in a 1988 plebiscite on his remaining in power. He had a year and a half between then and the handover of power to Patricio Aylwin's left-wing coalition to secure his impunity.[11] The most important feature of this was a sweeping amnesty enacted in 1978 which covered crimes committed in the regime's most brutal period between 1973 and 1978 including murder, injury and kidnapping. Undefeated and unreformed, the military retained a high degree of legitimacy (retaining seats on the National Security Council) and financial independence from the state. Indeed, Pinochet would remain head of the army until 1997. Though Aylwin campaigned for the presidency promising to undo the amnesty and punish human rights violations, Pinochet's famous threat of 'Touch one hair on the head of my soldiers, and you lose your new democracy' meant that any accountability measure would arrive stillborn.[12] Indeed, on two occasions in December 1990 and May 1993 when some measure of justice was mooted at national level, the army engaged in very public mobilizations. In March 1990 when Dorfman wrote this play, Chile might better have been characterized as a 'recovering authoritarian' than a transitional democracy[13]—it is worth remembering that for years after

---

[8] Jon Elster, *Closing the Books: Transitional Justice in Historical Perspective* (Cambridge UK, New York: Cambridge University Press, 2004) at 93.

[9] Mary Helen Spooner, *Soldiers in a Narrow Land: The Pinochet Regime in Chile* (Berkeley: University of California Press, 1999).

[10] Mark Ensalaco, "Military Prerogatives and the Stalemate of Chilean Civil-Military Relations," *Armed Forces and Society* 21 (1995): 255, Jorge Mera, "Chile: Truth and Justice Under Democratic Government" in *Impunity and Human Rights in International Law and Practice*, ed. Naomi Roht-Arriaza (New York: Oxford University Press, 1995), 171.

[11] De Brito, *supra* note 6, at 133.

[12] Jorge Correa Sutil, "'No Victorious Army Has Ever Been Prosecuted….': The Unsettled Story of Transitional Justice in Chile" in *Transitional Justice and the Rule of Law in New Democracies*, ed. A. James McAdams (Notre Dame, London: University of Notre Dame Press, 1997), 123 at 132.

[13] Alison Brysk, "Recovering From State Terror: The Morning After in Latin America," *Latin American Research Review* 38 (2003): 238, 238.

transition, there were still hundreds of political prisoners in captivity. In this climate, Aylwin was limited to creating the *Comision Nacional de Verdad y Reconciliacion* in April 1990 (usually known as the Rettig Commission after its President, Raul Rettig) with a limited remit to investigate political disappearances and extrajudicial executions perpetrated since the coup. Human rights activists criticized the Commission's mandate, which was limited in that it was only allowed to investigate crimes resulting in death, while it could not name perpetrators or even judge their actions. The amnesty remained in force.

This political context forms the backdrop for the play. A climate of fear still pervades—both Paulina and Gerardo visibly blanch when cars come to the house, fearing a visit from the army.[14] The lawyer Gerardo has just been appointed to the national truth commission, but he is acutely aware of its limitations. Fifteen years earlier when Paulina was tortured, Gerardo swore that only criminal justice would suffice as a response ('Some day, my love, we're going to put these bastards on trial.... Your eyes will be able to rove over each one of their faces while they listen to your story').[15] Now, however, he finds himself as one of the key figures of a truth commission he reluctantly recognizes as a shabby compromise. Even though he accepts the merit of publicizing its conclusions (in this he echoes Ignatieff's belief that truth commissions 'can narrow the range of permissible lies'),[16] he acknowledges that the process is 'limited',[17] falling short as it must of his wife's desire for retribution and his own earlier ideals of the rule of law as a young lawyer. Gerardo's participation in, and defence of, the TRC is shot through with the ambivalence Dorfman obviously feels for the impoverished opportunities for justice at the time. Though not dismissive of the value of historical inquiry and somewhat open to the idea of the commission as a necessary bridge between the repressive past and a better future, Gerardo is fully conscious of its inadequacy. His equanimity is born not of a belief in the reconciliatory potential of the commission nor of a rejection of the retributive impulse, but rather out of necessity. Admonishing Paulina for kidnapping Roberto, he claims:

> Do you want these people back in power? You want to scare them so they come back to make sure we don't harm them? You want the times back when these people decided our life and death?[18]

Indeed, Chilean President Aylwin would later concede that the national truth commission was a 'second-best option' to avoid destabilization by the outgoing military leadership.[19] Paulina too resents the restraints of the transition:

---

[14] Dorfman, *supra* note 1, at 1 and 8.

[15] *Id.* at 24.

[16] Michael Ignatieff, "Articles of Faith," *Index on Censorship* 25 (1996): 110, 114.

[17] Dorfman, *supra* note 1, at 6.

[18] *Id.* at 24.

[19] Sutil, *supra* note 12, at 131–133.

> Compromise, an agreement, a negotiation. Everything in this country is done by consensus, isn't it. Isn't that what this transition is all about? They let us have democracy, but they keep control of the economy and of the armed forces? The commission can investigate the crimes but nobody is punished for them? There's freedom to say anything you want as long as you don't say everything you want?[20]

In the later period surrounding the South African TRC, literature, conferences and practitioners would deliberately create a post hoc compensating, explanatory account of truth commissions. Roht-Arriaza argues that the (enforced) emphasis on truth required a retrospective explanatory theory to explain why it was so important,[21] while Gray contends that 'to minimize what is lost in this trade-off, advocates for commissions have developed jurisprudential theories designed to satisfy calls for justice in transitions'.[22] In contradistinction to Gerardo's disappointed legalism, the jurisprudence of justice was augmented and transformed by a willingness to modify and complement legalist impulses by drawing on normative discourse from the fields of ethics, medicine and theology.[23] Whereas at the time Dorfman wrote the play many considered TRCs 'a sop aimed at masking moral defeat',[24] arguments rejecting the morality and legality of TRCs became far less common due to the almost-hegemonic language of reconciliation.[25]

The Play as a Critique of the Modalities of Transitional Justice

Death and the Maiden anticipates these debates in what would later be labelled the 'truth versus justice' debate in its characters' contrasting attitudes to issues of accountability and reconciliation, an unhelpfully dichotomized debate where truth was rather simplistically aligned with reconciliation in contradistinction to a retributive recourse to law and where criminal accountability was narrowly deemed for the totality of justice. These attitudes are dictated not only by their personal beliefs, but by the dramatic situation of Paulina, Roberto and Gerardo as proxies for victims, the accused and the state. In refusing to take sides, Dorfman reminds us of the imperfection of these options in the compromised transitional

---

[20] Dorfman, *supra* note 1, at 26–27.

[21] Naomi Roht-Arriaza, "The New Landscape of Transitional Justice" in *Transitional Justice in the Twenty-First Century: Beyond Truth Versus Justice*, eds. Naomi Roht-Arriaza and Javier Marrizcuena (New York: Cambridge University Press, 2006), 1 at 3.

[22] David Gray, "An Excuse-Centered Approach to Transitional Justice," *Fordham Law Review* 74 (2005-06): 2621, 2688.

[23] Ruti Teitel, "Human Rights in Transition: Transitional Justice Genealogy," *Harvard Human Rights Journal* 16 (2003): 69, 81-82.

[24] Susan Dwyer, "Reconciliation for Realists," 13 *Ethics & International Affairs* 13 (1999): 81, 89.

[25] Richard A Wilson, *The Politics of Truth and Reconciliation in South Africa: Legitimizing the Post-Apartheid State* (Cambridge: Cambridge University Press, 2001), 171.

environment. In examining the interactions of all three, he demonstrates that the lines between what is truth and what is justice are blurred—not only can they be mutually constitutive, but the lack of one can compound the absence of the other.

Even if legal justice was politically permissible, the obvious limitations of the judiciary could only result in a tainted process. As Paulina puts it

> The judges? The same judges who never intervened to save one life in seventeen years of dictatorship? Who never accepted a single habeas corpus ever? Judge Peralta who told that poor woman who had come to ask for her missing husband that the man had probably grown tired of her and run off with some other woman? That judge? What did you call him? A judge? A judge?

Their disillusion with the courts reflected popular disaffection in Chile and was echoed by the later report of the Rettig Commission.[26] Throughout the Pinochet era, the Chilean courts refused *habeas corpus* proceedings, deferred to the decisions of military courts and reflected a deeply conservative ideology.[27] During transition, there was little change in the judiciary's composition or ethos. A few months before the play was written, the Supreme Court held unanimously that the self-amnesty law was not only valid but 'of compulsory application'.[28]

At various points in the play, Gerardo appears to believe in the reconciliatory potential of truth, speaking of the value of the 'moral sanction' his commission will issue,[29] its potential to 'close the book' on the past[30] and its preferability to the sort of untrammelled vengeance Paulina seems to desire.[31] This optimism and equanimity may in fact represent his deepest political convictions,[32] though Butt argues he is motivated more by political ambition than reason.[33] Aritzia similarly chides him for his cool lawyerly efficiency in controlling subversive discourse by extolling the virtues of moderation.[34] The greater ambivalence of Paulina can be

---

[26] "During the period in question, the judicial branch did not respond vigorously enough to human rights violations....this posture taken by the judicial branch during military rule was largely, if unintentionally, responsible for aggravating the process of systematic human rights violations... As a result, the people of this nation still do not have confidence that the judicial branch as an institution is committed to defending their fundamental rights." (Report of Chilean National Commission, 118–119).

[27] Sutil, *supra* note 12, at 126–7 and Lisa Hilbink, *Judges Beyond Politics in Democracy and Dictatorship: Lessons from Chile* (Cambridge: Cambridge University Press, 2007), 5.

[28] Cath Collins, *Post-Transitional Justice: Human Rights Trials in Chile and El Salvador* (Pennsylvania: Pennsylvania University Press, 2010), 102-103.

[29] Dorfman, *supra* note 1, at 11.

[30] *Id.* at 36.

[31] *Id.* at 26.

[32] David Luban, "On Dorfman's Death and the Maiden," *Yale Journal of Law and the Humanities* 10 (1998): 115, 118 and 120.

[33] John Butt, "Guilty Conscience?", *Times Literary Supplement*, February 28, 1992, 22, cited in Cited in Robert A Morace, "The Life and Times of Death and the Maiden", *Texas Studies in Literature and Language* 42 (2000): 135, 143.

[34] Pilar Zozaya Aritzia, "Alternative Political Discourses in Ariel Dorfman's *Death and the Maiden*" *Atlantis* 18 (1996): 453, 454–455.

contrasted with that of Roberto when he becomes the subject of Paulina's more retributive process. At various points, he parrots the convenient reconciliatory political discourse employed by the era's exiting authoritarians, hailing Gerardo as a man 'shutting the door on the divisions and hatreds of the past'[35] and as 'the voice of civilization'.[36] When faced with actual punishment, he pleads the language of repentance and impunity, begging to be left alone with the recriminations of his conscience and the need to end cycles of vengeance:

> I have three children, two boys, a girl. Are they supposed to spend the next fifteen years looking for you until they find you… Oh Paulina, isn't it time we stopped?[37]

However, it is in its treatment of Paulina as victim that the play is most prescient in its treatment of the truth versus justice predicament and the limitations thereof. At a time when theorists, practitioners and statesmen excitedly engaged in debates over punishment and reconciliation, restoration and closure, seeking all the while the best possible solutions to the dilemmas of transition, Dorfman seems to acknowledge the futility of justice for victims in the face of unspeakable brutality. Throughout the drama, Paulina articulates her dissatisfaction at the compromises of transition. In the play's most resonant lines, Paulina rejects the sacrifice of justice and recognition in the interests of mediating political change:

> And why does it always have to be the people like me who have to sacrifice, why are we the ones who always have to make concessions when something has to be conceded, why always me who has to bite her tongue, why?'[38]

However, when given the chance to impose her own accountability, the impossibility of closure and healing become apparent. As Barsky argues, Paulina wants personal liberation from her memories so she can resume her life.[39] The doctor who raped her has polluted Schubert, which in the play serves to represent art, civilization and all that Paulina values most highly, by using it to both facilitate and cloak his brutality.[40] As Motsemme notes, '[v]arious studies exploring the ways ordinary women speak about their traumatic pasts under violent regimes have consistently shown how they tend to place their narratives within everyday lived experience, rather than nationalist concerns'.[41]

At various points in the play, Paulina tests forms of transitional justice to recover this world, only to reject them. It is immediately apparent when Gerardo

---

35 *Id.* at 9.

36 *Id.* at 34.

37 *Id.* at 44.

38 *Id.*

39 Robert F Barsky, "Outsider Law in Literature: Construction and Representation in *Death and the Maiden*," *SubStance* 26 (1997): 66, 86.

40 David Schroeder, "Dorfman, Schubert, and Death and the Maiden," *Comparative Literature and Culture* 9 (2007): 1, 7, Luban, *supra* note 32, at 123.

41 Nthabiseng Motsemme, "The Mute Always Speak: On Women's Silences at the Truth and Reconciliation Commission," *Current Sociology* 52 (2004): 905, 909.

gives the news of his appointment that Paulina rejects the truth commission's limited mandate, evoking scepticism over its narrow remit to investigate violations that end only in death—Gerardo's categorization of only these crimes as those that are 'beyond repair' does not tally with Paulina's lived experience. In this way, the play mirrors an enduring problem of transitional justice, namely the characterization of certain kinds of violence as politically significant (those typically suffered by men) and other forms of violence as outside that difficult boundary (typically suffered, or suffered most, by women such as the sexual violation Paula endured, but also socio-economic and private violence).[42] As Bell contends, men 'predominantly, if not exclusively' negotiate transitions—one can see in the bonhomie of Gerardo and Roberto before Paulina kidnaps him and their collusion over a confession to placate her afterwards the types of elitist compromises that characterize the politics of transitional justice.[43] While men are assumed representative of the identities and interests present in the conflict, women are generally rendered invisible, irrelevant, other.[44] Throughout the play, the feminine voice of the thoroughly domesticated Paulina (she works in the home, makes margaritas and is patronized by her husband) is marked as other, opposed by Gerardo and Roberto's 'disembodied phallic voice of reason'.[45] At various points, both men ruminate on the unpredictability of women[46] and she is variously labelled 'sick', 'prototypically schizoid' and 'mad'.[47] What is perhaps most symbolic of the masculinist transitional discourse of the time is the fact that until Paulina's confrontation with Roberto, Gerardo had never asked her exactly what had happened to her during her torture. On two occasions, he admits that he never wanted to hear about it.[48] Paulina, by contrast, reacts against this indifference or wilful blindness and asserts the inseparability of her sexual anguish from the political anguish of Chile. Over time, women's experience of sexual violence has become better recognized in international law, most notably the statutes of the ad hoc tribunals and the UN Security Council's seminal Resolution 1325 on Women, Peace and Security.[49] National-level responses have also become more responsive than they

---

[42] Vasuki Nesiah, "Discussion Lines on Gender and Transitional Justice: An Introductory Essay Reflecting on the CTJ Bellagio Workshop on Gender and Transitional Justice," *Columbia Journal of Gender and Law* 15 (2006): 799, Fionnuala Ni Aolain, "Political Violence and Gender During Times of Recognition," *Columbia Journal of Law and Gender* 15 (2006): 829.

[43] Christine Bell, "Women Address the Problems of Peace Agreements" in Radhika Coomeraswamy and Dilruski Fonseka (eds) *Women, Peace-Making and Constitutions* (New Delhi: Women Unlimited, 2005), 96.

[44] Fionnuala Ni Aolain and Eilish Rooney, "Underenforcement and Intersectionality: Gendered Aspects of Transition for Women," *International Journal of Transitional Justice* 1 (2007): 338, 342.

[45] Andrew Munro, "Recalling Voice: *La Muerte y la Doncella*," *Ciberletras Journal of Literary Criticism and Culture*," 6 (2002): 1, 3.

[46] Dorfman, *supra* note 1, at 9.

[47] *Id.* at 17, 22, 30.

[48] *Id.* at 5 and 23.

[49] Security Council Resolution 1325, UN Doc. S/RES/1325, 31 October 2000.

were in the early 1990s. However, much remains to be done—Paulina's 'semiotically marked' progression from crouching in the corner on hearing the oncoming car to controlling the action is one that has yet to be fully realized in the world beyond the stage.[50]

Paulina will not be bound by the elitist compromises of men—in rejecting a unified, official discourse of compromise and forgiveness, she instead pursues a policy of individual retribution.[51] She affirms her desire to grant Roberto due process norms, denying Gerardo's claim that she is merely engaged in a revenge mission.[52] However, it soon becomes apparent that while Paulina can adopt the form of criminal trial, the substance of legal justice will elude her—Gerardo convincingly argues that her process replicates the legal abuses of the military regime,[53] while her circumstantial evidence (the memory of voice, mannerisms, shared love of Schubert) would never serve to secure a conviction in a court of law.[54] Paulina discounts legal justice and the wild revenge of raping Roberto (or having Roberto raped) and then appears to settle for truth and acknowledgement:

> I want him to confess. I want him to sit in front of that cassette recorder and tell me what he did—not just to me, everything to everybody—and then have him write it out in his own handwriting and sign it and I would keep a copy forever—with all the information, the names and data, and all the details. That's what I want.[55]

This echoes Nagel's observations on the division that exists between a victim's private, personal knowledge that she suffered a crime and the public acknowledgement that occurs when a person admits he committed it, wherein it becomes publicly sanctioned.[56] So desperate for closure is Paulina that she is willing to kill for it.

GERARDO: There's a problem, of course, you may not have thought of, Paulina. What if he has nothing to confess?
PAULINA: Tell him that if he doesn't confess, I'll kill him............
GERARDO: Paulina, you're not listening to me. What can he confess if he's innocent?
PAULINA: If he's innocent? Then he's really screwed.

However, after Gerardo and Roberto collude on a confession that mirrors Paulina's experience, Roberto's failure to make a genuine admission or demonstrate contrition prompts Paulina to threaten him with death. They freeze and the lights go down before the audience can learn whether she kills him or not. At a

---

50 Aritzia, *supra* note 34, at 453.

51 *Id.* at 456.

52 Dorfman, *supra* note 1, 22–23.

53 *Id.* at 20.

54 Barsky, *supra* note 39, at 78.

55 Dorfman, *supra* note 1, at 29.

56 Quoted in Lawrence Wechsler, *A Miracle, A Universe: Settling Accounts with Torturers* (New York: Pantheon, 1990), 4.

time when scholars and practitioners outlined theories about how trial or truth or restoration could approximate responses, Dorfman demonstrates that ritual and process and compromise have their limits. The rituals and procedures of civilized society, regardless of the ends to which they are directed or how morally compelling their employment is, can never respond adequately or proportionally to systematized past violations of human dignity. In the years since the play, optimism that transitional justice could constitute 'a universe of options for the transformation of society from a killing machine to a humane government' has been tempered by a more humbling acceptance that that no one tool or series of tools could on their own make the decisive shift towards a healed society.[57] It became apparent in even the best-funded and most publicly legitimate mechanisms applied since the play premiered that to pursue transitional justice is to entertain 'the near inevitability of imperfect justice'.[58] The reality is that the crimes that typify accountability between regimes such as the torture Paulina endured require the most severe response, but no punishment or acknowledgement can adequately communicate the appropriate scale of outrage. The experience of Paulina echoes Shklar's position that '[i]t is indeed doubtful that legal provisions can be devised for events of this sort. There are no civilised responses that are fitting, and certainly no legal norms can cope'.[59] Experience since the play's debut demonstrates that the intractable difficulties Dorfman presents do not admit of facile resolution. No state had ever undertaken process of trial that has prosecuted more than a fraction of those culpable. No truth commission was able to disclose what happened to a majority of the victims or secure itself from revisionist attack. No reparations process could adequately compensate more than a fraction of victims. To the suffering of individuals and the destruction of a wider society, transitional justice can only approximate a response, an illusory closure.

The Play as Transitional Justice

Having served as a cultural advisor to President Allende until being forced to leave after the coup, it was to this milieu that the exiled writer Dorfman returned. Various motivations for the play have been attributed by and to him—he cites a family's wilful amnesia over his friend's arrest and torture,[60] the need for a symbolic and public means of ending his exile at a time when many Chileans

[57] David J. Scheffer, "The Tool Box, Past and Present, of Justice and Reconciliation for Atrocities," 95 *American Journal of International Law* 95 (2001): 970, 970.

[58] Neil J Kritz, 'Where We Are and How We Got Here: An Overview of Developments in the Search for Justice and Reconciliation' in *The Legacy of Abuse: Confronting the Past, Facing the Future*, ed. Alice H. Henkin (Washington DC: Aspen Institute, 2002), 21 at 30.

[59] Judith N. Shklar, *Legalism, Morals, and Political Trials* (Cambridge, Massachusetts: Harvard University Press, 1964), 167.

[60] Larry Rohter, "Dorfman's 'Maiden' Cries Out," *New York Times*, March 8, 1992.

viewed migration as merely a personal choice[61] and above all the artist's impulse to engage the cultural processes of transition through a problematization of it:

> 'I felt that *Death and the Maiden* touched upon a tragedy in an almost Aristotelian sense, a work of art that might help a collective purge itself, through pity and terror, in other words to force the spectators to confront those predicaments that, if not brought into the light of day, could lead to their ruin'.[62]

This mission became all the more imperative in a time when a repressive censorship regime continued to punish criticism of Pinochetism with fines and jail sentences.[63] In addition, there was an observable phenomenon of self-imposed censorship by a society that 'denied what was happening in their country out of fear, guilt, confusion and a refusal to confront harsh realities'.[64] Chilean society as a whole appeared undecided on the merits of punishment given the risk it might reverse the social and economic progress being made.[65] Indeed, in the first workshop productions of the play in Santiago in 1991, the cast expurgated elements of the text due to fear of being associated with the play.[66] Because of its truncated remit, the Rettig Commission's report was itself censored in advance[67]—McClennen interprets the play as one about the silences of the real commission, not simply of torture survivors like Paulina but of exiles like Dorfman himself whose experiences would not be acknowledged in its report.[68]Rettig proved the catalyst for transforming Dorfman's 'aesthetic powerlessness'[69] into a self-conscious effort to reflect and influence the relatively muted contemporary debate on the past in Chile.[70] It allowed him to give Gerardo, hitherto an inchoate connubial figure in an as-yet unwritten fiction, a more resonant stake in the drama.[71]

Of course, Dorfman is not the only artist to employ drama to memorialize the past or interrogate the response to it. Because alternatives to current policy are difficult to conceive in the concrete legal world of compromise and power, art is one of the prime sites for counter-proposals. The plastic arts, literature, memorial

---

61 Sophia A. McClennen, "Torture and Truth in Ariel Dorfman's *La muerte y la doncella*," Revista Hispanica Moderna 62 (2009): 179 at 182–183.

62 Afterword in Ariel Dorfman, *Death and the Maiden* (Harmondsworth, Middlesex: Penguin Books, 1994), 74.

63 De Brito, *supra* note 6, at 149.

64 Carolyn Pinet, "Retrieving the Disappeared Text: Women, Chaos and Change in Argentina and Chile After the Dirty Wars," *Hispanic Journal* 18 (1997): 89, 89.

65 Sutil, *supra* note 12, at 123-4.

66 Pinet, *supra* note 64, at 96.

67 *Id.* at 95.

68 McClennen, *supra* note 61, at 183.

69 Morace, *supra* note 33, at 136.

70 "I found the characters trying to figure out the sort of questions that so many Chileans were asking themselves privately, but that hardly anyone seemed interesting in posing in public" (Ariel Dorfman, *The Resistance Trilogy* (London: Nick Hern, 1998), 146).

71 McClennen, *supra* note 61, at 182.

sculpture and poetry have often been employed in the service of critiquing both authoritarianism and its aftermath.[72] Literary and theatrical narrative offer the most valuable corrective to the potentially hegemonic official, public narrative of trials and truth commissions. Teitel posits that there is a distinct normative narrative structure of transitional justice, beginning in tragedy and ending in comic or romantic mode.[73] In the classical understanding, the tragedy is revealed through the process of trial, truth commission or administrative purge before which individual victims testify as proxies or symbols of larger collectives persecuted by the prior regime. She argues that coming to an agreed, official discourse of the past allows for unfavourable and instructive contrast between the liberal nature of the new rule of law and the repressive old lawless regime. As such, national truth commission reports present themselves as tragic accounts that end on a redemptive, comic note, where the burgeoning self-knowledge of victimization buttresses the liberalizing polity against reoccurrence. For example, even though it was implicitly designed to marginalize the experiences of torture survivors and exiles, the preamble to the law creating the Chilean National Commission on Truth and Reconciliation stated that 'the truth had to be brought to light… [because] only upon a foundation of truth [will] it be possible to meet the basic demands of justice and to create the necessary conditions for achieving true national reconciliation'.

The novel or the play, lacking the teleological impetus of the truth commission or trial, is neither directed nor compelled towards redemption, catharsis or even consolation. It can, however, give voice to the unacknowledged victim, to the vindications of the old regime transitional justice seeks to discredit, to the equivocacy and indeterminacy of transition that the truth commission report or trial verdict cannot. For example, in exploring the complex relationship between law and literature in testimony to crimes of apartheid before South Africa's Truth and Reconciliation Commission, Sanders contends that the greater ambiguity the novel allows invites a historical interpretation of its characters' acts exceeding what any commission or court may demand.[74] The novel or play can 'cut deeper' into the history of repression or violence, allowing more nuanced and even divergent understanding of the past, the process itself and the future. Similarly, Dube also finds fictional narratives useful 'precisely because they offer polysemic descriptions of transitional moments', thereby bearing witness to their inherently complicated nature.[75] Indeed, Barsky cites Paulina as a prime example of an 'outsider'

---

[72] Ksenija Bilbija et al (eds) *The Art of Truth-Telling about Authoritarian Rule* (Madison, Wis.: University of Wisconsin Press, 2005).

[73] Ruti Teitel, "Transitional Rule of Law" in *Rethinking the Rule of Law after Communism*, ed. Adam Czarnota et al (Budapest: Central European University Press, 2005), 279 at 288–292.

[74] Mark Sanders, *Ambiguities of Witnessing: Law and Literature in the Time of a Truth Commission*. (Palo Alto: Stanford University Press, 2007), 179.

[75] Siphiwe Ignatius Dube, "Transitional Justice Beyond the Normative: Towards a Literary Theory of Political Transitions," *International Journal of Transitional Justice* 5 (2011):177, 195.

to the legal process who serves as a metaphor for those excluded from the official, national process.[76] Because the Rettig Commission could not encompass the 'forest of narratives' submerged during repressive rule, in telling the symbolically potent stories of Paulina and Roberto, Dorfman was consciously trying to expose the facticity of the redemptive, stabilizing master narrative the Gerardos, Aylwins, Robertos and Pinochets attempted to manufacture.[77] The play ends in the sort of ambiguity a truth commission could never entertain, without repentance from Roberto, catharsis for Paulina or sage guidance from Gerardo for the future.

The purpose of the play was not simply to include the marginalized or subvert the national master narrative. It was also scripted to stimulate conversation about the issues the Chilean public seemed so keen to ignore. Just before the end, a giant mirror descends and audience becomes the fourth actor, 'forcing the members of the audience to look at themselves' for a few minutes. As Schroeder notes, this 'completely eliminates the distance between the audience and the play, making the audience part of the play, through self-consciousness being forced to address the issues of the play as virtual players'.[78] In the absence of a narrator telling the audience what to do or foreclosing available endings, the audience swaps the catharsis of resolution for the indeterminacy of reflection—it must ask itself where it stands on the guilt of Roberto, the pain of Paulina or the equanimity of Gerardo. While the audience stares in the mirror, 'selected moving spots flicker over the audience, picking out two or three at a time, up and down rows'. As McClennen notes, theatre is the most public form of literature and requires the most collective reception—the presumption must be that Dorfman may have intended the spotlights to linger on actual torturers in the audience or, perhaps less debatably, those complicit in the ancien regime.[79] Outside of Chile where the play found remarkably receptive audiences, Butt argues that the audience are ensnared 'in a vast moral trap' and must 'confront choices that most would presumably rather leave to the inhabitants of remote and less-favoured countries: the image of the play itself as a mirror set before the liberal conscience is central to the work'.[80]

If Dorfman's intention was to provoke debate or even a revision of his society's acquiescence to state-sanctioned impunity, he was not entirely successful. Chilean audiences were hostile to the very idea of reopening wounds so recently bandaged and the gender role reversal in the play, while some read it as an attack on the victims.[81] The play was ignored in Chile, 'a resounding failure among the public that it had attempted, secretly and in bad faith, to translate and express', as one critic put it.[82]

---

[76] Barsky, *supra* note 39.

[77] Pinet, *supra* note 64, at 90, 91 and 96.

[78] Schroeder, *supra* note 40, at 8.

[79] McClennen, *supra* note 61, at 185.

[80] Butt, as cited in Morace, *supra* note 33, at 143.

[81] *Id.* at 136.

[82] Brazilian literature critic Idelber Avelar, cited in McClennen, *supra* note 61, at 183.

Less direct and more allegorical works tended to work better,[83] though Collins does suggest that literature has had an impact in mobilizing public opinion towards accountability in the post-transitional context.[84] Not for the first time, Western liberals proved keener to vicariously engage with the vagaries of transition than the community most affected. The play proved immensely popular from the moment of its first foreign production in London in 1991. Soon dubbed 'the international play of the decade', within a year it had spread to forty countries, and was translated and adapted to suit the conditions of other transitional countries.[85] In this, it perhaps mirrored the 'dramatically compressed' temporal trajectory of transitional justice in the same decade as it captured the popular imagination.[86]

Conclusion

Death and the Maiden demonstrates Dorfman's pessimism over transitional justice policy in the earliest years of Chile's transition and his determination to revise the settlement. It is his voice we hear when Gerardo argues with Roberto that justice is impossible on account of the corruption of the courts. However, the passage of time in Chile would show that Paulina's desperate bid to circumvent the limitations of amnesty (what Aguilar calls 'the obsessive persistence of memory')[87] would in the long term prove to represent the trend of history, not her husband's studied stoicism. As the years went by, the compact between the new and old regimes would break down, driven by the campaigns of victims like Paulina and reform of the judiciary by the likes of Gerardo (indeed, early in the play Paulina teases him that he will be a future Minister for Justice).[88] As the Nineties passed into the Noughties, the Paulinas of this world would come together, no longer pursuing individual projects of justice, but instead making collective claims for accountability that would ultimately find willing allies in political parties and a reforming judiciary.[89] As Collins notes, a mix of gradualism and demand inflation coupled with reform of the judiciary in the late 1990s gradually altered the landscape for accountability—the courts began to find exceptions to the amnesty law, shifted its application from pre-emptive invocation at the start of trial to the end once culpability was established and exempted certain crimes from amnesty.[90] Progress towards accountability came less as a result of

---

83 Henry James Morello, "Masking the Past: Trauma in Latin American and Peninsular Theatre" (Phd Diss. University of Illnois, 2006), cited in McClennen, *supra* note 61, at 184.

84 Collins, *supra* note 28, at 131.

85 Morace, *supra* note 33, at 139 and 148.

86 Christine Bell, "Transitional Justice, Interdisciplinarity and the State of the 'Field' or 'Non-Field,'" *International Journal of Transitional Justice* 3 (2009): 5, 6–7.

87 Paloma Aguilar, "Transitional Justice in the Spanish, Argentinian and Chilean Case" (paper presented at Building a Future on Peace and Justice, Nuremberg, 3 June 2007), 32.

88 Dorfman, *supra* note 1, at 4.

89 De Brito, *supra* note 6, at 136.

90 Collins, *supra* note 28, at 81–99 and 124–126.

concerted state action, but rather as a result of periodic 'irruptions' such as cases, anniversaries and the mysteries of private agency.[91] The Pinochet proceedings in Europe in the late 1990s are believed by some to have inspired the judiciary to push for greater accountability, though this is disputed.[92] As the millennium approached, the military began to distance itself from Pinochet, successive left-wing governments became more assertive, and the military code of silence surrounding the old regime began to collapse.[93] By 2002, the first convictions for amnestiable crimes were recorded. In 2009, nearly two decades after *Death and the Maiden* premiered, 782 state agents were indicted or convicted for crimes, even if progress was slow and the amnesty remained intact.[94]

None of this was foreseeable at the time that play was written, however. In teasing out the relation between cultural expression, political transition, and the contours of justice in transitional situations, Dorfman could draw attention to what was lacking in Chile's response to the past. In Paulina, he could give expression to the as-yet inchoate collective voice of victimhood hitherto drowned out by the denials of the Roberto's and the placid accommodations of Gerardo. As the process of genuine accountability in Chile commenced and then accelerated, Morace could plausibly claim that the course of events might strip *Death and the Maiden* 'of virtually all its political and much of its dramatic urgency' and transform it into a mere spectacle.[95] Such judgments are inescapably subjective, but even if the play reflects contemporary Chile and transitional justice discourse less well than it initially did, the play continues to remind us of the dangers of marginalizing suffering, the role of art as a tool of oppression and as a tool of healing and the responsibility of art in holding a mirror up to political bargains. At the root of Dorfman's artistry is a radical uncertainty which allows multiple meanings and implications to live within his final script, but none to dominate except the idea of the imperfectability of justice.

Acknowledgments The author thanks Dr Jamie Rowen and Prof. Peter Rush for their useful comments.

Bibliography

1. Aguilar, Paloma. 2007. Transitional justice in the Spanish, Argentinian and Chilean case (paper presented at Building a Future on Peace and Justice, Nuremberg, 3 June 2007).
2. Aritzia, Pilar Zozaya. 1996. Alternative Political Discourses in Ariel Dorfman's *Death and the Maiden. Atlantis* 18: 453.

[91] Alex Wilde, "Irruptions of Memory: Expressive Policies in Chile's Transition to Democracy," *Journal of Latin American Studies* 31 (1999): 473.

[92] Kathryn Sikkink, *The Justice Cascade: How Human Rights Prosecutions are Changing World Politics* (New York: W.W. Norton & Co., 2011), David Sugarman, "Courts, Human Rights and Transitional Justice: Lessons from Chile," *Journal of Law and Society* 36 (2009): 280.

[93] Morace, *supra* note 33, at 135.

[94] Collins, *supra* note 28, at 138.

[95] Morace, *supra* note 33, at 135.

3. Arthur, Paige. 2009. How 'Transitions' Reshaped Human Rights: A Conceptual History of Transitional Justice. *Human Rights Quarterly* 31: 321.
4. Bell, Christine. 2005. Women address the problems of peace agreements. In *Women, peace-making and constitutions*, ed. Coomeraswamy Radhika, and Fonseka Dilruski, 96. New Delhi: Women Unlimited.
5. Bell, Christine. 2009. Transitional justice, interdisciplinarity and the state of the 'field' or 'non-field'. *International Journal of Transitional Justice* 3: 5.
6. Bilbija, Ksenija et al. (eds). 2005. *The art of truth-telling about authoritarian rule*. Madison, Wis.: University of Wisconsin Press.
7. Butt, John. 1992. Guilty conscience? *Times literary supplement*, February 28, 22.
8. Brysk, Alison. 2003. Recovering from state terror: The morning after in Latin America. *Latin American Research Review* 38: 238.
9. Collins, Cath. 2010. *Post-transitional justice: Human rights trials in Chile and El Salvador*. Pennsylvania: Pennsylvania University Press.
10. De Brito, Alexandra Barahona. 2001. "Truth, justice, memory and democratization in the Southern Cone". In *The politics of memory: Transitional justice in democratizing societies*, ed. Alexandra Barahona De Brito, Carmen González-Enríquez and Paloma Aguilar, 199. New York: Oxford University Press.
11. Dorfman, Ariel. 1991. *Death and the maiden*. London: Nick Hern Books.
12. Dorfman, Ariel. 1998. *The resistance trilogy*. London: Nick Hern.
13. Dorfman, Ariel. Whose memory? Whose justice? A mediation on when and how to reconcile. Paper presented at eighth annual Mandela lecture, July 31, in Johannesburg, South Africa.
14. Dube, Siphiwe Ignatius. 2011. Transitional justice beyond the normative: Towards a literary theory of political transitions. *International Journal of Transitional Justice* 5: 177.
15. Dwyer, Susan. 1999. Reconciliation for realists. *Ethics & International Affairs* 13: 81.
16. Elster, Jon. 2004. *Closing the books: Transitional justice in historical perspective*. Cambridge: Cambridge University Press.
17. Ensalaco, Mark. 1995. Military Prerogatives and the Stalemate of Chilean Civil-Military Relations. *Armed Forces and Society* 21: 255.
18. Gray, David. (2005–2006). An excuse-centered approach to transitional justice. *Fordham Law Review* 74:2621.
19. Hilbink, Lisa. 2007. *Judges beyond politics in democracy and dictatorship: Lessons from Chile*. Cambridge: Cambridge University Press.
20. Ignatieff, Michael. 1996. Articles of faith. *Index on Censorship* 25: 110.
21. Kritz, Neil. 2002. Where we are and How we got here: An overview of developments in the search for justice and reconciliation. In *The legacy of abuse: confronting the past, facing the future*, ed. Alice H. Henkin, 21, Washington DC: Aspen Institute.
22. Leebaw, Bronwyn. 2005. Human rights investigation and dialogue. *Human Rights and Human Welfare* 5: 71.
23. Luban, David. 1998. On Dorfman's Death and the Maiden. *Yale Journal of Law and the Humanities* 10: 115.
24. McClennen, Sophia A. 2009. Torture and Truth in Ariel Dorfman's *La muerte y la doncella*. *Revista Hispanica Moderna* 62: 179.
25. Mera, Jorge. 1995. Chile: Truth and justice under Democratic Government. In *Impunity and human rights in international law and practice*, ed. Naomi Roht-Arriaza, 171, New York: Oxford University Press.
26. Morace, Robert A. 2000. The life and times of death and the maiden. *Texas Studies in Literature and Language* 42: 135.
27. Morello, Henry James. 2006. Masking the past: Trauma in Latin American and Peninsular Theatre. PhD diss., University of Illinois.
28. Motsemme, Nthabiseng. 2004. The mute always speak: On women's silences at the truth and reconciliation commission. *Current Sociology* 52: 905.
29. Munro, Andrew. 2002. Recalling Voice: *La Muerte y la Doncella*. *Ciberletras Journal of Literary Criticism and Culture* 6: 1.

30. Neier, Aryeh. 2000. What should be done about the guilty? *New York Review of Books*, February 1, 34.
31. Nesiah, Vasuki. 2006. Resistance in the age of empire: Occupied discourse pending investigation. *Third World Quarterly* 27: 903.
32. Nesiah, Vasuki. 2006. Discussion lines on gender and transitional justice: An introductory essay reflecting on the CTJ bellagio workshop on gender and transitional justice. *Columbia Journal of Gender and Law* 15: 799.
33. Aolain, Fionnuala Ni. 2006. Political violence and gender during times of recognition. *Columbia Journal of Law and Gender* 15: 829.
34. Aolain, Fionnuala Ni. 2007. Underenforcement and Intersectionality: Gendered aspects of transition for women. *International Journal of Transitional Justice* 1: 338.
35. Orentlicher, Diane. 1991. Settling accounts: The duty to prosecute human rights violations of a prior legal regime. *Yale Law Journal* 100: 2537.
36. Pinet, Carolyn. 1997. Retrieving the disappeared text: Women, chaos and change in argentina and chile after the dirty wars. *Hispanic Journal* 18: 89.
37. Robert F Barsky. 1997. Outsider Law in Literature: Construction and Representation in Death and the Maiden. *SubStance* 26: 66, 86
38. Roht-Arriaza, Naomi. 2006. The new landscape of transitional justice. In *Transitional justice in the twenty-first century: Beyond truth versus justice*, eds. Naomi Roht-Arriaza and Javier Marrizcuena, 1, New York: Cambridge University Press.
39. Rohter, Larry. 1992. Dorfman's 'Maiden' Cries Out. *New York Times*, March 8.
40. Sanders, Mark. 2007. *Ambiguities of witnessing: Law and literature in the time of a truth commission*. Palo Alto: Stanford University Press.
41. Scheffer, David. 2001. The tool box, past and present, of justice and reconciliation for atrocities. *American Journal of International Law* 95: 970.
42. Schroeder, David. 2007. Dorfman, schubert, and death and the maiden. *Comparative Literature and Culture* 9: 1.
43. Shklar, Judith. 1964. *Legalism, morals, and political trials*. Cambridge: Harvard University Press.
44. Sikkink, Kathryn. 2011. *The justice cascade: How human rights prosecutions are changing world politics*. New York: W.W. Norton & Co.
45. Spooner, Mary Helen. 1999. *Soldiers in a narrow land: The Pinochet regime in Chile*. Berkeley: University of California Press.
46. Sugarman, David. 2009. Courts, human rights and transitional justice: Lessons from Chile. *Journal of Law and Society* 36: 280.
47. Sutil, Jorge Correa. 1997. 'No victorious army has ever been prosecuted…': The unsettled story of transitional justice in Chile. In *Transitional justice and the rule of law in new democracies*, ed. A. James McAdams, 123, Notre Dame, London: University of Notre Dame Press.
48. Teitel, Ruti. 2003. Human rights in transition: Transitional justice genealogy. *Harvard Human Rights Journal* 16: 69.
49. Teitel, Ruti. 2005. Transitional rule of law. In *Rethinking the rule of law after communism, ed.* Adam Czarnota et al, 279, Budapest: Central European University Press.
50. Teitel, Ruti. 2008. Editorial note—Transitional justice globalized. *International Journal of Transitional Justice* 2: 1.
51. Weaver, James and Colleran, Jeanne. 2011. Whose memory? Whose justice?: Personal and political trauma in ariel dorfman's death and the maiden. *Performance Research: A Journal of the Performing Arts* 16:31.
52. Wechsler, Lawrence. 1990. *A miracle, a universe: Settling accounts with torturers*. New York: Pantheon.
53. Wilde, Alex. 1999. Irruptions of memory: Expressive policies in Chile's transition to democracy. *Journal of Latin American Studies* 31: 473.
54. Wilson, Richard. 2001. *The politics of truth and reconciliation in South Africa: Legitimizing the post-apartheid state*. Cambridge: Cambridge University Press.

Chapter 6
Enacting Justice: The Role of Dah Theatre Company in Transitional Justice Processes in Serbia and Beyond

Olivera Simić and Dijana Milošević

Dah: Breathing, Creating and Embracing

Dah Theatre (Dah) was created in Belgrade by Dijana Milošević and Jadranka Andjelić in 1991, at the beginning of the fall of ex-Yugoslavia. At the time, Milošević and Andjelić were driven 'perhaps subconsciously, to oppose the destruction with creation; to create, in the midst of a world falling apart, a microcosmos of theatre'[1]. They envisioned that their theatre would last for fifteen to twenty years, but twenty-two years later, Dah is still engaged in vital cultural work.

Although much has changed in the former Yugoslavia in these two decades, many challenges remain the same—a lack of financial support for the work of theatre, for instance, and a determined denial of war crimes committed by one's own ethnic group. At the time when Dah was founded, there was no tradition of independent professional groups, no cultural understanding of what these groups were about and no financial support to enable their existence. Dah was a genuine pioneer in Serbia: it introduced many radically new ideas, including a theatre laboratory, theatre workshops and actor's training. At the time, a civil war was raging in the former Yugoslavia—a war for which the Serbian government of the time had an enormous responsibility. The circumstances in which to develop artistic projects could not have been less favourable. Paradoxically, it was precisely those circumstances that made the existence of Dah intensely meaningful and culturally essential—the theatre's performances acted as a way of opposing the violence that engulfed all of us living in the region at the time.

[1] Dubravka Knežević, 'Do poslednjeg daha', *Scena* no. 5/6, Sept/Dec 1995.

O. Simić (✉) · D. Milošević
Lecturer, Griffith Law School, Griffith University, QLD 4111 Gold Coast, Australia
e-mail: o.simic@griffith.edu.au

D. Milošević
e-mail: dijana.mlsvc@gmail.com

P. D. Rush and O. Simić (eds.), *The Arts of Transitional Justice*,
Springer Series in Transitional Justice 6, DOI: 10.1007/978-1-4614-8385-4_6

The first Dah project, *This Babylonian Confusion*, was a street performance named after Bertolt Brecht's poems. Dah recognized the relevance of Brecht's vision to its own work and used his words (but not characters) to describe the situation in Serbia. In this way, through Brecht, the troupe members could highlight the public silence about the wars raging in Bosnia and Herzegovina (BH) and Croatia—wars that the Serbian government had wholeheartedly denied. *This Babylonian Confusion* was the first play to speak publicly about what was happening in the region. Dah took to the streets with its performance to inform the citizens of Serbia that there was a war waged in their name. One of Brecht's poems, 'When Leaders Speak of Peace', mirrored the situation in Serbia particularly closely, acting as a startling reminder that the nationalist war and slaughter were, in fact, waged *in our name*:

> When the leaders speak of peace
> The common folk know
> That war is coming.
> When the leaders curse war
> The mobilisation order is already written out.[2]

The words of Bertolt Brecht had been carefully chosen by Dah to describe what was happening in Serbia: the Serbian government 'talked' about peace while 'preparing for' and 'engaging in' the war. Such was the resonance produced by Brecht's work, and such was the relevance of his words to the situation in Serbia that many people in the audience asked Dah if they had written the text for performance themselves. Brecht's poem spoke directly to the situation in Serbia, in which there was no narrative about the war because Serbia was not 'officially' at war and the media, controlled and censored by the government, did not report it. Yet, at the same time, the government was issuing drafts for mobilization: overnight, young men were drafted and forcibly conscripted to join the war effort. And at this time too, people began receiving news from their friends and relatives about terrible crimes happening in BH. In this context, Dah believed that it was fundamentally important for people of Serbia to have the war publicly spoken about and acknowledged in public forums and spaces. Dah was the first theatre in Serbia to say out loud what many people denied and did not want to hear about—'we are at war'.

This Babylonian Confusion was the only anti-war street performance to be staged in Serbia at the time. Yet the authors of the play did not intend to create an anti-war performance. At the time, the Dah troupe was working through their deeply personal need to oppose the ubiquitous violence around them. *This Babylonian Confusion* was a scream of rebellion against the silence of the people, the media blockade and the apparent indifference to the suffering of our closest neighbours in BH. It was a scream about the things that everyone knew were

---

2 Bertolt Brecht, 'When leaders speak of peace' in *Selected Poems* (New York: Harcourt Brace, 1975), 133.

coming but no one wanted to talk about. This performance was groundbreaking in both a personal sense and professional sense for Milošević:

> It [the play] marked the way for my theatre and concurrently kept me in the country, because I realised, due to the reaction of our audience, that there is an enormous need to break the silence and to talk about things that were happening. I realised that people around us needed our work and this was an incredible privilege for a young theatre group – to understand, in the very beginning, that its work was indispensable for someone.[3]

This was the beginning of Dah's work on truth, justice and reconciliation. Dah rejects any attempt to be categorized and does not see itself as a representative of an exclusively documentary, feminist or political theatre. It defines itself as a contemporary theatre which draws on the tradition of theatre laboratories and, as such, uses a variety of resources it considers useful—documentary and dramatic materials as well as their own texts—to give the fullest expression to the subject matter they are engaging with. As a troupe, Dah is interested in everyday life; Dah's members use the stage to work through the themes that preoccupy them. History is very important to Dah: its performances seek to create a full-blooded relationship with historical events. While Dah has been established by women and majority of the troupe members are women[4], it does not define itself as a feminist troupe. It also does not define itself as documentary theatre, although two recent performances that engage with the question of our responsibility to the past—*Crossing the Line* and *The Story of Tea*—draw extensively on historical facts and documentary material. In *Crossing the Line*, documentary material is used, for the first time, throughout the entire performance, while *The Story of Tea* incorporates documentary material about the real-life war crime committed in Štrpci.[5]

This chapter is based on Olivera Simić's interview with Dijana Milošević conducted in Belgrade in December 2011, as well as participant observation, email correspondence between the two authors and a series of informal conversations that the two authors have had over the past few years about Dah and its engagement with the themes of transitional justice. In this chapter, we focus on two of Dah's recent performances, *Crossing the Line* and *The Story of Tea*, which take on questions of accountability, truth, past war crimes and reconciliation. Through these two performances, we analyse the role of Dah in transitional justice processes—its work with survivors and the general community, as well as its possible contribution to the ongoing state court war crime trials for past injustices.

---

[3] Personal interview, Dijana Milošević, Belgrade, Serbia, 12 December 2011.

[4] Dah has four women and one man in its troupe.

[5] Members of the Revenges (Osvetnici) military unit, commanded by Milan Lukić, with logistical support from the Federal Republic of Yugoslavia, were responsible for the abductions and then murder of nineteen men on the Bosnian territory. Although Lukić was sentenced to twenty years of imprisonment by ICTY, his indictment did not include the massacre of nineteen men. Women in Black state that this situation exposes the limits of ICTY. Only one person has been charged and accused for this crime, see Dušan Komarčević, *Kreatori zločina i dalje na slobodi*, E-novine, 27 February 2012, available at, http://www.e-novine.com/drustvo/59890-Kreatori-zloina-dalje-slobodi.html (accessed 1 February 2013).

The role of Dah theatre in transitional justice processes.[6]

According to Milošević, dealing with the past is an essential prerequisite for healing and transformation to take place. Theatre plays a powerful role in this process of reckoning with the past, since artists have the power to speak out—and to be heard—in the public domain. As Milošević puts it, 'I feel that we lend our beings and our voices to the people whose voices we do not hear. I think that it is a huge responsibility as well as a privilege to work on these issues'. The Dah ensemble frequently gives interviews to local and international media, and as a result, its members have many opportunities to talk openly about what happened to *us* in the past and what is happening to *us* in the present. As Dolan argues, a theatre has very specific, material consequences, which, combined, produce a political intervention in an effort towards creating cultural change.[7] This cultural change, in turn, comes from people taking responsibility and holding themselves accountable for the events around them. Coming from Serbia and being of Serb origin,[8] the troupe wanted to talk about what was happening around them because of the personal urge felt by its members, but also because Serbia's government had initiated the war. As Milošević points out,

> In our name the most unspeakable atrocities have been committed regardless of the other sides' responsibility for the war. To us, this performance [*Crossing the Line*] was a path towards self-healing and reconciliation with our own people and with people from our former homeland. We are those, who were vulnerable, who felt guilty and who transformed our feeling of guilt into a feeling of responsibility. We are the ones, who lived here and did not support what was happening, but our voices have not been heard. We had an enormous need for our voices to be heard in the name of all those people who had not agreed to and who didn't support what was happening. It is the power of theatre to give that voice, to give voice to the voiceless.

Dah sees itself as a theatre that can open doors to victims to seek justice; it is also a space where people can reconsider their views. As a theatre, it employs techniques that allow the crossing of borders between the rational and the irrational, and between reality and metaphor: these techniques inherent to transformational and devised theatre can at times open up a much larger space for potential reconciliation than formal justice mechanisms. Through its work, Dah crosses not only ethnic lines, but also more insidious lines that divide people, who hold opposing or antagonistic views on a range of crucial matters. Dah's aim is to maintain direct contact with its audience. For this reason, its audience, as a rule, is positioned in a circle or in a way that makes members of the audience mirror each

---

[6] Siddiqui et al. and McNamee chapters in this volume both directly address the role of theatre in transitional justice: the former as a policy issue and the latter as a marker of a form of cultural expression that ties form to affect.

[7] Jill Dolan, *The Feminist Spectator as Critic* (Michigan: University of Michigan Press, 1991), 2.

[8] We would like to emphasize that both authors became aware of their ethnic origins in the beginning of the 1990s with the dissolution of Yugoslavia. As many Yugoslavs, we were raised in communist families where ethnicity was not discussed or in any way celebrated.

other—as in *The Story of Tea, The (play)*. Dah creates a shared space and a specific way of communicating with its audience, where people with different ways of thinking can meet and explore the same issue from different perspectives. Dah does not use the language of political propaganda; it seeks to problematize issues and to explore contradictions within them. Milošević sees Dah as fundamentally a truth-seeking mechanism:

One of the most important functions theatre can perform in the context of transitional justice is to inspire and encourage empathy and solidarity. In Serbia, according to Milošević, many people do not feel empathy towards victims of the recent past. In that sense, theatre can call out directly to peoples' emotions and, as a result, can help people accept what had happened: there is no genuine acceptance of the past without empathy for its many victims. *Crossing the Line* is a good example of the power of theatre to reach people. As Milošević explains,

> I think that the majority of people in Serbia do not accept the historical facts with respect to the wars of the 1990s in the way they have been documented in countless books, articles and media coverage. Yet these same people were deeply affected when they saw our performance. They understood that the stories we told on stage were true stories and that it did not matter who the victim was and where it came from, because the victim is a victim and the biggest victims in all wars are women. The fact that we are a political theatre, but not a member of any political party, and that we represent human stories, places our audience and the people who do not want to face the past in a defenseless position.

While the courtroom may use a theatrical form to show how justice should be carried out, any judicial system must look for clear-cut causes and consequences in order to reach its aims. The theatre, unlike the judicial system, does not seek resolution. It, by contrast, raises questions by presenting facts as well as different views and complexities inherent in a particular situation. Theatre does not offer any resolution, nor does it declare any 'verdict'. Theatre has the power to create a space where people meet other people, frequently with opposing views of history and the present moment. In this space, audience members are free to express and share their feelings and thoughts about the performance and about the traumatic past. In such a physical space, there is no hierarchy, contradiction can coexist and different views can be heard and respected. It is a space for open dialogue, not for preaching to the converted. The time and space that an audience shares in theatre is radically different from the time and space of the courts: in courts, people tend to assume predetermined adversarial positions with no possibility for meaningful interaction or communication. Time in the judicial context is linear; it is viewed as flowing sequentially and chronologically. In contrast, time is frequently not linear in the theatre, but multidirectional. Theatre can look simultaneously to the past, the present and the future; it can travel through temporal frames vertically or horizontally. Theatre can also predict certain future scenarios by drawing on intuition and the prophetic language of symbols and dreams; such tools and mechanisms are not recognized as legitimate in the courtroom.

Dah believes that there is space and time for cooperation between formal and informal justice mechanisms—between courts and theatres. Peru is a good example of such cooperation—there, the state's Truth and Reconciliation

Commission (TRC) invited the theatre group *Yuyachkani*, to create a performance about the political violence that occurred between 1980 and 1990 in their country.[9] After this performance, many common people, peasants and workers, who did not want to be witnesses in courts and did not want to testify even to the TRC, opened up for the first time to the assembly and spoke about their experiences. In that sense, it was important to document their testimonies and they gave these testimonies to the director of the theatre and its troupe after watching a performance. Dah had a similar experience with their play *Crossing the Line*. At the end of performances, people often felt compelled to tell their stories to the members of the troupe.[10] The importance of these stories is multifaceted. As Milošević puts it,

> We have an enormous respect for people, who tell us their stories after the performance, and these stories have significance to all of us. These stories give us lots of incentive to continue with this performance and with our work in general.

The Belgrade's city council, state institutions and relevant ministries do not want to finance *Crossing the Line*; their reactions to it have been negative and polarizing. Some state institutions told Dah that the theme of war and women survivors was 'not relevant any more', while others thought it was 'still not time to talk about these things'. The government does not want to turn to the past and crimes committed in 'our name'. The play was made with the support of a non-profit organization 'Reconstruction Fund for Women' (Belgrade) and a small grant given by Pro Helvetia (Switzerland). With this performance, Dah has never been invited to any of the state sponsored theatre festivals in its own country, although *Crossing the Line* was performed at various festivals across the world.

Violence Against Women: *Crossing the Line*

> 'In the dark time
>
> Will there also be singing?
> Yes, there will be singing. About the dark times'.[11]

Crossing The Line (2009) was written after an invitation from Women in Black (WiB), a feminist activist organization from Serbia. In 2007, WiB published a book titled *Women's Side of War*. It is an anthology with one hundred and twenty testimonies, notes and reminiscences written by women about the wars that were

[9] *Grupo Cultural Yuyachkani* is an activist theatre group, performing in reaction to, and in defiance of politics in Peru. The group has been established in 1971. See, http://hemisphericinstitute.org/cuaderno/yuyachkani/group.html.

[10] While Dah has not documented these stories so far, its members are reflecting on how they could do so in the future, but do not yet have a clear strategy regarding this material at the moment.

[11] Bertolt Brecht, 'Motto to the 'Svendborg Poems' [*Motto der 'Svendborger Gedichte*] (1938).

raging in former Yugoslavia between 1991 and 1999. The book encourages reflections on specific forms of women's suffering and their courage to overcome trauma and to reclaim normal life, as well as on the value of solidarity with women beyond the ethnic and religious boundaries and divisions. After reading the book for the first time while it was still in a manuscript form, the actors and Milošević agreed that, at the end, the primary victim of any war is a woman regardless of her ethnic or other affiliations. While preparing this play, the troupe dealt with questions of their country's and their personal responsibility for the atrocities committed by their fellow Serbs on orders from their political and military elites.

The performance of *Crossing the Line* posed many of the questions that were first articulated in *This Babylonian Confusion*. What is the responsibility of artists in relation to the terrors committed in 'their name'? Do artists have the moral right to perform while people around them are suffering terribly? Can theatre be a way of creating peace and bringing justice to the victims of war? The particularly pressing concern during the creation of *Crossing the Line* was whether the troupe had the right to speak on behalf of women who survived tragedies and who witnessed the darkest of times. While Dah uses a variety of methods in their plays, such as the language of symbols and metaphors, in this play the troupe used narrative form because they were dealing with authentic testimonies from women survivors about their experiences with war.

In agreeing to their book to be turned into a play, the WiB requested that Dah would not change any part of the text, that is, the Dah was required to use the authentic stories, faithfully recreated, in the play. The WiB condition posed an enormous creative challenge: to turn documentary material, which, as such, did not necessarily meet the criteria of a compelling dramatic text into living, breathing theatrical material. It was important to avoid falsifying the essential truth of these stories of women's suffering and courage and to avoid falling into hopelessness or

Fig. 6.1 Dah Theatre, original scene from *Crossing the Line*. Photographer Sarah DeLong. Reproduced with permission of Dah Theatre. Actresses: Sanja Krsmanović Tasić, Maja Vujović and Ivana Milenović Popović

into an overly stylized theatrical text. Minimalism turned out to be the only possible solution: only what was necessary, what had to be said and shown, was left in the play. After all, Dah was speaking in the name of women who either did not have a public voice themselves or could not reach many people through the public telling of their stories. It was important to Dah to perform this play across the entire region, but particularly in Serbia. In Serbia, the play functions as a direct confrontation with the past: a way of confronting the audience with what had been done in 'their/our' name.

It is important to note here that in Dah's performances, the spectators are not just anonymous audience members whom performers address from the stage. In many of Dah's performances, the audience members are also narrators and survivors of the stories that actors portray. Dah often organizes conversations with their audiences after a play. As the play has been performed in front of different audiences, including war veterans, Dah has never been able to predict the audience reaction. Yet, so far at least, audiences have invariably been supportive and emotionally affected. The common initial reaction is silence and a shared feeling of numbness. People seem visibly shaken by what they have seen and often stay in their seats for a few minutes without speaking before slowly moving around and engaging with others.

In December 2011, the first author, Olivera Simić, was in the audience watching a performance of *Crossing the Line*, which was staged as part of a regional festival, being mounted for the first time, called the 'Off Frame Festival of Socially Engaged Theatre'.[12] After the performance, the audience and actors gathered for a glass of wine and snacks provided by the Dah. Olivera found herself standing next to Novica, a war veteran from Serbia, who was conscripted by the Serbian government and sent to fight in BH. He was visibly shaken by the performance. Over the glass of wine in a relaxed and friendly atmosphere, Novica whispered to Olivera: 'It was so difficult to watch this performance. I feel terrible that some of my comrades may have committed those crimes. How can anyone do this? I have a wife and a daughter too'.

Milošević recalls that in one of their performances in the south of Serbia, there was an older man in the audience who was shaken by the play. After the play was over, the man addressed Milošević in front of the audience. 'I am shocked by these stories', the man said. 'Who were these monsters who did such terrible things—rape, torture etc.?' Milošević replied, 'I am sorry but I have to tell you that these people were your and my neighbors'. Despite the confrontational nature of the play, audiences have not responded negatively: no one attempted to intimidate the actors or to argue that the stories Dah used in the play were propaganda and lies. Dah believes that this was so because among the stories that were told were Serb stories too—stories of Serb women and their suffering. Dah sees their play and the

[12] The 'Off Frame Festival' has brought together organizations and authors who focus their work on socially engaged theatre in Serbia and the region. The festival aimed to create a space for discussions about life in post-conflict environments. 'Off Frame Festival', December 4–10, 2011, www.off-frame.org.

Fig. 6.2 Dah Theatre, original scene from *Crossing the Line*. Photographer Milan Petrović. Reproduced with permission of Dah Theatre

audience reaction as a form of public healing, and a vital step towards public recognition and acceptance of the crimes committed in 'our name'.

According to Milošević, the performance had a particularly cathartic effect on audiences in BH. The pain and loss experienced by the people in BH were publically recognized through this play, and to Dah, this process of shared recognition was of the utmost importance. Milošević*'s commented* about her emotional experience with the play *Crossing the Line* when it was performed in Bihać, BH, December 2009:

> I realised at one moment that the whole audience was weeping. I was very distressed and asked myself whether we are re-traumatising people or healing them? However, once we finished the play, we received standing ovations and talked to the audience. I realised then how important it was for them to publically hear their stories and in that way be acknowledged in their suffering.

For victims and survivors, the play offers the direct possibility of healing: seeing and hearing the stories becomes a public acknowledgement of the often unacknowledged and therefore dangerously invisible, crimes. And, of course, the play and the theatre troupe itself come from Serbia—which symbolizes the empathy felt by certain Serbian people towards Bosnian victims of war as well as their solidarity. Dah performed—and is still performing—beyond the Balkans. In other parts of the world, the play is perceived as a universal protest against the violence inflicted on women. The reactions outside of the Balkans are also emotional, but audiences, especially women, relate the stories less to the particular historical and geopolitical context, and more to violence against women more generally. While touring the USA, in Dah's conversations with youth after the play, the audience shared stories about domestic violence, rape in student campuses and violence against women. They saw the play as a voice against violence against women. What fascinates Milošević about playing this performance abroad is to see 'how *our* local story which is so rooted in our region, politics and history has become universal by using the language of theatre and art. It has cross intercontinental borders and became a unique story in that sense'.

Dah has no support from either city or the regional authorities to develop their play further or stage it more widely across the region. *Crossing the Line* has been performed in Croatia, Serbia, Macedonia, the United States, Slovakia, but not yet in Slovenia. Significantly, it is only very recently that Dah was invited to perform in Kosovo. Prior to that invitation, Milošević had shared her thoughts with me as to the reasons that *Crossing the Line* had not been welcomed to Kosovo:

> Our Albanian sisters from Kosovo were not happy with our performance because we gave more space to the Bosnian stories and because we perhaps did not emphasise more the horror they survived. However, we do not measure victimhood; it is not our aim. We tried to organise a performance there, but we have never been invited with this performance to Pristina because it is still probably not the time for us to go there and because we are in that sense incorruptible. We do what we believe in and we think that if people in Pristina had a chance to see the performance, many of them would open their hearts to the possibility of a dialogue.

However, to Dah's pleasant surprise, in May 2013, Milošević and Dah were invited by Kosovo theatre director Zana Hoxha Krasniqi, the organizer of the *Femmes Fatales*, the First Regional Female Artists Festival for Human Rights in Kosovo.[13] Zana has directed her own theatrical version of the WiB book *Women's Side of War* and at the festival, and it is planned that both performances will be played together. This development is regarded as a step of enormous importance and meaning for both directors since it heralds a new willingness to open the Kosovo space to a troupe from Serbia to perform a play of their own creation.

Facing the Past Together: *The Story of Tea*

The Story of Tea (2006) deals with issues of confronting the truth and how we react to someone close to us committing a crime. Dah used Anton Pavlovich Chekhov's *Three Sisters* as a dramatic template for their play—Chekhov's main theme in *Three Sisters* is the missed and lost chances in our life. *The Story of Tea* brings together true stories from the region with the Chekhovian themes in order to speak

[13] The Festival is held from 27–30 May 2013 in Oda Theater, Pristina, Kosovo.

Fig. 6.3 Dah Theatre, original scene from *The Story of Tea*. Photographer Jovan Cekić. Reproduced with permission of Dah Theatre. Actresses: Sanja Krsmanović Tasić, Maja Vujović, Aleksandra Jelić and Jugoslav Hadžić

about the treatment of truth and the chances squandered by the Serbian society. One of the true stories incorporated in the Dah play is the abduction of nineteen Muslim men of Yugoslav nationality from the Belgrade-Bar train at Štrpci station at the border of BH, Montenegro and Serbia. The men were kidnapped and murdered because they had Muslim names. Later, the murderers were caught and put on trial, but Serbia never issued a statement of condolence, which might have been seen as a way of apologizing to the families of people who were abducted and killed. The questions often asked by the audiences after seeing *Crossing the Line* are raised in *The Story of Tea* by the actors themselves: (Fig. 6.3)

> What kind of people could take out the bones from fresh graves and re-bury them again? What kind of man could sit in a dredger and take out somebody's bones? Where are all those people who did that? Where do they live? Are they possibly our neighbours?[14]

The question of the ongoing denial of past wrongdoings is prominent in both plays. A sense of disbelief that the people who tortured, raped and murdered were 'our people' has been strongly emphasized by both the audience and the actors. According to Logar and Bogosavljević, surveys conducted among the Serb population have highlighted three segments of society: the first group uncritically believes that all blame lies with the 'other side' and that Mladić, Karadžić and Milošević are victims of a global anti-Serb conspiracy[15]; the second group

[14] Dah Theatre, the line from *The Story of Tea*. Full transcript of the play on file with authors.

[15] Svetlana Logar and Srdjan Bogosavljević, *Vidjenje istine u Srbiji*, Rec 62(8) 15 (2001), available at http://www.b92.net/casopis_rec/62.8/pdf/005-034.pdf (accessed 12 January 2013).

believes that crimes were indeed committed by the Serbs and that the nation has to confront their reality and legacy; the third group thinks that the blame lies with the international community rather than Milošević. Members of the third group remain undecided about what truly happened and about the nature of the Serbian culpability.[16] This culture of denial is reflected in mainstream political discourse, where denial of war crimes is promoted as a normative and acceptable way of dealing with the legacy of the Serbian past.[17] To reflect on this culture of denial, at the end of the performance, all of the actors speak the following words in unison:

If I open my innards to
this truth recovery and
let the world listen to
the thrum of blood in my
heart, the gush of bile
in my spleen, the
susurrations of air in my
lungs, the drip, drip,
drip of urine in my
kidneys, the clatter of
corpuscles and platelets
in my arteries, when I
sound them all from deep
inside where the dead
reside, will I be healed?[18]

The whole performance takes place in the space between spectators, who are sitting in such a way that they face one another. At the beginning of the play, the audience is served nineteen cups of tea. The number of cups symbolizes the number of people abducted and murdered on the train in Štrpci. At the end of the performance, actors put the candles in those cups. After the actors leave the stage, the audience often stays in the theatre, sitting still, in the complete darkness, illuminated only by the nineteen candles, which nineteen people hold in the cups. In this way, Dah has created a space of memory, resembling a wake. The fact that people stay behind sitting, remembering and reflecting is important, as it signals the beginning of the potential healing (Fig. 6.4).

---

[16] Ibid. at 32.

[17] Jelena Obradović-Wochnik, *Strategies of Denial: Resistance to ICTY Cooperation in Serbia*, *in* War Crimes, Conditionality and EU Integration in the Western Balkans 29, 34 (Judy Batt & Jelena Obradović-Wochnik eds., 2009), *available at* http://www.iss.europa.eu/uploads/media/cp116.pdf (last visited March 1, 2013).

[18] David Duggan, a playwright. The text is a part of his play 'AH 6905'. Reproduced with permission of Dah Theatre.

Fig. 6.4 Dah Theatre, original scene from *The Story of Tea*. Photographer Jovan Cekić, Reproduced with permission of Dah Theatre. Actors: Sanja Krsmanović Tasić, Maja Vujović, Aleksandra Jelić and Jugoslav Hadžić

Inscribing the Present with the Past

Both performances, *Crossing the Line* and *The Story of Tea*, emphasize the role of art to memorialize the past: its ability to inscribe the present with tangible marks and traces of the past and to ensure that remembering, both public and private, is understood as an ongoing and indispensable cultural process. They both engage with the understanding that memory is elusive and tricky and that people often remember specific things and that they remember different things at different times. In Serbia, the audience and the troupe members grew up in the same country and have a shared history and, for the most part, very similar childhoods. However, as Milošević points out,

> but what you remember about that country is probably different from my memories. Art makes it possible for these different parts of memory to be documented. There is no such thing as only one truth and only one possible memory. There are many memories that coexist simultaneously and can all be truthful in that sense. Art can put these different remembrances in the same space next to each other without saying 'your memory is more worthy than mine'.

Dah has experienced ongoing threats because of its work. Twice, while touring with *Crossing the Line* in 2010, Dah's offices were burgled. Dah has received threatening letters and there was even an attempt to burn down the theatre. Despite these obstacles, Dah believes wholeheartedly that 'with our lives and voices we are demonstrating that it is possible to live a life with more humanity and dignity. We would like to see that our work can contribute to a better society'.

Acknowledgments We would like to thank Associate Professor Peter Rush for his helpful suggestions and valuable comments on earlier drafts of this paper.

Bibliography

1. Brecht, Berlot. 1975. 'When leaders speak of peace' in *Selected Poems*. New York: Harcourt Brace.
2. Brecht, Bertolt. 1938. 'Motto to the 'Svendborg Poems' [*Motto der 'Svendborger Gedichte*].
3. Duggan, David. 2005. Play 'AH 6905'.
4. Dolan, Jill. 1991. *The feminist spectator as critic*. Michigan: University of Michigan Press.
5. Knežević, Dubravka. 1995. 'Do poslednjeg daha', *Scena* no. 5/6, Sept/Dec 1995.
6. Komarčević, Dušan. 2012. *Kreatori zločina i dalje na slobodi*, E-novine, 27 February 2012. Available at, http://www.e-novine.com/drustvo/59890-Kreatori-zloina-dalje-slobodi.html.
7. Obradović-Wochnik, Jelena. 2009. *Strategies of Denial: Resistance to ICTY Cooperation in Serbia*. In War crimes, conditionality and EU integration in the Western Balkans, eds Judy Batt and Jelena Obradović-Wochnik, 29, 34. Available at http://www.iss.europa.eu/uploads/media/cp116.pdf.
8. Logar, Svetlana and Srdjan Bogosavljević. 2001. Vidjenje istine u Srbiji, Rec 62(8):15. Available at http://www.b92.net/casopis_rec/62.8/pdf/005-034.pdf.

Chapter 7
Culture, Theatre and Justice: Examples from Afghanistan

Nadia Siddiqui, Hadi Marifat and Sari Kouvo

> In Afghanistan we live in the streets of the dead, and we die in the streets of life.
>
> Poet, Afghanistan.

Introduction

After over 30 years of conflict, people in Afghanistan have learned to survive violence and endure hardship, but reaching beyond survival to lasting, positive social and political change—living in the streets of life, as it were—has proved difficult if not impossible for many in the country. That a poet captured this sentiment of the people is not surprising given the important role poetry has played in Afghanistan in elucidating and disseminating stories and narratives, attuned to what is actually happening in society.

This role is a distillation of why storytelling and cultural expression (including oral, written, visual and performative practices) in ongoing and post-conflict settings are crucial. Opportunities for portraying the truth about war and war-related experiences are not only important for individual healing, but they can also serve an important function in restoring collective memory and repairing the social fabric in which individuals are embedded.[1] Arts-based mechanisms for remembering and truth-telling may allow people to collectively share their stories and

---

[1] Shanee Stepakoff, "Telling and Showing: Witnesses Represent Sierra Leone's War Atrocities in Court and Onstage", *The Drama Review* 52, no. 1 (2008): 26.

N. Siddiqui (✉)
International Center for Transitional Justice, 5 Hanover Square, 24th Floor, New York, NY 10004, USA
e-mail: nsiddiqui@ictj.org

H. Marifat
Afghanistan Human Rights and Democracy Organization, Kabul, Afghanistan
e-mail: hadimarifat@gmail.com
URL: www.ahrdo.org

S. Kouvo
Afghanistan Analysts Network, Kabul, Afghanistan
e-mail: sari@afghanistan-analysts.org
URL: http://www.afghanistan-analysts.org

P. D. Rush and O. Simić (eds.), *The Arts of Transitional Justice*,
Springer Series in Transitional Justice 6, DOI: 10.1007/978-1-4614-8385-4_7,

create "meaning about what happened in the community".[2] In contexts like Afghanistan where human rights frameworks and transitional justice measures are nascent and contested by powerful national—and international—elites, grass-roots cultural expressions are among the only spaces for debating conflict and justice and in this sense may be a place for cultural as well as political change. Artists then not only help to tell what has happened and is happening, but can provide communities an outlet to develop solutions—to help people live rather than simply survive.

In examining post-conflict and transitional contexts through a frame of cultural expression, artists and activists are seeking to uncover "what would we know that we do not know now? Whose stories, memories and struggles might become visible? What tensions might performance behaviours show that would not be recognized in texts and documents?"[3] and perhaps more importantly help lay the bedrock in communities on which the social trust needed for dealing with legacies of conflict must stand. This chapter aims to situate cultural practices, in particular participatory theatre, within the context of arts-based and memory-related efforts to promote transitional justice, specifically truth-seeking, in Afghanistan. The text will explore the potential benefits and dangers of the use of these methodologies to promote transitional justice in societies during and after conflict.

While dressed in an academic form, this article draws on the practical work of the three authors. Sari Kouvo has followed Afghanistan and its transitional justice process for the European Union, the International Centre for Transitional Justice (ICTJ) and the Afghanistan Analysts Network.[4] Hadi Marifat is an Afghan human rights activist who has worked for the United Nations Assistance Mission in Afghanistan and Human Rights Watch. He is also a co-founder and current director of the Afghanistan Human Rights and Democracy Organization (AH-RDO), an all-Afghan led and run civil society organization whose aim is to develop a participatory theatre and arts-based transitional justice and gender platform in Afghanistan. Nadia Siddiqui was a member of the International Centre for Transitional Justice's Afghanistan and International Policy Relations teams. She worked closely to help research and develop ICTJ's early engagement with theatre in Afghanistan and develop and organize AHRDO's first international

---

[2] Beatrice Pouligny, "Understanding Situations of Post-Mass Crime by Mobilizing Different Forms of Cultural Endeavors" (panel contribution, 19th IPSA World Congress, Durban, South Africa, July 1, 2003).

[3] Diana Taylor, The Archive and the Repertoire: *Performing Cultural Memory in the Americas* (Durham, NC: Duke University Press, 2003), xviii.

[4] This chapter builds in part on Kouvo's previous publications including Sari Kouvo and Dallas Mazoori, "Reconciliation, Justice and Mobilization of War Victims in Afghanistan", *International Journal of Transitional Justice* 5, no. 3 (2011): 492–503; Sari Kouvo, "Transitional Justice in the Context of Ongoing Conflict: the Case of Afghanistan", ICTJ Briefing Report (New York: ICTJ, 2009); Fatima Ayub, Sar Kouvo, and Rachel Wareham, *Security Sector Reform in Afghanistan*, Initiative for Peacebuilding Report (Brussels: IfP, 2009); and Fatima Ayub, Sari Kouvo, and Yasmin Sooka, *Addressing Gender-Specific Violations in Afghanistan* (New York: ICTJ, 2009).

theatre and policy tour of the US and Europe. She also develops and directs art and design events around New York City.[5] The authors then are participant-observers and as such despite best efforts at distancing our personal engagement from the work, certain biases may remain. At the same time, our analysis benefits from the strength of our understanding not only of the theoretical frameworks of transitional justice in peacebuilding contexts, but also the practical complexities of using alternative methods for transitional justice in difficult conflict environments.

Cultural Expression and Transitional Justice

Catastrophes can pull societies apart; they can also shatter the ordinary divides and patterns that separate people. In these circumstances, new communities can emerge, where people in coming together find purposefulness and connectedness amid death, chaos, fear and loss.[6] Rebecca Solnit argues that in the aftermath of disaster, be it hurricane or bombing, the demolished status quo can create space "in which we are who we hope to be, do the work we desire, and are each our sister's and brother's keeper".[7] In contexts of prolonged conflict, however, as abuses and violence compound, survivors often find that their experiences are open-ended; they live with an event that "has no ending… no closure and therefore… continues into the present".[8] Performative arts in conflict and transitional settings can provide a bridge to "who we hope to be" by engaging with the "moral imagination", the capacity for individuals to stay grounded in the troubles of the real world, while simultaneously remain open to the possibilities of a better one.[9]

Theatre in particular as an art form serves a deeper purpose than storytelling alone: it functions as a vital act of transfer, transmitting social knowledge, memory, and a sense of identity through reiterated behaviours.[10] Performance can play a role in giving voice to the marginalized and in demanding the right to speak

[5] This chapter also builds in part on Siddiqui's previous publications including Nadia Siddiqui, "Theatre and Transitional Justice in Afghanistan", ICTJ Briefing Report (New York: ICTJ, 2010); and Nadia Siddiqui and Hjalmar Joffre-Eichhorn, "From Tears to Energy: Early Uses of Participatory Theatre in Afghanistan", in Transitional Justice, Culture, and Society, ed. Clara Ramirez-Barat (New York: Social Science Research Council, forthcoming).

[6] Rebecca Solnit, *A Paradise Built in Hell: The Extraordinary Communities that Arise in Disaster* (New York: Penguin Books, 2009), 3.

[7] Ibid.

[8] Shoshana Feldman and Dori Laub, *Testimony: Crisis of Witnessing in Literature, Psychoanalysis, and History* (New York: Routledge, 1992), 62.

[9] Cynthia E. Cohen, Roberto Gutierrez Varea, and Polly O. Walker, eds., *Acting Together: Performance and the Creative Transformation of Conflict,* vol. 1, Resistance and Reconciliation in Regions of Violence (Oakland, CA: New Village Press, 2011), 11.

[10] Taylor, *The Archive and the Repertoire*, 2.

publicly without fear.[11] It encourages present and forward looking understanding by making relationships central and acknowledging interdependence among people and societies; cultivating paradoxical curiosity through inquiry about identities, values and beliefs leading to understanding that is above simple dualities; making space for the creative act in contexts where political violence would make it seem that there are no options for cultural action and response; and finally, enabling risk-taking to allow people to examine possibilities of what a peaceful society could look like.[12]

Theatre then can be thought to work at the "interface between the creative and the political, calling together audiences of citizens to contemplate their society or its ways".[13] Framing theatre as an active and collective process connects it to the notion that "compassion is an unstable emotion. It needs to be translated into action, or it withers".[14] The idea here being to create a disequilibrium inside the spectator not only to empathize with the protagonist on stage, but also to prepare the way for concrete actions to address injustices and bring about transformation.

Having audiences actively participate in the transformation process is a central principle of community-based theatre. It offers participants an aesthetic instrument to analyse their past in the context of the present and to invent and shape their futures according to their needs, determined through participatory theatre exercises and games, without having solutions imposed on them by experts.[15] The underlying assumption is that people are all equipped to be actors and to take centre stage. The main theatrical focus is on dialogue, with the explicit aim of allowing participants to take control of situations rather than simply having things happen to them.

Community-based theatre is most closely identified with Brazilian theatre director Augusto Boal and his Theatre of the Oppressed, which became an international movement using his techniques as vehicles for participatory social change in the mid-twentieth century.[16] For Boal, many ordinary citizens feel powerless and are in fact blocked in the face of oppression and injustice. To

[11] Jonothan Neelands, "Acting Together: Ensemble as Democratic Process in Art and Life", *Research in Drama Education: The Journal of Applied Theatre and Performance* 14, no. 2 (2009); 180.

[12] Cohen et al., *Acting Together*, 11–12.

[13] John McGrath, "Theatre and Democracy", *New Theatre Quarterly* 18 (2002): 137–138.

[14] Susan Sontag, *Regarding the Pain of Others* (New York: Farrar, Straus and Giroux, 2003), 101.

[15] United Nations Assistance Mission in Afghanistan (UNAMA), "*Tears into Energy*: Community-based Theatre and Transitional Justice", unpublished report, April 2008.

[16] Boal developed the Theatre of the Oppressed based on his own experiences with dramatic performance and was heavily influenced in the pedagogical and political principles espoused by Brazilian educator, Paulo Freire, namely that the situation lived by participants should be understood, including its root causes, and that changing the situation should follow the precepts of social justice. The Theatre of the Oppressed is a form of popular, participatory and democratic theatre of, by, and for people engaged in a struggle for liberation. For more details see, Arvind Singhal, "Empowering the Oppressed through Participatory Theatre", *Investigación y Desarrollo* 12, no. 1 (2004): 138–163.

address this, he developed the Theatre of the Oppressed process whereby audience members, so-called spect-actors, can stop a performance and assume a protagonist role onstage to change the dramatic action, propose various solutions, discuss plans for change, and train themselves for social action.[17] The theatrical act itself becomes a conscious intervention and a rehearsal for social action, based on collective analysis.[18]

Among the components of Boal's approach are (1) Image Theatre, a basis for other participatory theatre work that asks participants to transform their own or others' bodies into representations of particular situations, emotions or ideas; and (2) Forum Theatre, which allows audience members to stop a scene or play showing a conflict that the characters do not know how to resolve/transform and suggest and try out possible solutions. "Joker" characters serve as neutral moderators between the actors and the spect-actors, setting up the rules of the event for the audience, facilitating the spect-actors' replacement of the protagonist on stage and summing up the essence of each proposed solution in the intervention. The term itself derives from the joker or wild card in a deck of playing cards, where that card is not tied to a specific suit or value, neither is the Theatre of the Oppressed joker tied to an allegiance to any one performer, spect-actor, or interpretation of events.[19]

Playback Theatre is another widely used technique in community-based theatre. Developed in the United States in 1975 by Jonathon Fox and Jo Salas, this method enables an audience member to tell a story from his or her life and then watch as actors and musicians immediately re-create the scene, giving it artistic shape and coherence.[20] Its main tenet is that human beings need to tell their stories in order to construct meaning. Any story that is significant to the teller, whether happy or sad, mundane or transcendental, can be a part of a performance. Playback Theatre celebrates individual experience and the connections between people through their stories. Similar to Theatre of the Oppressed, this methodology is open to both professional actors and those with no acting experience, promoting the idea that artistic expression is the domain of all people.

A Playback Theatre performance usually includes a variety of short and long forms to respond to audience input, with the three most common being "fluid sculptures", short, abstract sounds and movements expressing the spectators' emotional states; "pairs", an improvisation based on spectators' experiences of simultaneously occurring conflicting emotions; and "stories", in which audience members share longer personal stories of their pasts. Improvised music is an essential element as well and an array of different instruments are usually available for the performers to experiment with. Finally, there is a conductor, playing the

---

[17] UNAMA, "*Tears into Energy*".

[18] Singhal, "Empowering the Oppressed", 146.

[19] Ibid., 148.

[20] Bev Hosking and Christian Penny, "Playback Theatre as a Methodology for Social Change" (paper presented at the DevNet Conference, Wellington, New Zealand, December 2000).

role of host and interviewer, who helps to frame and shape the stories told by the audience, thereby effectively co-creating them.

Unlike Theatre of the Oppressed, Playback Theatre was not originally devised with an explicit political agenda in mind, but both methodologies have in recent years been utilized to raise social justice concerns in post-conflict and transitional contexts, including Burundi,[21] the Democratic Republic of Congo,[22] Kosovo[23] and, recently, Afghanistan. The use of these theatre forms within these contexts is not entirely surprising as the connection between cultural expression and transitional justice is inherent given that a central tenet of transitional justice is to give voice to the victims of trauma and human rights violations.

Transitional justice measures—from trials to truth-seeking—aim to provide forums for testimony in an effort to bring accountability and uncover truth in violent contexts where both have been absent. As such, these mechanisms require voices from communities that have in many cases had their means of expression silenced. Catherine M. Cole argues, for instance, that the South African Truth and Reconciliation Commission's (TRC) live public hearings were in effect performances and were *effective*; however, imperfectly, in facilitating transition from a racist, totalitarian state to a nonracial democracy because they were *affective*.[24]

Despite this, official transitional justice initiatives, through mandate and resources, can only include a select and limited number of victims to participate, leaving a larger number individuals and groups to feel excluded and thus certain truths to remain taboo.[25] Furthermore, in criminal justice settings, participants are constrained in their responses given the structures of formal proceedings and may face adversarial questioning of their experiences. Rather than set the scene and express themselves freely, victims must confine their explanations to the questions asked as their testimonies are requested to demonstrate culpability (or not) of the accused.

At the same time, in the absence of any formal processes for justice and truth, communities will seek their own means for remembering conflict and violations of the past. Recent research in Colombia indicates, for instance, that a number of arts-based initiatives have been endeavoured locally by members of conflict affected

[21] Search for Common Ground, "Burundi Update", June 2008 http://www.sfcg.org/programmes/burundi/burundi_update.html.

[22] Search for Common Ground, "Centre Lokole/Search for Common Ground's Participatory Theatre for Conflict Transformation", http://www.ceri-sciencespo.com/themes/re-imaginingpeace/va/base/Congo_1173192498.pdf; and Search for Common Ground, *Participatory Theatre for Conflict Transformation: Training Manual* (Kinshasa: Search for Common Ground, n.d.).

[23] Jonathan Chadwick, "Working in Kosovo on a Participatory Theatre Project on Missing Persons", AZ Theatre, http://www.aztheatre.org.uk/index.php?page=war-stories-kosovo.

[24] Catherine M. Cole, "Performance, Transitional Justice, and the Law: South Africa's Truth and Reconciliation Commission", *Theater Journal* no. 2 (2007): 179.

[25] Ksenija Bilbija and others, eds., *The Art of Truth Telling About Authoritarian Rule* (Madison: The University of Wisconsin Press, 2005), 3.

regions in the absence of a formal, national process.[26] These unofficial and alternative truth-seeking initiatives serve to "repudiate past violence… demand remembrance… and insist that violence not be repeated".[27] While these unofficial processes can present stories about specific communities or groups, they cannot alone guarantee political enlightenment, but rather they lay the groundwork for bonding and interactivity within the community.[28] This is still important in bringing divided communities together and in helping to activate what William Ury terms the "third side", that is, the surrounding community within a conflict which can serve as a container for escalating violence.[29] As people contribute to a process of dialogue and remembrance, an impulse arises from the relationships linking each member and every other member in the community.[30] Thus, in utilizing their own forms of expression and traditions for commemoration and mourning, tellers of truths form in effect informal networks of "watchdogs against new encroachments… speak[ing] their truths to power, to themselves, to their compatriots, to anyone who might be listening".[31]

These networks can begin grass-roots processes for justice and accountability, but cannot in and of themselves capture the "complex truths" inherent in a broader historical narrative of a given conflict—a narrative necessary for rebuilding a more just society.[32] Cultural expression outside of formal proceedings informs transitional justice processes aimed at capturing a national record because they are densely packed with meaning, having been "polished" by centuries of transmission from one generation to the next.[33] This meaning may not be apparent in literary or historic documents or straightforward testimony alone, but rather found in performed, expressive behaviours. Examples of the use of performative input into formal processes can be found particularly within official truth-seeking efforts. This was evident within the South African TRC, where "some truths could be contained within the commission's mandate and procedures [and] other truths constantly erupted in the live, embodied experience" of its public hearings.[34] Officials in charge of Peru's TRC enlisted the Lima-based theatre collective,

---

[26] See Marcela Briceño-Donn and others, eds., *Recordar en conflicto: Iniciativas no oficiales de memoria en Colombia* (Bogotá: ICTJ, 2009).

[27] Bilbija and others, eds., *The Art of Truth Telling About Authoritarian Rule*, 3.

[28] Rustom Bharucha, "Between Truth and Reconciliation: Experiments in Theatre and Public Culture", *Economic and Political Weekly* 36, no. 39 (2001): 3767.

[29] William Ury, *The Third Side: Why We Fight and How We Can Stop* (New York: Penguin Books, 1999), 7.

[30] Ibid., 14.

[31] Bilbija and others, eds., *The Art of Truth Telling About Authoritarian Rule*, 3.

[32] Judy Barsalou, *Trauma and Transitional Justice in Divided Societies*, Special Report (Washington, D.C.: USIP, 2005), 1.

[33] Cynthia E. Cohen, "Creative Approaches to Reconciliation,'' in *The Psychology of Resolving Global Conflicts: From War to Peace*, ed. Mari Fitzduff and Christopher E. Stout (Westport, CT: Greenwood Publishing Group, 2005), 3: 72.

[34] Cole, "Performance, Transitional Justice, and Law", 186.

Grupo Cultural Yuyachkani, to help with outreach. The Yuyachkani collective had been performing in Peru for 30 years prior to partnering with the TRC, with the aim of "imagining Peru"[35] as a coherent nation despite the pervasive violence of the civil war through "cultural engagement with the indigenous and *mestizo* populations and with complex, transcultured (Andean-Spanish) ways of knowing, thinking, remembering".[36] Yuyachkani's goal was to serve as a mediator and conduit to the public hearings between the government-operated TRC and rural populations—for whom until recently, the state was seen as an enemy of the people. The theatre group not only acted out the TRC's itinerary, but also used the performances to transform ordinary public spaces temporarily into places for ritual and reflection. This not only highlighted the transition from previous periods of conflict to the new democracy, but did so in a manner that was "participatory for the community"[37] and sought to foster individual transformation.

Taken together then, creative expression, in particular theatre practices, can serve a variety of functions in transitioning contexts including: as a way of providing some modicum of individual and/or collective healing (if it is appropriately connected to and followed up with psychosocial counselling); as a complement to and outreach tool for formal transitional justice mechanisms; and as an informal, independent documentation and truth-seeking device in the absence of any formal transitional justice processes. With this in mind, we will explore further the complex context of Afghanistan, with a special focus on uses of participatory theatre methodologies as part of a fragile grass-roots transitional justice movement.

Conflict and the Nascent Transitional Justice Process in Afghanistan

As a result of over three decades of conflict, most Afghans have lived with conflict, violence and predatory political leaderships all their lives or have been forced to flee their country because of these factors. Hopes that grew in the country after the United States-led military intervention in 2001 for a more peaceful and just future have been shattered with the re-emergence of abusive leaders, corrupt institutional structures, and recurrent violent conflict. Lack of accountability has enabled warlords—politico-military leaders with continued links to illegal armed groups—to become part of the new national and community elite. Many of these leaders are alleged perpetrators of war crimes or other serious human rights violations and their continued access to power contributes to an atmosphere of fear. As a consequence, transitional justice issues are politicized and highly sensitive in

[35] Francine A'ness, "Resisting Amnesia: Yuyachkani, Performance, and the Postwar Reconstruction of Peru", *Theatre Journal* 56, no. 3 (2004): 400.

[36] Taylor, *The Archive and the Repertoire*, 192; A'ness, 399.

[37] A'ness, 399.

Afghanistan.[38] Opportunities for expressing opinions about past and present violations are diminishing by the day and public space in which to talk about the legacies of war or other issues that may challenge country elites is fast disappearing.

The effort to promote justice and accountability for past—and present—war crimes and human rights violations has been fraught with challenges. In 2004, the Afghanistan Independent Human Rights Commission (AIHRC) published its report *A Call for Justice*: *A National Consultation on Past Human Rights Violations in Afghanistan*, which presented the findings of how Afghans wanted to deal with the legacies of past abuse in the country.[39] In an effort to bolster and support the AIHRC's work, *A Call to Justice* was originally slated to be released in conjunction with a United Nations (UN) prepared report documenting war crimes in Afghanistan. This, however, did not happen as the UN decided to suppress the release of their own report, claiming that the information detailed within it would risk destabilizing the political situation in Afghanistan and pose security threats to UN staff in the country.[40]

Even without the UN's supporting report, the AIHRC's national consultation sent a very strong message to both the Afghan government and the international community that Afghans wanted accountability for war crimes or at the very least that known perpetrators of war crimes be removed from official positions of power. It also resulted in the drafting of an action plan for Peace, Justice and Reconciliation, popularly called the Transitional Justice Action Plan, by a commission comprised of representatives from the office of President Hamid Karzai, the AIHRC and the UN Office of the High Commissioner for Human Rights (OHCHR), with support from European diplomatic missions. The action plan outlined a five-point strategy focusing on symbolic measures (memorialization), documentation and truth-seeking, institutional reform, vetting and accountability based on recommendations from the AIHRC national consultation. Although the President's office participated in drafting the plan, it was by no means easy to ensure its passage in the Afghan Cabinet. The action plan was approved in December 2005, but only after references to criminal accountability for war crimes had been watered down. The final version does, however, include references to accountability in the preamble and calls, as one of its final action points, for the

[38] For a more in depth analysis of transitional justice in Afghanistan, see Ahmad Nader Nadery, "Peace or Justice? Transitional Justice in Afghanistan", *International Journal of Transitional Justice* 1, no. 1 (2007): 173–179; and Patricia Gossman, Gossman Patricia, "Disarmament and Transitional Justice in Afghanistan", ICTJ Case Study (New York: ICTJ, 2009).

[39] Afghanistan Independent Human Rights Commission (AIHRC), *A Call for Justice: A National Consultation on Past Human Rights Violations in Afghanistan* (Kabul: AIHRC, 2004).

[40] See, Angélique Mounier-Kuhn, "Le «mapping report» sur l'Afghanistan: histoire d'un dossier escamoté", *Le Temps*, October 2, 2010, http://m.letemps.ch/Page/Uuid/aadd4d4e-cd9b-11df-a30b-a70320d5cebf/Le_mapping_report_sur_lAfghanistan_histoire_dun_dossier_escamotė; and Sari Kouvo, "Facts for Reconciliation: Human Rights Documentation Needed", *Afghanistan Analysts Network*, October 10, 2010, http://aan-afghanistan.com/index.asp?id=1217.

establishment of a commission to make recommendations to the President about how to approach accountability. To date, only a few of the action points have been implemented. The action plan has been publicly launched (though it took one year for the President to do so), a national day for victims of war crimes was announced and has been celebrated annually, a Presidential advisory panel on senior political appointments has been established, and the AIHRC recently finalized a massive war crimes documentation and mapping exercise in Afghanistan, though has not yet released the report.[41]

This minimal implementation of the action plan has still resulted in backlash in the country including counter-action against its launch by some of the former warlords elected to Parliament. In the name of national reconciliation, an ad hoc parliamentary commission drafted a law that provided blanket amnesty for all those involved in the last two and a half decades of Afghan conflict crimes. The law effectively also amounted to self-amnesty for its drafters. After only a few changes, the law was adopted by the President's office and it was published in the Official Gazette in December 2008.

The adoption of the National Stability and Reconciliation Law, often called the Afghan Amnesty Law, was in many ways a death-blow to the formal transitional justice process in Afghanistan. It solidified the power of warlords, and particularly, the factional commanders from the Civil War era within the Afghan government structures. It did so without any forceful reactions by the United Nations or the wider international community, suggesting that while there *in general* can be no amnesty for war crimes under international law, *exceptions* are possible and Afghanistan is one of them. While there was not broad international condemnation of the Afghan Amnesty Law, Afghan civil society, especially Kabul-based civil society networks, spoke out against it. The key argument raised was that it is not the role of the government to forgive, but that citizens, especially victims, need to make this decision.[42]

Afghan civil society has remained largely reactive in its approach to political and security developments; however, the past few years have seen a new form of engagement for transitional justice increasingly adapted to the Afghan context and less internationally driven. In early 2009, the Transitional Justice Coordination Group (TJCG), a loose network of 25 Afghan and international civil society organizations, was established and it has been a driving force in the efforts to establish a national network for war victims in Afghanistan.[43] The Civil Society and Human Rights Network developed a training manual for transitional justice published in 2011, the first such manual to have been drafted in Dari and not

---

[41] See, Patricia Gossman, "Kabul's Stealth Attack on Human Rights", *New York Times/ International Herald Tribune*, December 26, 2011, http://www.nytimes.com/2011/12/27/opinion/kabuls-stealth-attack-on-human-rights.html.

[42] Similar sentiments were expressed in the Afghanistan Research and Evaluation Unit's field research on Afghan opinions about justice and reconciliation, see: http://www.areu.org.af/ResearchProjectDetails.aspx?contentid=2&ParentId=2&ResearchProjectId=27&Lang=en-US.

[43] For further analysis see, Kouvo and Mazoori, "Justice, Reconciliation and Mobilization".

translated from English, and has conducted regional trainings about transitional justice. The Afghan Civil Society Forum Organization conducted and published a research on Afghans' opinions about and definitions of violence and justice covering a 60-year period of Afghan history (1958–2008).[44] The last few years have also seen several new organizations picking up subjects relating to the links between ending the conflict and justice.

The declining security situation and increasing attention to both local- and national-level reintegrations have also resulted in civil society refocusing its attention from advocating for—or expecting—the establishment of a formal transitional justice process to focusing on how justice elements can be integrated in conflict-resolution at the local levels and in the nascent peace process. There is then an increasing focus on consultation, community-based dialogues and—what will be discussed below—cultural and theatre initiatives. The TJCG, for example, organized a photo exhibition focusing on conflict and justice for National Victims' Day in 2010, and a number of groups have held several short-story competitions focusing on issues of peace and conflict.

Cultural Expressions and Theatre as a Means to Discuss Conflict and Justice

Afghanistan has a long-existing tradition of poetry, oral storytelling and performance. Poetry and oral storytelling have for centuries reflected the history, tradition, myths, religious epics, daily lives, emotions and pride of landscape in Afghanistan. They also reflect a love in Afghan culture for stories and the rituals around performing, listening and remembering details. These forms also served as a medium for sharing ideas about societal change. Some of the very first poems written in Persian Dari in the ninth century had a political bent, and modern political poetry in Afghanistan dates back to the early twentieth century where it was connected with the "Constitutional" movement of the time led by intellectuals, writers, poets, and social activists with an aim to ensure complete political freedom and a constitutional system in Afghanistan.[45] Following this, in the so-called democracy decade (1963–1973), political poetry was incorporated into left and right wing ideologies and into the workings of newly established Communist and Islamic political organizations and political parties.[46]

Modern Afghan theatre, also borne out as a practice in the early twentieth century, was started by a few men who had studied in Europe in the 1930s and

[44] Afghan Civil Society Forum Organization, *A First Step on a Long Journey: How People Define Violence and Justice in Afghanistan (1958–2008)*, (Kabul: ACSFO, 2011).

[45] Partaw Naderi, "Poetry and Politics" (lecture, Iowa City Public Library, Iowa City, IA, October 27, 2006).

[46] Ibid.

returned to Afghanistan to make translations of the Western canon; train actors in romantic acting styles; direct and produce these plays; and spread their work to other cities.[47] Over the course of 20 years since starting this work, the group had interested other prominent Afghans on the importance of theatre enough to have developed about a dozen playwrights whose works dealt with relevant social, political, economic, domestic and religious problems facing society.[48] By 1960, Kabul housed two public theatres subsidized by the Ministry of Press, Information and Culture and by the municipality.

As political unrest escalated through the later 1970s in Afghanistan, left-wing Communist movements utilized creative expression, in particular poetry, to introduce concepts of proletarian revolution, the peasant, socialism and Lenin for the first time.[49] It was the Communist People's Democratic Party of Afghanistan, who rose to power through coup in 1978, that most closely linked creative expression to political and ideological structures than ever before in the country. Opposition mujahideen groups followed suit, using arts to frame their own narratives. As such, artists were persecuted depending on their political beliefs (or lack thereof) under the Communist regime as well as by the competing mujahideen groups who fought for power in the 1980s. As a result, artists, like many other Afghan citizens fled the country. Despite this, so-called resistance poetry was still being written by Afghan poets in exile in Pakistan and Iran during this period. The final death knell for cultural production in Afghanistan came with the ascendancy of the Taliban in the 1990s who made clear through the destruction of cultural sites and execution of traditional storytellers, Sufis, poets, artists and musicians that Afghanistan was not a place for any kind of expression beyond the religious.[50]

The fall of the Taliban has seen the gradual reemergence of cultural production and expression, though arts practices do not hold the importance they once had, superseded by practical aspects of individual and national survival.[51] Traditional storytelling is a rare commodity and storytellers even more so—the great stories of Afghanistan's past are not entirely forgotten, but additional themes of war, terror, loss and small gains, are now part of the repertoire.[52] While these new themes are realities far removed from the magic of fairy tales traditionally told, they do serve as "safety valves to relieve tensions caused by oppression and venting a society's animosities as well as expressing its aspirations".[53]

[47] George H. Quimby, "Theatre in Iran and Afghanistan", *Educational Theatre Journal* 12, no. 3 (1960): 203.

[48] Ibid.

[49] Naderi, "Poetry and Politics".

[50] Wahid Omar, "From Storytelling to Community Development", in Telling Stories to Change the World: Global Voices on the Power of Narrative to Build Community and Make Social Justice Claims, eds. Rickie Solinger, Madeline Fox, and Kayhan Irani (New York: Routledge, 2008), 194.

[51] Naderi, "Poetry and Politics".

[52] Omar, "From Storytelling to Community Development", 194.

[53] Ibid.

Few traditional storytellers remain in Afghanistan, but the need to tell long silenced stories may explain the resurgence of theatre, despite its being a relatively newer arts practice in the country, particularly in its participatory forms. There have been a number of advancements in theatre including: the reopening of the destroyed Kabul Theatre in 2002; the establishment of the Afghan Theatre Festival in 2004 in conjunction with Kabul Theatre, Kabul University, the Afghan Ministry of Culture and other international institutions; and the growing number of women's theatre groups. The theatre practices in Afghanistan cover a range of styles, including staged works and participatory exercises, and topics, such as social justice and public health concerns.[54] They offer windows to explore experience as well as serving as subtle mechanisms for change.

Given Afghanistan's low levels of literacy, theatre and other unwritten means of outreach are useful for communication and interaction that can foster public understanding, engagement and participation around justice related topics. While the use of participatory theatre techniques to broach legacies of war and accountability specifically is a recent innovation, it has already helped create positive impulses for peacebuilding and promotion of transitional justice in Afghanistan.

Theatre processes oriented around transitional justice began in earnest in Kabul in 2008, first initiated jointly by the AIHRC and the United Nations Assistance Mission in Afghanistan (UNAMA) and followed up with support from ICTJ. The work consisted of introducing both traditional and participatory theatre techniques, including Theatre of the Oppressed and Playback Theatre, to Afghan human rights activists interested in developing cultural approaches to transitional justice in country. In 2009, this group of activists went on to formally establish AHRDO whose aim is to build a theatre and arts-based transitional justice and gender platform in Afghanistan.

AHRDO has been a driving force behind a series of war victims-centred theatre endeavours that included Theatre of the Oppressed and Playback Theatre initiatives with different war victim communities around the country as a means of documenting experiences of conflict. The overarching goal of this work is to use theatre to create a space for war victims of Afghanistan to come together and analyse the past, in the context of the present in order to initiate grass-roots strategies for how to deal with the truth of the past and become active protagonists in shaping a more peaceful and just society. One recent project, the development of a new theatre piece called *Infinite Incompleteness*, sought to better connect the disparate stories of victims and bring them to a wider audience in Afghanistan and abroad. The point was to have these experiences and stories acknowledged as part of the culture of Afghanistan and be included as part of ongoing discussions for national stability.

Infinite incompleteness was developed based in part on the request from victims' groups involved in AHRDO-run participatory theatre workshops that a theatrical work be created based on their own experiences. This provided the perfect

[54] Nicole Estvanik, "Global Spotlight", *American Theatre Magazine*, February 2012.

opportunity for AHRDO to recognize its own goal to produce and stage a nonfiction performance piece using real words and stories from war victims in Afghanistan. In order to collect these stories and develop a script, AHRDO utilized different participatory methods including Playback Theatre and Documentary Theatre in which pre-existing documentary material serves as a basis for performance and is most often based on people's actual words and experiences, with victims' groups from across Afghanistan. The AHRDO team invited victims' groups to participate in a total of 20 workshops in different parts of the country. With consent, 120 stories were told and a total of 10 were carefully selected, edited and arranged in a basic storyline. The piece was written with consideration to Afghanistan's ethnic and linguistic diversity (three local languages are utilized in the script); different phases of conflict (1978–present); and the equal promotion of both men and women's experiences. These real stories were complemented by a parallel storyline consisting of a series of fictional actions and events carried out by the characters in order to create a narrative that is set in the past, present and, ultimately, future of the country. Contemporary Afghan and Iranian poetry and music were incorporated into the piece in an effort to promote an atmosphere that would resonate with the original target audience, the countless victims of war in Afghanistan.

Infinite incompleteness premiered in December 2010 at the French Cultural Center in Kabul for an audience of nearly 250 Afghans and included a post-performance discussion in honour of Human Rights Day and Afghanistan's National Victim's Day. The piece was also performed at the National Victims' Conference organized by the TJCG in March and in December 2011. The fact that the play covers violations from all three phases of the conflict and is performed in all the local languages resonated well with the audience of the National Victims' Conference and resulted in a spontaneous sharing of testimonies wherein people from different parts of the country came forward to make known what had happened to them and their families. The piece has been staged several more times in Afghanistan and toured the United States to promote victims' concerns around justice issues in Afghanistan.

AHRDO also completed another larger-scale project using participatory theatre techniques to engage women on the creation of legislation from the community level up to help promote women's rights in Afghanistan. The purpose was to collect information on how to increase women's political participation, strengthen women's participation in law making, and identify and categorise legal problems women face. This programme was conducted in Kabul, Mazar-i-Sharif, Jalalabad, Bamiyan, and Herat. AHRDO staff analysed the findings from the theatre initiatives and based on major trends and recommendations identified by the women participants, drafted a final report, *Afghan Women after the Taliban: Will History Repeat Itself*? which was released to coincide with International Women's Day in March 2012.[55] The report was also distributed and discussed with Afghan parliamentarians, local officials and the international community.

[55] AHRDO, *Afghan Women After the Taliban: Will History Repeat Itself?* (Kabul: AHRDO, 2012).

While this work in Afghanistan signals, in a small, targeted way, that participatory theatre has the capacity to explore the legacies of conflict and to establish spaces for discussion for grass-roots action, there are a number of challenges Afghan practitioners face when carrying out this work. One of the most practical challenges is gaining access to theatre participants and spaces to conduct workshops. Many of the communities in which AHRDO works are very poor, and for some local authorities, partners and participants, their "support" to theatre projects is contingent on receiving funds. AHRDO is an officially registered NGO in Afghanistan and because of the influx of international funding for human rights and justice initiatives, it is not lost on victim communities that there could or should be monetary incentive for their participation beyond what AHRDO can provide. This makes it difficult to get to conversations about the true objectives of the processes for grass-roots, participatory, and transformative action.

Further complicating matters is the international community's rush to co-opt and fund any burgeoning creative practice for their own programming agendas.[56] As one Afghan artist noted, "I was trying to generate some genuine street art, but before it had even taken root I was contacted by a contractor for the American government working on a gender awareness project who wanted to use graffiti to raise consciousness of women's rights".[57] Newer practices like theatre or even street art are not indigenous to the context and take time to develop organically, to "Afghanize". Participatory theatre methodology seems to resonate as a practice within the communities AHRDO has worked with and has begun the process of Afghanizing, as evidenced by theatre participants requesting that their own stories be developed into a stage play, incorporating traditional Afghan symbols and poetry; women participating in a Theatre of the Oppressed workshop of their own accord developing and altering theatre games to better reflect the Afghan context; and perhaps most tellingly, people in Yakowlang in Bamiyan Province organizing themselves more formally in a victims' shura or council within their community.

Without this process, using these creative forms for political, human rights or development campaigns may not be particularly effective as the community at large may not know how to engage with them. Exploiting these processes without letting them take hold within the culture also undermines Afghan creative collaboration as it forces civil society to compete for funds rather than work together to develop a community of practice. The victims' group in Yakowlang is a stark example of this. The group came together organically around an idea, but then very quickly worked to attract donors and project funding, rather than build slowly and connect to a broader community.

This leads to perhaps the crux of the challenge in using participatory theatre methodologies in Afghanistan: the existing community itself. This presents itself

---

[56] This is in some ways inevitable as Afghanistan remains a very poor country and like others who are able to work, local activists need to make money (in some cases by capitalizing on donor ideas) to support large extended families.

[57] Jason Burke, "Kabul's Graffiti Guerrillas Put the Writing on the Walls", *The Guardian*, June 12, 2011, http://www.guardian.co.uk/world/2011/jun/12/kabul-grafitti-guerrillas-walls.

in difficulties in engaging men and women together within theatre initiatives, developing language and conceptual constructs that make sense to largely illiterate and uneducated populations, and in such a divided context bringing members of different ethnic groups together.

In an effort to start grappling with the idea of Afghanistan as a coherent nation, a requirement of each AHRDO theatre initiative is the inclusion of individuals from differing social and ethnic groups, who have lived through different periods of conflict and comprised of both men and women. This goes for the AHRDO staff that facilitates the initiatives as well. That a group of Playback Theatre actors, for example, who performed a variety of stories together consisted of diverse representations of Afghanistan and had men and women sharing the stage had considerable symbolic value, with many audience members expressing approving astonishment that something they thought "impossible" was actually happening in their community. At the same time, AHRDO staff may have to endure abuse and derision when first entering into a community because of their approach, introducing members of different groups to each other. This, coupled with the difficult personal narratives presented and other nonperformance-related duties within AHRDO, can take a physical and emotional toll on theatre staff.

The biggest hurdle for AHRDO practitioners, however, stems from the legacy war victims carry of decades of exclusion and deprivation of space to participate within the public sphere. Despite acknowledging the importance of empowerment, participation and learning—benefits participants feel theatre begins to provide—many war victims do not really believe in the idea of grass-roots, peaceful, people-led change in general or the transformative potential of theatre in particular.

Theatre allows them to communicate about the past often for the first time in a space where all experiences matter. This in particular creates impetus to participate; however, most war victims have yet to see anything in their country change through these actions and thus do not think that anything can or rather that they themselves can be the catalysts for such change. In Afghanistan, as in other contexts, the marginalized and excluded have lengthy grievances, but rarely if ever get "mad *together*… hopes and grievances [are] narrowly conceived, which blunt[s] a sense of common predicament".[58] In a context where there is no political will from either the international community or national government for transitional justice, the people themselves are going to have to come together to demand it. This is perhaps where participatory theatre best fits within the realm of grass-roots movements in Afghanistan—in helping chip away at a narrowly conceived community to a view to common predicament across divides and eventually to getting mad together to bring positive, lasting change.

These cultural shifts take time, and the very fact that people in the end are willing to engage in these creative processes indicates that having a space to share experiences and ideas is important and serves as a first step towards action. While

---

[58] Katherine Boo, *Behind the Beautiful Forevers: Life, Death, and Hope in a Mumbai Undercity* (New York: Random House, 2012), 237.

many theatre participants initially are unable to imagine an Afghanistan in the future—free of conflict and injustice in a broad sense—they are able to engage in games and create short performances based on their own immediate situations that required both actors and audience to take on new roles and attempt different solutions to resolve conflicts. This was seen in the process using theatre to develop legislative strategies to improve women's rights: women did have concrete recommendations for how their rights could be better protected. These workshops and performances then, being participatory in nature, perhaps have allowed those involved to begin to awaken from what Diana Taylor terms "percepticide", the metaphorical (and sometimes all too literal) blinding of the population on behalf of those, usually members of abusive political regimes, who have an interest in hiding the truth from view.[59] In Afghanistan, percepticide means being "too busy surviving" to consider what a future without impunity could look like or to demand one's rights.

In order for this consciousness to have more lasting effect, and potentially turn into positive social action, it needs to be sustained and supported outside of the theatre context and in communities at large. As one theatre activist reported, "Participatory theatre… is a very useful and effective means which would need to be accompanied by complementary means in order to mobilize civil society on transitional justice".[60] This view recognizes that participatory theatre is but one method of raising transitional justice issues and unless accompanied by other initiatives is unlikely to trigger significant change. It also underscores the importance of various human rights and justice networks working closely with each other and with artistic communities as well.

Individual theatre practices may not in and of themselves provide more permanent healing, but they can help lead to renewed cultural production and community life which can foster and sustain agency and closure. Through this sustained cultural production, through continuous questioning of the status quo, artists and activists can begin to breakdown the barriers and hierarchy that stifle innovation and prevent active engagement in issues concerning the community. Helping to reclaim, re-evaluate, and re-appropriate the cultural means of production can be a way to develop new norms for rights and justice at a local level, to allow individuals the ability to "feel recognized once more as people, not only as victims".[61]

In serving as conduits to other isolated, indigenous justice movements in the country connecting communities to one another, theatre and arts practitioners can in effect help to propel a third side from the ground up. Creating and upholding a continuum of this nature in a context that is marked by constant violent ruptures is

---

[59] Diana Taylor, *Disappearing Acts: Spectacles of Gender and Nationalism in Argentina's 'Dirty War'* (Durham, NC: Duke University Press, 1997), 72.

[60] ICTJ Assessment, "Transitional Justice Theatre Training of Trainers Project", unpublished report, August 2009.

[61] Pouligny, "Understanding Situations of Post-Mass Crime". See note 3.

not an easy task and can result in positive cultural initiatives being short-lived as both institutions and individual's burn out without strong community support and collaboration. To combat this then, just as artists and activists before them, AH-RDO and other members of the human rights and creative sectors in Afghanistan need to not only start conversations within and between communities, but help them get angry together, and work to a common goal.

Conclusions

Context is important when considering judicial and artistic/theatrical methods for truth-seeking and accountability: if one approach is relatively weak, the other may become more central to national healing.[62] This is certainly the case in Afghanistan, where impunity is rampant and the space for accountability continues to shrink. Formal transitional justice mechanisms, beyond documentation, seem a long way off, but an arts-based approach may be suitable even when large-scale, public discussion about the past is not yet possible. Theatre provides for the expression, both verbal and embodied, of collective feelings in the public realm. In a repressive environment, self-articulation is itself an act of defiance aimed at the established order, a rebellion against official attempts at silencing alternative accounts of history. Performance in this type of setting can serve not only to denounce but to defamiliarize the violence people live with every day, exposing its absurd and dehumanizing effects in a way that is coherent.[63]

Participatory theatre methodologies can be seen as possible tools for enriching grass-roots efforts to deal with the painful truth of the past because they can create spaces for discussion and allow for local ownership of the process of remembering, by taking into account its religious, ethical, cultural, social, and psychological dimensions, addressing individual and collective needs.[64] This is important as approaches to memory that privilege the individual fail to do justice to the cumulative and collective nature of trauma suffered by communities, literate or not.[65]

The work in Afghanistan thus far using participatory theatre methodologies has created fragile spaces for discussion about legacies of conflict, has begun to connect these discussions to higher level policy arenas, and has provided a start to building networks of victims. It has also allowed for female participation, providing a modicum of agency to victims in general and women in particular. These

---

[62] Cambodia is one place where the arts served as the main vehicle for victims of the genocide to communicate their experiences, because the tribunal was slow to start. See Stepakoff, "Telling and Showing", 23–24. Colombia is another context where the arts are used as a main vehicle for truth and memory, see note 24.

[63] A'ness, "Resisting Amnesia", 400.

[64] Ly Daravuth, "Notes on Pchum Ben" (working paper, Recasting Reconciliation through Culture and the Arts, Coexistence International, Waltham/Boston: Brandeis University, 2005), 4.

[65] Taylor, *The Archive and the Repertoire*, 193.

are small, fragile gains and worth building on, even if their sustainability is far from certain.

One of the biggest challenges comes in sustaining momentum and developing agency for change within communities that for too long have felt themselves powerless in the face of oppression and conflict. Those that do let theatre in have no real means of supporting it on their own, and practitioners run the risk of raising hopes they are certainly unable to fulfil. Building a truly grass-roots movement will require even deeper engagement with communities all over Afghanistan, putting further burden on theatre practitioners. A possible way to alleviate this while still continuously engaging communities would be to link participatory theatre work more closely with activities of other civil society networks as well as other arts initiatives, allowing for communities to understand the full scope of a justice movement and participate in different ways, both locally and in a broader national fora. It could also build a more robust and proactive civil society.

Rather than focus only on sending messages from communities directly to government and international audiences, it may also be useful to work laterally to connect more citizens to each other. Indeed, the actions of those closest to us, rather than government policy or expert opinion, are what most influence behaviours.[66]

Attempting to bring people together in this way may help to capture the power latent in communities but repressed because of prolonged conflict and corrupt regimes, breaking the silence on injustice "through a thousand acts of construction to build a better world, a thousand acts that declare that there is a much, much better way of organizing and deciding our lives together".[67]

In urging ordinary Afghans to begin organizing together, civil society needs to do the same, collaborating to develop a proactive network of citizens working for justice. This is fragile work in Afghanistan and can be easily taken apart or politicized along religious or ethnic lines. The arts serve as a way to begin pushing the bounds of what is deemed possible and the use of a largely symbolic tool—the production of a play—in place of more traditional transitional justice approaches can crucially preserve safety for activists who would otherwise be at risk. The fact that, at least in Afghanistan, the transformative potential of theatre in all its forms is for the most part underestimated and sometimes even ridiculed may be a comparative advantage. It may empower people, particularly women, to participate in the creation of an outlet where what happened to them individually and collectively can be dealt with openly and respectfully, and it may consequently keep their struggle for justice alive creatively.

[66] Carne Ross, *The Leaderless Revolution: How Ordinary People Will Take Power and Change Politics in the 21st Century* (New York: Blue Rider Press, 2011), xviii.

[67] Ibid., xxvi.

Bibliography

1. Afghan Civil Society Forum Organization (ACSFO). 2011. *A first step on a long journey: How people define violence and justice in Afghanistan* (1978–2008). Kabul: ACSFO.
2. Afghanistan Human Rights and Democracy Organization (AHRDO). 2012. *Afghan women after the Taliban: Will history repeat itself*? Kabul: AHRDO.
3. Afghanistan Independent Human Rights Commission (AIHRCi). *A call for justice: A national consultation on past human rights violations in Afghanistan*. Kabul: AIHRC.
4. A'ness, Francine. 2004. Resisting amnesia: Yuyachkani, performance, and the postwar reconstruction of Peru. *Theatre Journal* 56(3): 395–414.
5. Ayub, Fatima, Sari Kouvo, and Rachel Wareham. 2009. *Security sector reform in Afghanistan*. Initiative for Peacebuilding Report, Brussels: IfP.
6. Ayub, Fatima, Sari Kouvo, and Yasmin Sooka. 2009. *Addressing gender-specific violations in Afghanistan*. ICTJ Long Report, New York: ICTJ.
7. Barsalou, Judy. 2005. *Trauma and transitional justice in divided societies*. Special Report, Washington, D.C.: USIP.
8. Bharucha, Rustom. 2001. Between truth and reconciliation: Experiments in theatre and public culture. *Economic and Political Weekly* 36(39): 3763–3773.
9. Bilbija, Ksenija, Jo Ellen Fair, Cynthia E. Milton, and Leigh A. Payne eds. 2005. *The art of truth telling about authoritarian rule*. Madison: The University of Wisconsin Press.
10. Boo, Katherine. 2012. *Behind the beautiful forevers: Life, death, and hope in a Mumbai undercity*. New York: Random House.
11. Briceño-Donn, Marcela, Félix Reátegui, María Cristina Rivera, and Catalina Uprimny Salazar, eds. 2009. *Recordar en conflicto: Iniciativas no oficiales de memoria en Colombia*. Bogotá: ICTJ.
12. Burke, Jason. 2011. Kabul's graffiti guerrillas put the writing on the walls. http://www.guardian.co.uk/world/2011/jun/12/kabul-grafitti-guerrillas-walls. *The Guardian* June 12, 2011.
13. Chadwick, Jonathan. Working in Kosovo on a participatory theatre project on missing persons. AZ Theatre, http://www.aztheatre.org.uk/index.php?page=war-stories-kosovo.
14. Cohen, Cynthia E. 2005. Creative approaches to reconciliation. In *The psychology of resolving global conflicts, from war to peace*, vol. 3, ed. Mari Fitzduff, and Christopher E. Stout, 69–102. Westport: Greenwood Publishing Group.
15. Cohen, Cynthia. E., Roberto Gutierrez Varea, and Polly O. Walker, eds. 2011. Acting together: Performance and the creative transformation of conflict. *Resistance and reconciliation in regions of violence,* vol. 1. Oakland: New Village Press.
16. Cole, Catherine, M. 2007. Performance, transitional justice, and the law: South Africa's truth and reconciliation commission. *Theatre Journal* 59(2): 167–187.
17. Daravuth, Ly. 2005. Notes on pchum ben. Working paper, *recasting reconciliation through culture and the arts, coexistence international*. Waltham/Boston: Brandeis University.
18. Estvanik, Nicole. 2012. *Global spotlight*. USA: American Theatre Magazine. February.
19. Feldman, Shoshana, and Dori Laub. 1992. *Testimony: Crisis of witnessing in literature, psychoanalysis, and history*. New York: Routledge.
20. Gossman, Patricia. 2009. *Disarmament and transitional justice in Afghanistan*. ICTJ Case Study, New York: ICTJ.
21. Gossman, Patricia. 2011. Kabul's Stealth attack on human rights. *New York times/ International herald tribune*, 26 Dec 2011. http://www.nytimes.com/2011/12/27/opinion/kabuls-stealth-attack-on-human-rights.html.
22. Hosking, Bev, and Christian Penny. 2000. Playback theatre as a methodology for social change. Conference paper, DevNet Conference, Wellington, New Zealand, December 2000.
23. ICTJ Assessment. 2009. *Transitional justice theatre training of trainers project.*: Unpublished report, August 2009.

24. Kouvo, Sari. 2010. Facts for reconciliation: Human rights documentation needed. *Afghanistan analysts network*, 10 Oct 2010. http://aan-afghanistan.com/index.asp?id=1217.
25. Kouvo, Sari. 2009. *Transitional justice in the context of ongoing conflict: the case of Afghanistan*. ICTJ briefing report, New York: ICTJ.
26. Kouvo, Sari, and Dallas Mazoori. 2011. Reconciliation, justice and mobilization of war victims in Afghanistan. *International Journal of Transitional Justice* 5(3): 492–503.
27. McGrath, John. 2002. Theatre and democracy. *New Theatre Quarterly* 18: 133–139.
28. Mounier-Kuhn, Angélique. 2010. Le ≪ mapping report » sur l'Afghanistan: histoire d'un dossier escamoté. *Le Temps*, 2 Oct 2010. http://m.letemps.ch/Page/Uuid/aadd4d4e-cd9b-11df-a30b-a70320d5cebf/Le_mapping_report_sur_lAfghanistan_histoire_dun_dossier_escamote.
29. Naderi, Paraw. 2006. Poetry and politics. Iowa City: Lecture, Iowa City Public Library, 27 Oct 2006.
30. Nadery, Ahmad Nader. 2007. Peace or justice? Transitional justice in Afghanistan. *International Journal of Transitional Justice* 1(1):173–179.
31. Neelands, Jonothan. 2009. Acting together: Ensemble as democratic process in art and life. *Research in Drama Education: The Journal of Applied Theatre and Performance* 14(2): 173–189.
32. Omar, Wahid. 2008. From storytelling to community development. In *Telling stories to change the world: global voices on the power of narrative to build community and make social justice claims*, eds. Rickie Solinger, Madeline Fox, and Kayhan Irani, 193–200. New York: Routledges.
33. Pouligny, Beatrice. 2003. Understanding situations of post-mass crime by mobilizing different forms of cultural endeavors. Panel contribution, 19th IPSA world congress, Durban, South Africa, 1 July 2003.
34. Quimby, George H. 1960. Theatre in Iran and Afghanistan. *Educational Theatre Journal* 12(3): 200–204.
35. Ross, Carne. 2011. *The leaderless revolution: How Ordinary people will take power and change politics in the 21st century*. New York: Blue Rider Press.
36. Search for common ground. 2008. Burundi update. June 2008. http://www.sfcg.org/programmes/burundi/burundi_update.html.
37. Search for common ground. Centre Lokole/Search for Common Ground's Participatory Theatre for Conflict Transformation. http://www.ceri-sciencespo.com/themes/re-imaginingpeace/va/base/Congo_1173192498.pdf.
38. Search for Common Ground. *Participatory Theatre for Conflict Transformation: Training Manual*. Kinshasa: Search for Common Ground, n.d.
39. Siddiqui, Nadia. 2010. *Theatre and transitional justice in Afghanistan*. ICTJ briefing report, New York: ICTJ.
40. Siddiqui, Nadia, and Hjalmar Joffre-Eichhorn. From tears to energy: Early uses of participatory theatre in Afghanistan. In *Transitional justice, culture, and society*, ed Clara Ramirez-Barat. New York: Social Science Research Council, forthcoming.
41. Singhal, Arvind. 2004. Empowering the oppressed through participatory theatre. *Investigación y Desarrollo* 12(1): 138–163.
42. Solnit, Rebecca. 2009. *A paradise built in hell: The extraordinary communities that arise in disaster*. New York: Penguin Books.
43. Sontag, Susan. 2003. *Regarding the pain of others*. New York: Farrar, Straus and Giroux.
44. Stepakoff, Shanee. 2008. Telling and showing: Witnesses represent sierra leone's war atrocities in court and onstage. *The Drama Review* 52(1): 17–31.
45. Taylor, Diana. 2003. *The archive and the repertoire: Performing cultural memory in the Americas*. Durham, NC: Duke University Press.
46. Taylor, Diana. 1997. *Disappearing acts: Spectacles of gender and nationalism in Argentina's 'dirty war'*. Durham, NC: Duke University Press.

47. United Nations Assistance Mission in Afghanistan (UNAMA). 2008. Tears into energy: Community-based theatre and transitional justice. Unpublished report, April 2008.
48. Ury, William. 1999. *The third side: Why we fight and how we can stop*. New York: Penguin Books.
49. Winterbotham, Emily. 2012. *Healing the legacies of conflict in Afghanistan: Community voices on justice, peace and reconciliation*. Kabul: AREU.

Chapter 8
The Bleak Visions of *Literary Justice* for Survivors of Srebrenica: Examining the Fictional Narratives of Srebrenica Genocide in Light of the Insights from Transitional Justice

Ajla Demiragić and Edin Hodžić

The (Un)Reality of Genocide and the Truth of Fiction: An Introduction

Among the core justifications for, and underlying ideas behind, transitional justice are enabling a society devastated by mass violence to move forward, at the same time honouring the victims and remembering the past injustices or atrocious crimes as a means of preventing their occurrence in the future.[1] While the principal goal remains producing a societal shift from patterns of human rights violations and heinous crimes towards the future founded on the rule of law and universal condemnation of past atrocities, a goal perhaps conducted in the spirit of reconciliation, text and narrative seems to be the primary medium. Storytelling in transition is commonly accorded important, often gigantic, functions:

> By means of story, we can learn the terrible and noble dimensions of what happened, we can put names to faces, dimension to places and events, gain a sense of the humanity of the victims and the victimizers, relive the events of history in their fearsome detail: story provides that.[2]

[1] See generally Neil J. Kritz, ed., *Transitional Justice: How Emerging Democracies Reckon with Former Regimes*, Vol. 1 (Washington: USIP Press, 1995); see also Martha Minow, *Between Vengeance and Forgiveness: Facing History after Genocide and Mass Violence* (Boston: Beacon Press, 1998).
[2] Harold Scheub, 'Now for a Story', in *The Art of Truth-Telling about Authoritarian Rule*, ed. Ksenija Bilbija et al. (Madison: University of Wisconsin Press, 2005), 13.

A. Demiragić (✉)
Faculty of Philosophy, University of Sarajevo, Franje Rackog 1, 71000 Sarajevo, Bosnia and Herzegovina
e-mail: demiragic.ajla@gmail.com

E. Hodžić
Analitika—Center for Social Research, Kaptol 3, 71000 Sarajevo, Bosnia and Herzegovina
e-mail: edin.hodzic@analitika.ba

P. D. Rush and O. Simić (eds.), *The Arts of Transitional Justice*,
Springer Series in Transitional Justice 6, DOI: 10.1007/978-1-4614-8385-4_8,

Indeed, '[w]e read [transitional narratives] not only to discover truth, but also to discover order' in the chaos of past experiences.[3] Ultimately, as Ruti Teitel aptly explains, transitional justice narratives are structured as forward-looking tragedies with a resolution whereby '[t]he country's past suffering is somehow reversed, culminating in a happy ending of peace and reconciliation'.[4]

One of the principal characteristics of transition from the violent past towards a peaceful future is often the sheer cacophony of narratives: court decisions, truth-telling bodies' reports, historians' accounts, testimonial literature, media reports, documentaries, and works of literary or cinematic fiction—they all coexist, mutually communicate, often collide. In such a multitude of stories of the violent past, even the conventional distinction that is often postulated—that between document and fiction, between transitional justice mechanisms *per se* and artistic engagements with past atrocities—does not seem to be entirely plausible, at least when seen from inside the transition itself. Indeed, at the level of the medium of text, '[a]ny representation of trauma is to a certain degree "fictitious" in its attempt to recreate a narration beyond the collapse of language and meaning the traumatic experience originally produced'.[5] Moreover, even horrors described in court rulings and reports of various truth-telling institutions are often rightfully described as *unspeakable,*[6] unimaginable, even beyond the human condition.[7]

Leaving this ontological uncertainty of transitional stories aside, the relationship between *dealing with the past* and *fictionalizing the past* is generally described as beneficial and complementary. Indeed, fiction is seen as particularly suitable for serving the goals of transitional justice: the *untimeliness* of literature gives it a 'unique ability to look back and look forward simultaneously, reinterpreting the past and forecasting possible futures'.[8] Shoshana Felman also speaks of the post-WWII 'historical necessity of involving literature in action, of creating a new form of *narrative as testimony* [however imperfect] not merely to record, but to rethink and, in the act of its rethinking, in effect to transform history by bearing literary witness to the Holocaust'.[9]

---

[3] Theresa Godwin Phelps, *Shattered Voices: Language, Violence, and the Work of Truth Commissions* (Philadelphia: University of Pennsylvania Press, 2004), 125.

[4] Ruti Teitel, *Transitional Justice* (New York: Oxford University Press, 2000), 109.

[5] Martina Kopf, 'The Ethics of Fiction: African Writers on the Genocide in Rwanda', *Journal of Literary Theory* 6 (2012), 72.

[6] See e.g. Priscilla B. Hayner, *Unspeakable Truths: Transitional Justice and the Challenge of Truth Commissions* (New York and London: Routledge, 2011).

[7] Writing about the possible tasks of the Holocaust fiction, for example, Lang asserts that the 'Holocaust seems so thoroughly unreal that we need to bring it down to the human realm'. Berel Lang ed., Writing and the Holocaust (New York: Holmes & Meier, 1988), 92, quoted in Daniel R. Schwarz, *Imagining the Holocaust* (New York: St. Martin's Press, 1999), 37.

[8] Oscar Hemer, '*Writing Transition: Fiction and Truth in South Africa and Argentina*' (PhD diss., University of Oslo, 2011), 13.

[9] Shoshana Felman, 'Crisis of Witnessing: Albert Camus' Postwar Writings', *Cardozo Studies in Law and Literature* 2 (1991), 198.

Fictional narratives are seen as having the potential to support transitional justice efforts, in that they may open and shape public discourse regarding the causes and consequences of grave violence. As a characteristic voice of this understanding of the specific social role of fiction, Nadine Gordimer writes ecstatically about a new form of critical realism that is necessary in South Africa in that it can 'describe a situation so truthfully … that the reader can no longer evade it'.[10] It is also argued that fictional narratives can bring about richer, more complex and more disturbing forms of justice unburdened by the demands and limitations of the juridical or normative realm and by the dual imperatives of truth and reconciliation that permeate transitional justice discourse.[11] In this vein, it is indeed important to note a certain level of contradiction, or at least potential contradiction, between the legal and the literary means of dealing with the past. As Felman so perceptively explains, while juridical approaches to societal trauma aim to bring about *closure*, fiction is there to further open up the horrifying events and explore them in their deeper meaning and implications.[12]

It is also contended that fiction can fill the gaps and shortcomings in the core design of the transitional justice toolbox, illuminating the often neglected, complex questions of the 'here and now' of a transition, or the 'reality of the transitional'.[13] This is where fiction can make a major contribution, as it can 'offer polysemic descriptions of transitional moments, thereby bearing witness to these moments' complicated nature'.[14] Finally, fictional narratives can also function as transitional justice mechanisms in their own right. Apart from their truth-telling function, they can also be conceived as specific, disturbing artistic memorials of the atrocious past. Furthermore, one can imagine that fiction, just like any normative transitional justice mechanism, can serve the goal of translating and representing the victims' (otherwise unshareable) pain in language, thereby reversing the silencing that was the principal mechanism of oppression.[15] As African writer Boubacar Boris Diop put it, 'perhaps *only* fiction can treat this subject [of

---

[10] Nadine Gordimer, *The Essential Gesture: Writing, Politics and Places*, ed. Stephen Clingman (New York: Knopf, 1988), 298–299.

[11] Some of these virtues of fiction, both assumed and neglected, are usefully reviewed and illustrated in Sephiwe Ignatius Dube, 'Transitional Justice beyond the Normative: Towards a Literary Theory of Political Transitions', *International Journal of Transitional Justice* 2 (2011), 177–197.

[12] She writes: 'Literature is a dimension of concrete embodiment and a language of infinitude that, in contrast to the language of the law, encapsulates not closure but precisely what in a given legal case refuses to be closed and cannot be closed. It is to this refusal of the trauma to be closed that literature does justice'. Shoshana Felman, *Juridical Unconscious. Trials and Traumas in the Twentieth Century* (Cambridge: Harvard University Press, 2002), 8.

[13] Dube, 'Transitional Justice', 195.

[14] Ibid., 195.

[15] Godwin Phelps, *Shattered Voices*, 45–51.

genocide], by engaging the power of human imagination to make a move towards understanding, something which the reading of bare facts perhaps cannot do'.[16]

Ultimately, in this perspective, works of fiction thematizing past violence can contribute to providing a basis for a statewide dialogue on the past, which is, according to Osiel, the principal criterion for evaluating a country's transitional justice efforts.[17] Nonetheless, it is important to emphasize that these potential or assumed 'functions' of fiction in transition are not necessarily mutually exclusive. As Martha Minow contends, the '(a)rt of the unthinkable should disturb as well as commemorate'.[18]

A Note on Focus and Main Questions

Against the background of such a rich spectrum of assumed functions of fiction in transitional justice contexts, in this chapter, we examine how fictional literature speaks to transitional justice efforts in Bosnia and Herzegovina (hereinafter BiH). We do this by looking at a set of narratives that have emerged after the genocide in Srebrenica. In particular, one of the crucial questions we ask is: What are the visions of *survivors*—those located between, even defining the space between, the past and the future[19]? Admittedly, our principal question seems ill-founded at first glance. After all, '[t]his is genocide, this incomprehensible loss of past and future life, individual and collective'.[20] Nonetheless, we focus on examining literary elaborations of transitional justice for those who survived, for their place between past and present, between memory and forgetting.

This chapter is by no means an exhaustive examination of literary production thematizing Srebrenica genocide, which is indeed extremely rich, ever increasing and often hard to trace.[21] The narratives we have selected belong to the *literature*

[16] Boniface Mongo-Mobussa, *Désir d'Afrique* (Paris: Gallimard, 2002), 189, quoted in Audrey Small, 'The Duty of Memory: A Solidarity of Voices after the Rwandan Genocide', *Paragraph* 30 (2007), 88.

[17] Mark Osiel, *Mass Atrocity, Collective Memory, and the Law* (New Brunswick: Transaction Publishers, 1997), 3.

[18] Minow, *Between Vengeance*, 142.

[19] Indeed, '…the body of the witness is the ultimate site of memory of individual and collective trauma…', Felman, *Juridical Unconscious*, 9.

[20] Aleksandar Hemon, 'Srebrenica Web', *Dani*, July 1, 2005, accessed 21 January 2012, http://www.ex-yupress.com/dani/dani121.html.

[21] Very often, these works are published by their authors or in very limited number of copies. In addition, the system of legal deposit in national libraries of BiH and Republika Srpska is not fully effective, so the current national bibliography of BiH is incomplete and has rather limited coverage.

of trauma and, for the purposes of our analysis and interpretation, are treated above all as 'social products',[22] that is, they are stories that are capable of producing certain societal effects and participating in the formation of post-war identities. Naturally, not all of these narratives participate equally in the process of public 'standardization' of the story of Srebrenica. With some notable exceptions,[23] the majority of these narratives remain relatively unknown in the public sphere of BiH. Although we consulted the entire body of literary works on Srebrenica known to us, we engage primarily with those being closest to 'social products' in the above sense. In addition, a crucial factor in selecting the works to be examined in this paper is our thematic focus: we analyze the works that describe and explore the fates of survivors, visions of forgiveness, violent past and better future, as well as the ideas of justice *after* genocide.

Although extremely important autobiographical prose works on the Srebrenica genocide have been produced,[24] we do not examine testimonial literature as such. We interrogate first and foremost how arts, literature and film in particular, responded to the challenges of witnessing the unimaginable and utterly undescribable horror of the Srebrenica genocide, as well as, more importantly for our purposes, the 'afterlife' of the survivors. At the same time, we endeavour to tackle a crucial question formulated by Kali Tal: 'What happens when a survivor's story is retold (and revised) by a writer who is not a survivor? How are survivor's stories adapted to fit and then contained within the dominant structure of social, cultural and political discourse?'[25]

---

[22] Advancing their thesis of 'social life as storied', Margaret Somers and Gloria D. Gibson emphasize that narratives need to be treated as social products, in that '... stories guide action; that people construct identities (however, multiple and changing) by locating themselves or being located within a repertoire of emplotted stories; that "experience" is constituted through narrative...'. M. Somers and G. Gibson, 'Reclaiming the epistemological "Other": Narrative and the social constitution of Identity', in Social Theory and Politics of Identity, ed. Craig Calhoun (Cambridge: Blackwell, 1994), 38–39, quoted in Steph Lawler, 'Narrative in Social research', in *Qualitative research in action* ed. Tim May (London: Sage publication, 2002), 244.

[23] Such as the oratorio *Srebrenica Inferno*, which has been featuring prominently during the central July commemoration and burial of the newly identified victims of genocide, Abdulah Sidran's poem *Tears of the Mothers of Srebrenica*, which was initially published in the most widely circulated newspaper in the Federation of BiH, or a bestselling novel *When it Was July*.

[24] Examples include writings by Emir Suljagić *Razglednica iz groba* (Postcards from the Grave) (Sarajevo: Civitas, 2005) or (factual) novels based on survivors' testimonies such as Mihrija Feković-Kulović's *Živjeti i umirati za Srebrenicu* (Living and Dying for Srebrenica) (Sarajevo: Connectum, 2009) or Sadik Salimović's *Put smrti: Srebrenica-Tuzla: prema istinitim događajima* (The Path of Death: Srebrenica-Tuzla: Based on True Events) (Sarajevo: Udruženje pokret majki enklava Srebrenica i Žepa, 2008).

[25] Kali Tal, Worlds of Hurt: Reading the Literatures of Trauma, accessed 15 April 2011, http://www.kalital.com/Text/Worlds/Chap1.html

A Brief Note on Normative Transitional Justice in BiH

What does it mean to examine fictional works in the context of transitional justice, in particular in BiH? In many other states, including South Africa and Argentina, fictional accounts of the violent past can, and indeed sometimes are, compared with normative, official narratives, such as those of truth commissions.[26] In BiH, however, fiction can mostly be seen as an anticipation of normative transitional justice, having in mind that a Bosnia-specific, comprehensive and ambitious transitional justice strategy has just been drafted, with still uncertain prospects of its being adopted, let alone consistently implemented.[27] In such circumstances, fictional works that thematize the 1992–1995 war and its consequences are necessarily set against the background of the uncertain, cacophonous and ethnically divided field of Bosnia's transitional justice.

Despite more than 15 years of engagement of a wide range of actors in this field, progress is still not substantial in BiH, at least when seen from the perspective of thc goals of transitional justice. While prosecutions, with a myriad of problems and delays, continue at all levels,[28] truth telling beyond the courts is still underdeveloped and mostly unofficial, confined to individual, mainly mono-ethnic initiatives of various NGOs.[29] Disputes even over minimal, forensic truth still permeate public discourse and manipulation with numbers of victims on all sides continues, along with negationism and denial of genocide in Srebrenica in particular.[30] Divisions permeate the field of cultural production as well, in particular when it comes to artistic works thematizing the recent war in BiH. Such works, as a rule, remain confined to the parts of the state where they were produced (Federation of BiH or Republika Srpska).[31]

Genocide in Srebrenica undoubtedly and understandably received most attention in the various justice and documentation efforts. Nonetheless, most, if not all,

---

[26] See generally Hemer, *Writing Transition.*

[27] For full text of a working draft of the strategy (in local languages), see Ministry for Human Rights and Refugees of BiH and Ministry of Justice of BiH, *Transitional Justice Strategy for BiH 2012–2016*, 2012, accessed 08 July 2012, http://www.mpr.gov.ba/aktuelnosti/propisi/konsultacije/Strategija%20TP%20-%20bosanski%20jezik%20fin%20doc.pdf.

[28] See e.g. Alejandro Chehtman, 'Developing Bosnia and Herzegovina's Capacity to Process War Crimes Cases: Critical Notes on a "Success Story"', *Journal of International Criminal Justice* 3 (2011), 547–570.

[29] See generally Graeme Simpson, Edin Hodzic and Louis Bickford, Looking Back, *Looking Forward: Promoting Dialogue through Truth-Seeking in Bosnia and Herzegovina*, accessed 8 July 2012, http://www.undp.ba/upload/publications/Looking%20back,%20looking%20forward.pdf. See also Dragan Popović, *Transitional Justice Guidebook for BiH*, UNDP BiH (2009), esp. 147–151, accessed 27 February 2012, http://www.undp.ba/upload/publications/Vodic%20kroz%20tranzicijsku%20pravdu%20u%20BiH.pdf.

[30] See e.g. Paul B. Miller, 'Contested Memories: The Bosnian Genocide in Serb and Muslim Minds', *Journal of Genocide Research* 3 (2006), 311–324.

[31] See e.g. Jasmila Zbanić, 'Filmovi, zabrane i radost', accessed 28 February 2012, Radio Sarajevo http://www.radiosarajevo.ba/novost/74532/jasmila-zbanic-filmovi-zabrane-i-radost.

non-fiction or normative documents on Srebrenica have a typically narrow, investigative focus on clarifying the chain of events in the massacre of more than 8,000 Bosniak men in this former Bosniak enclave in mid-July 1995. They are prevalently concerned with examining the role of particular actors—such as the role of the UN in the Report of the Secretary General,[32] the role of the Dutch batallion within the UN forces in the case of the NIOD report,[33] or the responsibility of the Republika Srpska military and police in the report of the Government of Republika Srpska's Srebrenica Commission.[34] Perhaps surprisingly, it was only the ICTY Trial Chamber in the Krstic case that devoted some attention to considering, however, cursorily, the visions of survivors and their future after genocide. The Krstic chamber established that '[i]n a patriarchal society, such as the one in which the Bosnian Muslims of Srebrenica lived, the elimination of virtually all the men has made it almost impossible for the Bosnian Muslim women who survived the take-over of Srebrenica to successfully re-establish their lives'.[35] Furthermore, '[b]y killing all the military aged men, the Bosnian Serb forces effectively destroyed the community of the Bosnian Muslims in Srebrenica as such and eliminated all likelihood that it could ever reestablish itself on that territory'.[36] And, even more disturbingly, the Trial chamber in Krstic prophetically states that:

> 'by killing the leaders and defenders of the group and deporting the remainder of it, the VRS and General Krstic had assured that the Bosnian Muslim community of Srebrenica and its surrounds would not return to Srebrenica nor would it reconstitute itself in that region or indeed, anywhere else'. Moreover, 'what remains of the Srebrenica community survives in many cases only in the biological sense, nothing more. It's a community in despair; it's a community clinging to memories; it's a community that is lacking leadership; it's a community that's a shadow of what it once was'.[37]

The ICTY's portrayal of the survivors is a monolithic vision of community, even of its individual members, as entities without future. In this sense, while transitional justice is perhaps forward-looking at the level of the meta-narrative, in which the ICTY is one of the principal actors providing for justice, even truth and reconciliation,[38] the future of the survivors themselves seems deprived of any felicitous resolution. In a search for possible literary alternatives, in the next

[32] UN General Assembly, Report of the Secretary-General Pursuant to General Assembly Resolution 53/35, 'The Fall of Srebrenica', 15 November 1999, A/54/549.

[33] See e.g. Alexander Moens, 'Lessons for Peacekeepers: Srebrenica and the NIOD Report', *Canadian Foreign Policy Journal* 3 (2003), 141–158.

[34] See Popović, *Transitional Justice*, 60–63.

[35] Prosecutor v. Radislav Krstić, ICTY Case No. IT-98-33-T, (2 August 2001), para. 91.

[36] Ibid., para. 597.

[37] Ibid., para. 592. In text quotes refer to the prosecution argument.

[38] See e.g. Diane F. Orentlicher, That *Someone Guilty Be Punished: The Impact of the ICTY in Bosnia* (New York: Open Society Institute, 2011), 39–42, accessed 21 January 2012, http://www.soros.org/initiatives/justice/articles_publications/publications/that-someone-guilty-20100707/that-someone-guilty-20100708.pdf.

section, we examine if, and in what ways, the literary imagination of the Srebrenica genocide and its aftermath is different, deeper, more elaborate or more disturbing than this legal imagining of the ICTY.

Reflections of Genocide in Bosnian Fiction

Introductory Remarks

Although Srebrenica remains 'an obsessive topic of the public space in Bosnia and Herzegovina on which political myths are built',[39] it appears that the grand theme of genocide has been introduced into the BiH cultural and artistic realm gradually and rather cautiously. Once it became a matter of artistic production, however, the topic of the genocide in Srebrenica experienced a literary boom of a sort. After *Novel on Srebrenica*[40] was published in 1999, the next decade witnessed the publication of such diverse literary works as the poem *The Srebrenica Inferno,*[41] the novels *When it Was July,*[42] *Srebrenica City,*[43] *People, be Wondered,*[44] several prose works of Mirsad Mustafić,[45] a collection of children's stories *The Father's Embrace: Stories on Srebrenica,*[46] works of poetry such as Abdulah Sidran's *Tears of the Mothers of Srebrenica,*[47] *Srebrenica* by Ferida Duraković, *Potočari, Bosnia by* Ajla Terzić, *Srebrenica, Potočari* by Šejla Šehabović, as well as a number of collections of poems[48]; finally, the topic of Srebrenica was explored in

---

[39] Enver Kazaz, interview by Omer Karabeg, *Magazin plus*, 26 June 2010, accessed 20 May 2011, http://www.magazinplus.eu/index.php.kultura/2482-kada-ce-biti-napisan-prvi-roman-o-srebrenici

[40] Isnam Taljić, *Roman o Srebrenici*, 5th ed. (Srebrenica: Općina Srebrenica, 2007).

[41] Džemaludin Latić, *Srebrenički inferno: pismo Danteu Alighieriju iz Bosne*, 3rd ed. (Sarajevo: Connectum, 2006).

[42] Nura Bazdulj-Hubijar, *Kad je bio juli* (Zagreb, VBZ, 2005).

[43] Osman Arnautović, *Srebrenica city* (Tuzla: Infograf, 2007).

[44] Đidana Sarić, *Čudi se, svijete* (Sarajevo: Grafički promet d.o.o, 2006).

[45] Mirsad Mustafić, *Krvava šamija* (Tuzla: Off-Set, 2006), *Rastanak u Potočarima* (Tuzla: Off-Set, 2007), *Samrtni zvuci srebrenog grada* (Tuzla: Off-set, 2009), *Posljednji vapaj enklave* (Tuzla: Off-set, 2012).

[46] Fuad Kovač, ed., *Očev zagrljaj: priče o Srebrenici* (Sarajevo: Behar, 2006).

[47] Abdulah Sidran, *Suze majki Srebrenice* (Sarajevo: Bemust, 2009).

[48] For example, V. Bajramović, *Srebrenica nakraj srca* (Sarajevo: self-publishing, 2010.); Z. Muratović, *Srebrenica je vrisak do neba* (Sarajevo: self-publishing, 2005); M. Salihbeg Bosnawi, *Srebrenica je zvijezda padalica* (Sarajevo: self-publishing, 2000); S. Šahović, *Krvava Srebrenica.* (Sarajevo: Zonex ex Libris, 2006).

two plays—*Apparitions from the Silver Age*[49] and *Crocodile 'Lacoste'*,[50] and in one film—*Belvedere*,[51] directed by Ahmed Imamović.

As was the case with many fictional narratives on the Shoah,[52] the vast majority of literary works on Srebrenica could also be said to be plagued with the necessity of offering a realistic depiction of the traumatic event and its aftermath. Nonetheless, when speaking of the imperative of using 'the appropriate "genre"',[53] one can note a rather interesting formal diversity in terms of genre, a mixing of the so-called high and low literary forms, and the presence of a rather diverse set of fictional models. It was relatively early in the development of this specific sub-genre of *literature of genocide* that the radically stylized and aestheticized literary forms depicting the tragedy of Srebrenica have been produced: for example, the poem *Srebrenica Inferno*, written in Dante-like tercines, or the play *Apparitions from the Silver Age*, with a complex metaphorical apparatus and rather challenging intertextual connections. On the other end of the spectrum lie the narratives belonging to popular fiction, such as the epistolary novel *When it Was July* or the crime novel *Srebrenica City*.

Despite this richness of form, what marks the majority of narratives on Srebrenica is a certain ideological–aesthetical uniformity, manifested in the lack of critical reconceptualizations of given ethno-national and other identity roles. Although some of these narratives are attempted to be built as polyphonic, dialogical forms in the Bakhtinian sense,[54] they are rarely such as they are fixed within clear ethno-ideological identities and points of view. In most instances, focalization as well as the narrative perspective is fixed. The commonly used narration in first person suggests a clear relationship between the narrator and the character. Although narration in this manner should create the mask of an authentic, truthful survivor's account, such a storytelling strategy is more often than not burdened by a predefined, one-dimensional role model of a victim with which to emotionally identify.[55]

---

[49] Almir Bašović, *Priviđenja iz srebrnog vijeka* (Sarajevo: Oko, 2004).

[50] This award-winning play by Zlatko Topčić has still not been published, but it was set on scene in 2011 at The Chamber Theatre 55 from Sarajevo and directed by Sulejman Kupusović.

[51] *Belvedere*, directed by Ahmed Imamović (Sarajevo: Comprex, 2010), DVD.

[52] See generally Schwarz, *Imagining Holocaust.*

[53] Examining, inter alia, the issue of viability of representing Holocoust in a different narrative model, Hayden White identifies the prevalence of 'the kind of rule that stipulates that a serious theme—such as mass murder or genocide—demands a noble genre, such as epic or tragedy, for its proper representation'. *Figural Realism: Studies in the Mimesis Effect* (Baltimore: The John Hopkins Univ. Press, 1999), 31.

[54] See generally Mikhail M. Bakhtin, *Problems of Dostoevsky's Poetics*. Ed. and trans. C. Emerson. (Minneapolis: University of Minnesota Press, 1984).

[55] As Renata Jambrešić Kirin explains, analysing testimonial literature on the war in Croatia, '[p]ersonal experience relies on ideological patterns in order to get an acceptable interpretation within a wider community, whereas the reception of these interpretations, adaptations, artistic works etc. is often realized through intensive emotional identification, which forms the basis for building the common identity markers'. 'Svjedočenje i povijesno pamćenje: o pripovjednom posredovanju osobnog iskustva', *Narodna umjetnost* 2 (1995), 180.

This overwhelming uniformity is best seen in the presentation of characters. Consider the image of survivors. As will be shown below, almost all narratives on Srebrenica portray them in accordance with the dominant media representations, primarily in a superficial and one-dimensional way. This is clearly not in accordance with the 'reality of the transitional' in Bosnia, where the community of survivors of Srebrenica, just like any victim community, is heterogeneous and diverse, displaying various degrees of political contextualization, and mobilization, of their individual and collective traumas.[56]

Common Characteristics and Narrative Patterns

Survivors of Srebrenica in these narratives are typically women, elderly and children. However, women in particular are depicted using the same pattern: an unnamed Bosniak woman (or a woman with a typical ethnic name) who is inevitably a mother and a wife, that is, a widow. They are presented as figures of survivors who barely live, mechanically performing routine everyday functions, deformed mentally and physically by the devastating loss. They are deeply melancholic,[57] essentially incapable of terminating the never-ending mourning process and starting to heal. Nonetheless, there is an important nuance to this one-dimensionality of characters, especially when seen through the lens of transitional justice. In some narratives, they are depicted as being *above* earthly considerations of transitional justice, not merely incarnating the 'social value of suffering'.[58] In such perspectives, the loss and the figure of a victim/survivor are extremely idealized: Fatima as righteous[59] in the *Apparitions from the Silver Age*, Ruvejda as a patient and self-sacrificing sister who tirelessly takes care of her disabled brother and her sick sister in *Belvedere*. Alternatively, the characters of (female) survivors are depicted as having lost any trace of scruple, while almost the only characteristic that is left in them is the animalistic instinct of survival and self-protection; a scene from *The Novel on Srebrenica* is particularly telling:

---

[56] See e.g. Craig Evan Pollack, 'Intentions of Burial: Mourning, Politics, and Memorials Following the Massacre at Srebrenica', *Death Studies* 2 (2003), 125–142.

[57] In *Mourning and Melancholia* (1917), Freud describes melancholia 'as an enduring devotion on the part of the ego to the lost object. A mourning without end, melancholia results from the inability to resolve the grief and ambivalence precipitated by the loss of the loved object, place, or ideal" as cited in David L. Eng and David Kazanjian, 'Introduction', in *Loss. The Politics of Mourning*, eds. David L Eng and David Kazanjian (Los Angeles, London: Univ. of California Press, 2003), 3.

[58] Ruti Teitel, 'Transitional Justice as Liberal Narrative', in Experiments with Truth: Transitional Justice and the Process of Truth and Reconciliation: Documenta 11, Platform 2, ed. Okwui Enwezor et al. (Ostfildern-Ruit: Hatje Cantz, 2001), 241, as cited in Dube, 'Transitional Justice', 185.

[59] Bašović, *Priviđenja iz*, 9.

> I am looking at the female creatures in a hurry. These creatures have after a long, too long period of waiting, tasted real food. They gained strength to attack the trucks which brought food to them. No one can handle them ... Instinct of survival rules over the mass of women who for too long only had death before their eyes. .... They step on each other. They choke. They let their children's hands leave their fists. .... They even throw their babies away from their chests. It is not known that a female dog would discard her puppies.[60]

Most characters in this subgenre are depicted as holders of patriarchal and ethno-national values. For example, in the introductory verses of *Srebrenica Inferno*, depicting the horrific scene of suffering of the unnamed Bosniak woman and her family and of her little girl being taken away from her, the woman speaks out the last message to her daughter: 'My dear child, save the face of your proud father'.[61] In *When it Was July*, aunt Zejna will condemn Mirza's decision to get engaged to Biljana, a Serb: 'Poor Mirza, you must be out of your mind, you do not intend seriously to marry a chetnik, you know how much suffering they inflicted upon us...'[62]

At the same time, the narratives often portray women as uneducated housewives. Even if they had a career before the war, they do not wish or cannot work anymore. In the opening scene of *Belvedere*, at her sister's suggestion that she should apply for the post of a teacher at the local school, Ruvejda replies: 'I'm no good for a teacher or children anymore and children are not what they used to be'. The main characters are usually reduced to caregivers—apart from their duties of care for others and the search for their missing men, they have no function or purpose whatsoever. This is not to be confused with feminist reconceptualizations of the notion of caring labour, which comes to be understood as an active principle giving rise to 'a "rationality of care", exemplifying many alternative ideals of reason recently formulated by feminists'.[63] Rather, the taking care of others in these narratives is usually described as a set of mechanical, automatic gestures, empty skills deprived of any value in a patriarchal scheme, not least because they are necessary and taken for granted.

In the majority of these narratives, then, most of, primarily female, the characters of survivors of Srebrenica are portrayed as those to whom 'nothing, either bad or good, can happen any more'.[64] They are 'more dead than all the dead of

---

[60] Taljić, *Roman o*, 150–151 (Unless otherwise indicated, all citations from selected narratives are translated by the authors).

[61] Latić, *Srebrenica Inferno*, 11–12.

[62] Bazdulj-Hubijar, *Kad je bio*, 153.

[63] Sara Ruddick, *Maternal Thinking. Toward the Politics of Peace* (New York: Ballantine Books, 1989), 46.

[64] The verse from Abdulah Sidran's acclaimed poem *Uzevši kost i meso* (Taking the Bone and Flesh Away), from his collection of poems *Sarajevski tabut* (The Coffin of Sarajevo), published in 1993 in besieged Sarajevo.

their kin',[65] while Srebrenica 'resembles an open grave the most',[66] in which 'neither dead nor living can dwell…'.[67] Nonetheless, an important contradiction can be noted: that between the survivors' general lack of interest in life and future after genocide, on the one hand, and their painstaking efforts at identifying the mortal remains of their missing family members. The identifications and burial are, however, normally not depicted as potentially opening the way towards healing and a new future for survivors. Rather, the struggle to find the information on mortal remains of their loved ones is often presented as the single remaining issue worth living for.

A generational motif also dominates the narratives of the Srebrenica genocide. Commonly, there is a tension, sometimes even a conflict, between the survivors and the first *post-memory generation*—those who were born after the trauma, as well as those who experienced the traumatic event as children. They are depicted as facing a double marginalization, because they are excluded not only from the wider society, but also from the small community of survivors.[68] At the same time, they are normally accorded the role of those who carry the desire for change and for life that would not be entirely organized around the routine activities of remembrance and the search for the missing relatives. Such a wish, however, turns out to be ill-founded, as it most often ends up in another form of futile escapism, as in the case of Adnan, the young son of Zejna in *Belvedere*, who decides to change his life by entering a reality show[69] or the young girl Zarfa from *Srebrenica City*, who chooses the desperate path of revenge.

The motif of isolation of survivors from wider society is another dominant characteristic of literature on Srebrenica genocide. In most of these works, the story is set in the space of a refugee camp[70] or abandoned houses. Such closed semantic spaces do not allow for transformation of characters to occur. They are typically located at the periphery or even in very isolated, distant places becoming ghettos of a sort, unwanted reminders of the war and its disturbing heritage. In such a milieu, except for the novels *When it Was Ju*ly and, to a certain extent, *Srebrenica City*, the majority of the depicted characters do not cherish any hope for the future. In this sense, the verses of the poem *The Tears of the Mothers of Srebrenica* are more than illustrative:

---

[65] *Belvedere*, dir. Imamović. accessed 10 January 2012, http://belvederemovie.com/.

[66] Taljić, *Roman o Srebrenici*, 33.

[67] Sidran, *Tears of*, 5.

[68] This tension is particularly thematized in novels *When it was July* and *Srebrenica City*, where the respective central characters are a young boy Mirza and a teenager girl Zarfa.

[69] In particular, through a series of contrapuntal scenes his attempt to live a life of an ordinary teenager is presented in parallel with his aunt's painstaking search for the truth. For example, while the women are visiting the post-mortem identification centre, he is making a set of weights; while they are attending a silent protest they participate in every month on the eleventh day, he is going to an internet café.

[70] For example, the very title of Imamović's movie is taken from the name of the real refugee camp near Gorazde in eastern Bosnia.

… And you say:
Look to the future!
And we
Do not see it at all
At any place in any way
Nor do we see that it
Watches us
By any eye
Let alone that it sees us
And cares about us
We do not have a future
Of any kind
We have the present
Which a human eye
Cannot even look at[71]

Finally, another set of motifs in the fictional narratives of Srebrenica genocide is the overwhelming sense of distrust in justice and its mechanisms, and the emphasis on what transitional justice fails to achieve, rather than on its possible successes. The majority of these literary works exhibit a considerable distrust in the very possibility of closure. In all these narratives, achieving a form of closure is conceived as possible, if at all, only on the micro-level, be it a necessity to forgive and move on against all odds[72] or blind revenge replicating the cruelness of the crime.[73] Except for *When it Was July* and, to a certain extent, *Srebrenica Inferno* and its motif of an inter-religious dialogue as a way out from vicious cycles of victimization, no other narrative suggests the strategies of 'dealing with the past'. Rather, they force the protagonists of the story to remain indefinitely trapped in the nightmares and the incorrigible losses of the past, or to undertake the desperate path of the final self-destruction as the only way of ending the hopeless transition.[74]

---

[71] Sidran, *Tears of*, 11.

[72] Examples are the main character of *When it Was July*, Mirza and his decision to marry a Serb girl as a somewhat simplistic and superficial step towards restoring 'brotherhood and unity', or the illustrative conversation of the woman survivor of Srebrenica with Maria in Ravenna, at the end of Srebrenica Inferno.

[73] In *Srebrenica City*, the main female character chooses the path of revenge as the only viable form of justice.

[74] In *Belvedere*, for example, the main character Ruvejda activates a bomb to kill both herself and the man she suspects to be connected with the slaughter of her family; in *Crocodile Lacoste*, the killing of both herself and her father is the only way out for the woman who had found out about the heinous crimes her father committed.

The Realities and the Fiction of the 'Transitional'

How, then, do these fictional narratives of Srebrenica speak to normative transitional justice and, in particular, *the reality of the transitional* in Bosnia?

As a first step, one should critically reassess the omnipresent motif of the powerlessness of the victims in literature of Srebrenica genocide, with its many layers and paradoxes. In contrast to the literary images of the powerless community of survivors of Srebrenica, one can note a still vital symbolic power they enjoy in the divided public sphere of BiH, in particular in relation to cultural production. Indeed, among the fictional narratives of Srebrenica, there seems to be a tendency of confirming their 'authenticity' or 'adequacy' by getting either formal support or recognition from leading victim associations. This was the case, for example, with *Belvedere*, which was, as the introductory credits show, supported not only by various state institutions, but also by the women from the Movement of the Mothers from the Enclaves of Srebrenica and Zepa.[75] The latter have not only symbolically supported the film, but also took part in it as actors in various scenes of protests and gatherings in support of the search for the missing. This fictionalization of real characters adds another dimension to the imperative of a realistic and truthful presentation of trauma of Srebrenica. Moreover, another victim association[76] has proven to be a very efficient censorship institution of a sort when it managed to urge state authorities not to allow Angelina Jolie to film her *In the Land of Blood and Honey* on original locations in BiH.[77] These seemingly symbolic gestures are at the same time an expression of a somewhat counterintuitive and paradoxical control of otherwise powerless survivors over both their traumatic experience and its fictional reconstructions, which also comes to be seen as a deeply politicized act.

In effect, the majority of fictional narratives on Srebrenica have participated in the process of memorialization of, and testifying about, genocide using strategies of cultural coping that lead to the codification of trauma, but also to its

---

[75] The association was officially formed in 1999, but their activism goes back to 1996, when they organized their first protests demanding serious investigations into the fate of their missing men. On this association and their trajectory from a small grass root organization to a powerful transitional justice actor see Olivera Simic, 'What Remains of Srebrenica? Motherhood, Transitional Justice and Yearning for the Truth', *Journal of International Women's Studies* 4 (2009).

[76] Association 'Women-Victims of War'. See more about the organization at www.zena-zrtva-rata.ba.

[77] Initially, after a fierce protest by a representative of The Association of Women-Victims of War over the then still unconfirmed information that the film would feature a love story between an imprisoned Bosniak woman and a Serb army officer, the Ministry of Culture of the Federation of Bosnia and Herzegovina has refused to issue an authorization for shooting the film on the territory of this Bosnia's entity. See e.g. Belma Bećirbašić 'Trgovanje emocijama žrtve' *Dani*, 22 October 2010, 30.

'mythologization'.[78] Indeed, as Jasmina Husanović explains, 'the challenges of mythologization are understandably considerable: it is necessary to protect, in the state of an overwhelming block, an immense loss of life and meaning, and mythologization does that grandiosely, at the same time hiding the still present political trauma'.[79]

In an attempt at drawing the contours of a framework for understanding and explaining the endurance of dominant thematic patterns and motifs in fictional prose of Srebrenica, one should consider the important issue of the sequencing or timing of normative transitional justice in relation to fictionalizing the horrifying past. Normative transitional justice interventions are usually undertaken as soon after the tragic event as possible, with a temporally limited mandate and in a hopeful attempt to urgently shape and sanitize the public sphere and set the boundaries of the unacceptable discourse on the past in transition.[80] In BiH, especially having in mind the limited reach and societal impact of war crimes trials at all levels,[81] an official, coordinated and concerted project of dealing with the past has not yet been conceived of, let alone initiated. In such circumstances, trapped between the extremes of political appropriation of Srebrenica genocide by Bosniak political elites, and denial and revisionism among the Bosnian Serb leadership,[82] the extra-literary imperative of simplistic, repetitive, even screaming *truthfulness* becomes hard to ignore and resist.

A second dimension of the problematic of timing is that it may well be that different and diverse approaches to storytelling about genocide necessarily emerge over time. Such diversification of storytelling on the violent past is particularly important. While it is true that the above-mentioned broader, political considerations necessarily influence and shape cultural production in this field, different, more imaginative approaches would, in turn, be much more effective at the individual level. Writing about the literature of Holocaust, Daniel Schwarz reminds that 'as we move from the Holocaust, the matrix of naturalistic verisimilitude becomes less effective … than illuminating distortions, parables, and mythic history *because* the memoirs and diaries for survivors and historical novels have become part of our felt knowledge'.[83] It is, however, questionable that the Srebrenica genocide, which is dealt with in a complex web of juridical proceedings, scattered documentary evidence, competing documentation efforts and fully

[78] Kali Tal considers 'mythologization', along with 'medicalization' and 'disappearance', one of the principal strategies of cultural coping with a traumatic event: 'Mythologization works by reducing a traumatic event to a set of standardized narratives (twice- and thrice-told tales that come to represent "the story" of the trauma) turning it from a frightening and uncontrollable event into a contained and predictable narrative'. Tal, *Worlds of Hurt*, Chap. 1.

[79] Husanović, *Između traume*, 65.

[80] Cf. Hayner, *Unspeakable Truths*, 215–216.

[81] See e.g. Lara Nettelfield, *Courting Democracy in Bosnia and Herzegovina: The Hague Tribunal's Impact in a Postwar State* (Cambridge: Cambridge University Press, 2010), Chap. 5.

[82] See e.g. Miller, *Contested Memories*.

[83] Schwarz, *Imagining Holocaust*, 141.

fledged denial projects, has indeed become part of the universally 'felt knowledge' in BiH. Hence, however strong and counterproductive the numbing effect of the repeated and horrifying stories of Srebrenica, it is probably still early for symbolism and parables about the Bosnian genocide.

Instead of a Conclusion: Towards Literary Transitional Justice

Can transitional justice for Srebrenica begin in fiction? As things stand now, fictional narratives on Srebrenica genocide remain painful, descriptive and repetitive. They do not only resist closure implicit in transitional justice efforts; they seem to go even deeper into hopelessness. The above-elaborated patterns in literary and cinematic representations of Srebrenica can be said to be the fictional reflections of the actual building blocks in the project of mythologization of genocide which permeates public discourse in BiH, in particular among Bosniaks. This is why it is not surprising that in such fictional narratives, there are no imaginary conversations between perpetrators and survivors, there is no single survivor who carries hope, at least for future generations, the time does not pass by for Srebrenica, while the survivors, at least in the 'reality of fiction', are hopelessly murdered with a delayed effect. In other words, in fictional accounts of Srebrenica, surviving genocide is still, as a rule, understood as a contradiction in terms.

Fiction on Srebrenica has not managed to distort, explore and dissect, or to critically examine the juridical approaches to genocide, but have merely and passively reproduced it in an artistic form. Even more so, fictional narratives of Srebrenica continue to depict survivors almost exclusively as prisoners of the past, incapable of healing. What they in effect do is not give voice to those deprived of the voice, as Teresa Godwin Phelps would suggest,[84] but rather offer a very limited insight into their overwhelming voicelessness. In many ways, then, one of the somewhat neglected victims of genocide in Srebrenica is also literary imagination. This is why fictional literature of Srebrenica can be seen primarily as a potential area and subject of transitional justice interventions, rather than as the often assumed field of freedom of artistic imagery and exploration of both the unspoken and taken for granted in transition.

Epilogue

Fiction could perhaps, as a first step at least, indicate ways out of the overwhelming voicelessness and incorrigible 'otherness' of the victims of Srebrenica, towards more constructive engagements with the past, literary empathy, voice and agency. One could, with Damir Arsenijević, identify rare examples of works that

[84] See generally Godwin Phelps, *Shattered Voices*.

could be considered different, innovative, perhaps even emancipatory literary practices.[85] For example, Šejla Šehabović portrays survivors in a way that enables us to see them in a different light—as human beings, emphasizing their 'normalcy', closeness and familiarity (whereby the poet also actively participates in the act of commemoration)—and to feel connection and solidarity with them. In this way, the dominant narratives of incorrigible distance and ghettoization of the survivors are reversed.[86] In his novel thematizing war in Bosnia generally, Mirsad Sijarić[87] also offers an alternative strategy, in that he dissects the mind and soul of the likes of Radovan Karadžić, writing even in first person in a valuable attempt to explore the main character's earthly, everyday and possibly diabolic dimensions, both the banality and the peculiarity of evil. However important, these examples remain rare, marginal and marginalized exceptions with limited relevance to approaches to dealing with Srebrenica genocide itself. In this sense, we would have to agree with Enver Kazaz that a novel on Srebrenica still needs to be written,[88] i.e., that a new, richer and more imaginative practice of literary and artistic transposition of Srebrenica still needs to emerge.

A comprehensive account of the possible innovative literary approaches to Srebrenica and *literary transitional justice* in BiH is beyond the scope of this paper. However, let us conclude by indicating some of the contours of such a possible paradigm shift.

First, it would be necessary for such narratives to follow the lines of the above-noted exceptions and start emphasizing the notions of empathy, solidarity with, and humanity of the victims in order to combat the overwhelming feeling of numbness towards the atrocities of Srebrenica.[89] Moreover, what is needed is not only 'emphatic witnessing', but also and no less important, promoting and cultivating emphatic *reading* and *listening*—keeping in mind that the literature of trauma is not only 'unspeakable' but also often 'unreadable', or impossible to be heard.[90]

Second, organized efforts at the level of cultural production and cultural policy should be undertaken in order to both cultivate this kind of writing, reading and

---

85 See generally Damir Arsenijević, *Forgotten Future: The Politics of Poetry in Bosnia and Herzegovina* (Baden-Baden: Nomos, 2010).

86 Šehabović, *Srebrenica. Potočari*, English translation and a convincing analysis of the poem are found in: Damir Arsenijević 'Mobilising Unbribable Life: The Politics of Contemporary Poetry of Bosnia and Herzegovina', in *Toward a New Literary Humanism*, ed. Andy Mousley (New York: Palgrave Macmillan, 2011), 166–180.

87 Mirsad Sijarić, *Još jedna pjesma o ljubavi i ratu* (Another Song of Love and War) (Sarajevo: Connectum, 2008).

88 Kazaz, interview by Omer Karabeg.

89 For example, as Titus Levy elaborates, this kind of an emphatic response in what essentially is a trauma narrative is one of the notable qualities of Kazuo Ishiguro's novel *Never Let Me Go*. See Titus Levy, 'Human Rights Storytelling and Trauma Narrative in Kazuo Ishiguro's Never Let Me Go', *Journal of Human Rights* 10 (2011), 1–16.

90 Cf. Martina Kopf, 'Trauma, Narrative and the Art of Witnessing', in *Slavery in Art and Literature: Approaches to Trauma, Memory and Visuality*, eds. Birgit Haehnel and Melanie Ulz (Berlin: Frank and Timme, 2010).

listening and pose and thematize the difficult questions regarding the relationship of fiction with the realities of survivors, their diverse stories and experiences.[91]

Thirdly, and in the same vein, thematic variety in the literature of genocide and transition in general should be supported. Such an intervention would enable writers to go beyond repetitive, descriptive and painful variations of hopelessness.

And finally, literary projects thematizing more complex embodiments of femininity and masculinity—and not only one-dimensional mothers, soldiers and war veterans—would also be beneficial as they would enable literary steps beyond the often ethno-centric narratives of hopelessness and continuous victimization.

All in all, the diversification of narratives on Srebrenica genocide would be welcome not only for the sake of the future, but also and above all for the seemingly indefinite here and now of transition which still remains imprisoned in the same concentration camp, almost 20 years after the end of hostilities in BiH.

Acknowledgments We would like to thank Louis Bickford for valuable and detailed comments on an earlier draft and anonymous reviewers for their insightful comments. We are also grateful to the editorial team for their helpful guidance and patience.

Bibliography

Primary sources

1. Arnautović, Osman. 2007. *Srebrenica ity*. Tuzla: Infograf.
2. Bajramović, Velid. 2010. *Srebrenica nakraj srca*. Sarajevo: Self-publishing.
3. Bašović, Almir. 2004. *Priviđenja iz srebrnog vijeka*. Sarajevo: Oko.
4. Bazdulj-Hubijar, Nura. 2005. *Kad je bio juli*. Zagreb: VBZ.
5. *Belvedere*. 2010. *Directed by Ahmed Imamović*. Sarajevo: Comprex, DVD.
6. Feković-Kulović, Mihrija. 2009. *Živjeti i umirati za Srebrenicu*. Sarajevo: Connectum.
7. Kovač, Fuad ed. 2006. *Očev zagrljaj: priče o Srebrenici*. Sarajevo: Behar.
8. Latić, Džemaludin. 2006. *Srebrenički inferno*: pismo D*anteu Alighieriju iz Bosne*. Sarajevo: Connectum.
9. Muratović, Zumber. 2005. *Srebrenica je vrisak do neba*. Sarajevo: self-publishing.
10. Mustafić, Mirsad. 2006. *Krvava šamija*. Tuzla: Off-Set.
11. Mustafić, Mirsad. 2007. *Rastanak u Potočarima*. Tuzla: Off-Set.
12. Mustafić, Mirsad. 2009. *Samrtni zvuci srebrenog grada*. Tuzla: Off-set.
13. Mustafić, Mirsad. 2012. *Posljednji vapaj enklave*. Tuzla: Off-set.
14. Šahović, Sulejman. 2006. *Krvava Srebrenica*. Sarajevo: Zonex ex Libris.
15. Salihbeg Bosnawi, Melika. 2000. *Srebrenica je zvijezda padalica*. Sarajevo: Self-publishing.
16. Salimović, Sadik. *Put smrti: Srebrenica-Tuzla*: *prema istinitim događajima*.
17. Salimović, Sadik. 2008. Tuzla: Harfograf.
18. Sarić, Điđana. 2006. Čudi se, svijete. Sarajevevo: Grafičar promet.

[91] An example of such a project is a valuable and much cited two-year literary initiative Le Devoir de memoir, which resulted in publication of nine works by African writers thematizing the Rwandan genocide. The results of this project are valuable literary works, exhibiting a variety of sentiments—from hope to hopelessness, from continuous suffering to dreams of a better future. See generally Small, *The Duty of Memory*.

19. Sidran, Abdulah. 2009. *The Tears of the Mothers of Srebrenica*. Trans. Ahmed Ananda, and Lejla, Ananda. Sarajevo: Bemust.
20. Suljagić Emir. 2005. *Razglednica iz groba*. Sarajevo: Civitas.
21. Taljić, Isnam. 2007. *Roman o Srebrenici*. Srebrenica: Općina Srebrenica.

Secondary Sources

22. Arsenijević, Damir. 2010. *Forgotten future: The politics of poetry in Bosnia and Herzegovina*. Baden–Baden: Nomos.
23. Arsenijević, Damir. 2011. Mobilising unbribable life: The politics of contemporary poetry of bosnia and Herzegovina. In *Toward a new literary humanism*, ed. Andy Mousley, 171–178. New York: Palgrave Macmillan.
24. Bakhtin, Mikhail M. 1984. *Problems of Dostoevsky's poetics*. Trans. C. Emerson ed. Minneapolis: University of Minnesota Press.
25. Chehtman, Alejandro. 2011. Developing bosnia and Herzegovina's capacity to process war crimes cases: Critical notes on a 'success story'. *Journal of International Criminal Justice* 3: 547–570.
26. Dube, Siphiwe Ignatius. 2011. Transitional justice beyond the normative: Towards a literary theory of political transitions. *International Journal of Transitional Justice* 2:177–197.
27. Eng, David L., and Kazanjian, David. 2003. Introduction. In *Loss. The politics mourning*, ed. Eng, D.L., and Kazanjian, D., 1–25. Los Angeles: University of California Press.
28. Felman, Shoshana. 1991. Crisis of witnessing: Albert Camus' Postwar writings. *Cardozo Studies in Law and Literature* 2:197–242.
29. Felman, Shoshana. 2002. *Juridical unconscious. Trials and traumas in the twentieth century*. Cambridge: Harvard University Press.
30. Godwin Phelps, Theresa. 2004. *Shattered voices. Language, violence, and the work of truth commissions*. Philadelphia: University of Pennsylvania Press.
31. Gordimer, Nadine. 1988. The essential gesture: Writing, politics and places, ed. Stephen Clingman. New York: Knopf.
32. Hemer, Oscar. 2011. *Writing transition: Fiction and truth in South Africa and Argentina*. PhD dissertation, Oslo: University of Oslo.
33. Hemon, Aleksandar. 2005. The Srebrenica web. *Dani*, 1 July 2005. http://www.ex-yupress.com/dani/dani121.html.
34. Husanović, Jasmina. 2010. Između traume, imaginacije i nade. Kritički ogledi o kulturnoj produkciji i emancipativnoj politici. Beograd: Fabrika knjiga.
35. Jambrešić-Kirin, Renata. 1995. Svjedočenje i povijesno pamćenje: o pripovjednom posredovanju osobnog iskustva. Narodna umjetnost 2: 165–185.
36. Kazaz, Enver. 2010. Interview by Omer Karabeg. *Magazin plus*, June 26. http://www.magazinplus.eu/index.php.kultura/2482-kada-ce-biti-napisan-prvi-roman-o-srebrenici.
37. Kopf, Martina. 2010. Trauma, narrative and the art of witnessing. In *Slavery in art and literature: Approaches to trauma, memory and visuality*, eds. Birgit Haehnel, and Melanie Ulz, 47. Berlin: Frank and Timme.
38. Kopf, Martina. 2012. The ethics of fiction: African writers on the genocide in rwanda. *Journal of Literary Theory* 6: 65–82.
39. Kritz, Neil J. (ed.). 1995. *Transitional justice: How emerging democracies reckon with former regimes*, vol. 1. Washington: USIP Press.
40. Lang, Berel (ed.). 1988. *Writing and the holocaust*. New York: Holmes and Meier.
41. Levy, Titus. 2011. Human rights storytelling and trauma narrative in Kazuo Ishiguro's never let me go. *Journal of Human Rights* 10:1–16.
42. Miller, Paul B. 2006. Contested memories: The Bosnian genocide in Serb and muslim minds. *Journal of Genocide Research* 3: 311–324.

43. Minow, Martha. 1998. *Between vengeance and forgiveness. Facing history after genocide and mass violence*. Boston: Beacon Press.
44. Moens, Alexander. 2003. Lessons for peacekeepers: Srebrenica and the NIOD report. *Canadian Foreign Policy Journal* 3: 141–158.
45. Orentlicher, Diane F. 2011. *That someone guilty be punished: The impact of the ICTY in Bosnia*. New York: Open Society Institute. http://www.soros.org/initiatives/justice/articles_publications/publications/that-someone-guilty-20100707/that-someone-guilty-20100708.pdf.
46. Nettelfield, Lara. 2010. *Courting democracy in Bosnia and Herzegovina: The Hague Tribunal's impact in a Postwar state*. Cambridge: Cambridge University Press.
47. Pollack, Craig Evan. 2003. Intentions of burial: Mourning, politics, and memorials following the massacre at Srebrenica. *Death Studies* 2:125–142.
48. Popović, Dragan. 2009. *Transitional justice guidebook for BiH*. Sarajevo: UNDP BiH. http://www.undp.ba/upload/publications/Vodic%20kroz%20tranzicijsku%20pravdu%20u%20BiH.pdf.
49. *Prosecutor v. Radislav Krstić*. 2012. ICTY Case No. IT-98-33-T, 2 Aug 2001. Ministry for human rights and refugees of BiH and ministry of justice of BiH. *Transitional Justice Strategy for BiH 2012-2016*. http://www.mpr.gov.ba/aktuelnosti/propisi/konsultacije/Strategija%20TP%20-%20bosanski%20jezik%20fin%20doc.pdf.
50. Ruddick, Sara. 1989. *Maternal thinking. Toward a politics of peace*. New York: Ballentine Books.
51. Scheub, Harold. 2005. Now for a story. In *The art of truth-telling about authoritarian rule*, ed. Ksenija Bilbija et al., 10–14. Madison: University of Wisconsin Press.
52. Simpson, Graeme, Hodzic, Edin, and Bickford, Louis. 2012. *Looking back, looking forward: Promoting dialogue through truth-seeking in Bosnia and Herzegovina*, UNDP 2012. http://www.undp.ba/upload/publications/Looking%20back,%20looking%20forward.pdf.
53. Small, Audrey. 2007. The duty of memory: A solidarity of voices after the Rwandan genocide. *Paragraph* 30: 88–100.
54. Somers, Margaret, and Gloria D. Gibson. 1994. Reclaiming the epistemological ''other'': Narrative and the social constitution of identity. In *Social theory and the politics of identity*, ed. Craig Calhoun, 37–10. Oxford: Blackwell.
55. Schwarz, Daniel R. 1999. *Imagining the holocaust*. New York: St. Martin's Press.
56. Tal, Kali. 1996. *Worlds of hurt: Reading the literatures of trauma*. Cambridge MA: Cambridge UP. http://www.kalital.com/Text/Worlds/index.html.
57. Teitel, Ruti G. 2000. *Transitional justice*. New York: Oxford University Press.
58. Teitel, Ruti G. 2001. Transitional justice as liberal narrative. In *Experiments with truth: Transitional justice and the process of truth and reconciliation: Documenta 11, platform* 2, ed. Okwui Enwezor et al., 241–257. Ostfildern-Ruit: Hatje Cantz.
59. White, Hayden. 1999. *Figural realism: Studies in the mimesis effect*. Baltimore: The Johns Hopkins University Press.
60. UN General Assembly. 1999. Report of the secretary-general pursuant to general assembly resolution 53/35, "the fall of Srebrenica" 15 Nov 1999, A/54/549.
61. Zbanić, Jasmila. 2012. Filmovi, zabrane i radost. Last modified Feb. http://www.radiosarajevo.ba/novost/74532/jasmila-zbanic-filmovi-zabrane-i-radost.

Chapter 9
Memorial Culture in the Former Yugoslavia: Mothers of Srebrenica and the Destruction of Artefacts by the ICTY

Olivera Simić

Introduction

I would not wish anyone to live with these memories regardless of religion, race or colour. No one knows how difficult it is to live without family and only with memory.[1]

In July 1995, Srebrenica, a small town in the east of Bosnia and Herzegovina (BiH), became the site of a genocide that was carried out over just four days, when members of the Serbian forces slaughtered thousands of Muslim men and boys. During the war in BiH, Srebrenica was an isolated enclave which hosted thousands of Bosnian Muslims who had fled their homes as a result of attacks by Serb forces. In 1993, the UN Security Council 'demanded' that Srebrenica should be treated as a 'safe area' by 'all parties and others concerned' and thus should be 'free from any armed attack or any other hostile act'.[2] Despite proclaiming Srebrenica as one of the six 'safe zones' in BiH protected by the UN peacekeeping mission (UNMBIH), this town proved to be among the most unsafe places in the world.[3] Only a few months after the promulgation of Srebrenica as a 'safe area',

[1] Personal interview, Hatidža Mehmedović, Srebrenica, 9 December 2011.
[2] United Nations Security Council Resolution 819 (1993) on the situation in Bosnia and Herzegovina. See, S/Res/819/1993, 16 April 1993.
[3] Laura Silber and Allan Little, *The Death of Yugoslavia* (Penguin Books, 1996), 274.

O. Simić (✉)
Griffith Law School, Griffith University, QLD, 4111 Brisbane, Australia
e-mail: o.simic@griffith.edu.au

P. D. Rush and O. Simić (eds.), *The Arts of Transitional Justice*,
Springer Series in Transitional Justice 6, DOI: 10.1007/978-1-4614-8385-4_9

on 11 July 1995, Bosnian Serb forces entered Srebrenica, looted the small town and, in only four days, executed between 7,000 and 8,000 men and boys.[4]

Since 1996, when reports first emerged alleging that a massacre had wiped out the male population that had sought refuge in and around Srebrenica, the local, non-for-profit organization 'Mothers of Srebrenica see also Mothers of Srebrenica[5] (Mothers) galvanized local and international community to unearth the truth about the events of 1995 and to bring those responsible to justice. To achieve their goals, the Mothers use a variety of methods, including symbolic demonstrations, peaceful marches, public gatherings and speeches, as well as media exposure.

Similar to the Mothers of the Plaza de Mayo and the Federation of Mothers from Ayacucho,[6] these women demand that the truth be revealed about the disappearances and murders of their family members, predominantly their sons and husbands. Through their activism, they demonstrate that while they are victims of the war, they are also survivors.[7] They have been actively engaged in political mobilization at a grassroots level, using the ironically and sadly privileged place that they occupy as mothers who have lost their children, and often their whole families.

I have met with the Mothers in public settings, such as conferences and forums, and also privately, in their offices, when I was interpreting for an international agency that wanted to find out more about their work, and when I was travelling

---

[4] Estimates of the number of people killed in Srebrenica differ and are highly contested. The number 8,372 is adopted from the 'Preliminary List of People Missing or Killed in Srebrenica' compiled by the Bosnian Federal Commission of Missing Persons. The number was increased from the original 8,106 on 21 December 2008. See, Srebrenica Genocide Blog, http://srebrenica-genocide.blogspot.com/2008/12/update-8372-victims-of-srebrenica.html. Radislav Krstić, a Serb officer, was convicted for genocide and sentenced to 46 years of imprisonment by the International Criminal Tribunal for the former Yugoslavia, the first conviction for genocide by the Tribunal. See, The *Prosecutor v. Radislav Krstić*, Judgement, Case No. IT-98-33-T, 2 August 2001, para. 84.

[5] Four associations bring survivors together in Srebrenica: Mothers of Srebrenica, Women of Srebrenica, Association of Mothers of Srebrenica and Podrinja and Association of Mothers of Srebrenica and Žepa Enclaves. In this paper, I use 'Mothers' to refer to the association based in Potočari-Srebrenica.

[6] The Mothers of the Plaza de Mayo is an association of Argentine mothers whose children "disappeared" during the period of military dictatorship in Argentina from 1976 until 1983. The Mothers have gathered in order to find their missing sons and daughters, many of whom were tortured and killed. For detailed analyses of this association, see, Marguerite Guzman Berjano, *Revolutionizing Motherhood: The Mothers of the Plaza de Mayo* (Wilmington, DE: Scholarly Resources, 1994); Diana Taylor, 'Making a Spectacle: The Mothers of the Plaza de Mayo' (2001) 3 (2) *Journal of the Association for Research on Mothering: Mothering, Fathering and a Culture of Peace*, 97-109. The Federation of Mothers from Ayacucho is an organization of Peruvian mothers who promotes peace and raise human rights awareness.

[7] Meredeth Turshen and Clotilde Twagiramariya, *What Women Do in War-time: Gender and Conflict in Africa* (Zed Books, 1998); Krishna Kumar, *Women and Civil War: Impact, Organizations and Actions* (Lynne Rienner, 2001; Cynthia Cockburn, *The Space Between Us: Negotiating Gender and National Identities in Conflict* (Zed Books, 1998).

with a group of scholars who visited the Srebrenica graveyard.[8] To someone who was born and lived most of my life in the region, these encounters have been incredibly important, but also uncomfortable and painful. I have often felt anger and helplessness, which was absorbed and muted by the pain I sensed everywhere around me during these encounters.

Although I have met with members of the Mothers several times, I always feel nervous before I am about to meet and speak with one of them. Hatidža Mehmedović, the founder of Mothers, is a warm and brave woman of 62 years of age. She is well known in the Federation of BiH[9] as having lost two sons, her husband, two brothers and other male family members in the Srebrenica massacre. In the project '1,000 Women for Nobel Peace Prize', Hatidža was nominated for her tireless work for missing persons and for her support to all of the mothers whose children and family members were killed in the Srebrenica genocide.

Although I had encountered Hatidža on several occasions, I did not know her personally, so a good friend of mine from Sarajevo, Selma, told me that she would 'find out' Hatidža's cell phone for me. After I received Hatidža's phone number, I postponed calling her for several days, hoping that I would find a way to travel to Srebrenica and sit down and talk to her over the coffee, as the custom of my country prescribes. I felt embarrassed to call a woman who had lost her whole family in genocide and to talk to her over the phone about artefacts from the mass graves that the International Criminal Tribunal for the Former Yugoslavia (ICTY) had apparently destroyed. It seemed to me deeply inappropriate and disrespectful to instigate a conversation about anything related to genocide over the phone.

For days, I tried to find a way to get to Srebrenica from Banjaluka, my home city and the place where I resided while I was doing fieldwork in BiH in November and December of 2011. It is a paradox that many people told me how complicated it would be to get to Srebrenica from anywhere in BiH, even Sarajevo, while for Ratko Mladić[10] and the Serb army, it was not complicated at all. Nonetheless, for me, the travel logistics proved complicated. After all of my travel arrangements fell apart, I mentioned to another of my interviewees, Belma Zulčić, someone who knows Hatidža personally, that I wanted to talk to Hatidža but felt uncomfortable doing so over the phone. Belma encouraged me to call Hatidža anyway and volunteered to phone her first to give her notice to expect my call.

---

[8] Olivera Simić, 'Remembering, Visiting and Placing the Dead: Law, Authority and Genocide in Srebrenica' (2009) 13 *Law Text Culture*, 273-311; Olivera Simić, 'A Tour to a Site of Genocide: Mothers, Bones and Borders' (2008) 9 (3) *Journal of International Women Studies*.

[9] The Federation of Bosnia and Herzegovina is one of two entities in BiH. The vast majority of the population in this entity are Bosniaks (Bosnian Muslims).

[10] Ratko Mladić is a Bosnian Serb former military leader accused of committing war crimes during Bosnian war. Mladić was accused by the ICTY of being responsible for the Srebrenica massacre. His trial began on June 3, 2011 and according to some predictions expected to finish in 2016. See, *The Prosecutor v Ratko Mladic*, Case No. IT-09-92-I, 1 June 2011; Jesse Wieten, 'Mladic trial still expected to end in 2016', *News*, 11 April 2013, http://news.xinhuanet.com/english/world/2013-04/11/c_132301640.html.

When I finally called Hatidža, the first thing I told her was that I apologized for not being able to come to Srebrenica to meet her personally and to talk with her face to face. I told her that there were no buses to Srebrenica from Banjaluka or Belgrade (the two cities in which I was based during my visit) and that I had not been able to arrange someone to drive me there. Indeed, I did not have anyone to turn to in Banjaluka to ask to give me a ride to Srebrenica. Banjaluka is the political and economic centre of the Republika Srpska (RS) and a city that is still in denial of genocide. Srebrenica is about a five-hour drive from Banjaluka, and it is only possible to travel there by car. However, as there are no public transport options, it is extremely difficult, and generally impossible, to organize, for example, school excursions or any other sort of group tour to Srebrenica. It is also not possible for individuals to travel from Banjaluka to Srebrenica on public transport to pay their respects to those killed in genocide.

It is dangerous to talk about genocide in Banjaluka, let alone express any sorrow or acknowledgement of the horror that happened there in July 1995. I have hardly heard any solidarity or empathetic comments from my friends and acquaintances regarding Srebrenica. At the bare mention of this small town, most people in Banjaluka react with anger, rage and hatred. Persistent rumours circulate in Banjaluka that the massacre at Srebrenica did not happen; that the people allegedly killed now live in Canada or US, vote in elections for ultra-nationalist Bosniak parties, and even attend their own memorial service each year in Srebrenica; that the famous documentary that was broadcast across the world showing the execution of six unarmed men by the Scorpions, the Serbian paramilitary unit, was a fake montage made by those who hate the Serbs[11]; that the people shown dead in that footage were acting, and after the cameras stopped rolling, they got up and walked away in freedom; that the victims of the Srebrenica massacre killed each other; that then President of BiH Alija Izetbegovic 'needed' Srebrenica to provoke the international community and NATO into bombing the Serb army in BiH to end the war.[12]

These are just some of the dreadful rumours that I have heard over the last few years from Serbs in my hometown who deny the genocide. I even heard a few who

---

[11] In June 2005, the authentic video was publically broadcasted in Serbia and around the world which shows the 'Scorpions', a paramilitary Serb group, taking six Bosniak men into the wood near Srebrenica to be shot. Nataša Kandić, the executive director of the Humanitarian Law Centre in Belgrade, had managed to secure a copy of home video that the Scorpions made of their participation in executions of Bosniak men and boys after the fall of Srebrenica in 1995. The tape was used by the ICTY as an evidence material. See, Daniel Williams, 'Srebrenica video vindicates long pursuit by Serb Activist', *Washington Post*, 25 June 2005, http://www.washingtonpost.com/wp-dyn/content/article/2005/06/24/AR2005062401501.html; Institute Research for Genocide Canada, 'Natasa Kandic-Eyewitness Testimony', http://instituteforgenocide.org/?p=1126; Tim Judan and Daniel Sunter, 'How video that put Serbia in dock was brought to light', *The Guardian*, http://www.guardian.co.uk/world/2005/jun/05/balkans.warcrimes.

[12] NATO bombed positions of the Serb army not because of Srebrenica, but massacre at Markale market in Sarajevo in August 1995.

said that they would ‘kill them all’ again because this was rightful revenge for what the Bosniaks did to Serbs in Bratunac between 1992 and 1995.[13]

I apologized and told Hatidža that I felt uncomfortable talking over the phone but that Belma had encouraged me to call. I said to her that I had been writing about and following the work of Mothers for a long time, and I had travelled several times to the Srebrenica graveyard and Memorial Room. She politely thanked me for my interest in her story and started to speak. Once she started to talk, I could not stop her. I was stunned by this woman’s wisdom, bravery and pride. I sat in silence, with a knot in my stomach, while I listened to Hatidža recount the loss of her whole family in genocide. I was sitting in front of my phone and stared at it, completely frozen, worried that my breathing might interrupt the flow of Hatidža’s talk. I wanted to ask many questions, but I interrupted her only twice during our twenty-five-minute talk. Hatidža spoke for ten minutes, without taking a breath, as she talked of her shock and rage at the ICTY who destroyed the artefacts. I was moved by the absence of any expression of vengeance, by her humanity and by her sincere goodwill towards all people in BiH, especially children, regardless of their ethnicity.

At the end of our talk, I wished her ‘all the best’, but as soon as I hung up the phone I felt embarrassed for using these words. The phrase ‘sve najbolje’ is commonly used when saying goodbye in BiH. But how could I say ‘sve najbolje’ to Hatidža, a mother who is still searching for the bones of her killed children? What else could I say? What does wishing ‘sve najbolje’ means to Hatidža? It does not mean as assumed, to have good health and prosperity since she now faces, as she says, ‘a life of a victim and endless sorrow’. In the case of Hatidža, perhaps ‘sve najbolje’ means wishing her luck to find the bones of her dead children and her other relatives before she dies because as she puts it, ‘time passes away too quickly’. As Leydesdorff argues, ‘news of a body being found became good news, because it made a decent burial possible.’[14] Likewise, Šehida Abdurahmanović who lost a husband during the war and a dozen of relatives in Srebrenica genocide notes how identification of a body is important for survivors, ‘…when someone manage to identify his relative, we say to him ‘You are the lucky one’.’[15]

When Hatidža mentioned her two sons who were killed in the genocide, and how she does not have ‘anything’ (artefacts) from the younger one, I did not make any remarks or ask any questions. Immediately after I hung up, I regretted that I had not asked her something about her children, especially what their names were or how old

[13] Naser Orić was the first and only indictee for crimes against the Serb population in Srebrenica. In 2006, Orić, a former Bosnian army commander was found guilty of failing to prevent war crimes, and sentenced to two years in prison by the ICTY. On 3 July 2008, he was released from prison acquitted from the charges brought against him due to a lack of evidence that he bore criminal responsibility. See, *Prosecutor v. Naser Orić,* Case No. IT-03-68-A, Appeal Judgment, 3 July 2008.

[14] Selma Leydesdorff, *Surviving the Bosnian Genocide* (Indiana University Press, 2011), 8.

[15] Marija Taušan, ‘Masovna stratišta of Kravice do Pilice’, 10 July 2012, *BalkanInsight*, http://www.balkaninsight.com/en/article/masovna-stratista-od-kravice-do-pilice.

they were when they were killed. I felt numb, rendered speechless by Hatidža's story of the genocide, of BiH and destroyed artefacts. I was not even sure whether it was appropriate, but I felt an urge, almost an obsession, to find out more about her children, at least their names and age. For a moment or two, I wanted to call her again and ask these questions but I did not. I could not. I decided to write a letter to Belma about my feelings and my regret at not telling Hatidža that I felt sorrow, shame and guilt for a genocide that was committed in my name. I asked Belma whether she knew the name of her children, so I could mention them in my writing.

Azmir was born in 1974 and Almir in 1977. In November 2007, almost the whole skeleton of one of Hatidža's sons was found, but DNA analysis could not establish which son's skeletons had been found. There was no clothing on the skeleton, nor any other marks that could help with establishing identity. At the same time, a piece of the skeleton of Hatidža's husband, Abdulah, was also found. In May 2010, Hatidža was told that her other son had been found too. Unfortunately, only four bones belonging to the lower extremities were found, along with pieces of green trousers that Hatidža recognized as Azmir's. In a mass grave, an artefact was also found which Hatidža could identify as an amulet Azmir had with him at the time of killing. Thus, Hatidža could finally, thanks to those artefacts, establish that the skeleton that was first found in 2007 must have belonged to her younger son, Almir. Only after this identification could Hatidža bury both sons.

She decided to bury her two sons and her husband on 11 July 2010, even though she had only a few bones from the skeletons of Azmir and her husband. She was afraid of waiting any longer, in case something happened to her and then there would be no one to bury her sons and husband, because the majority of her and her husband's family had been killed. Even today, Hatidža's painful memories follow her. She often thinks about how her younger son, Almir, might have been nude at the time of killing, and she fears he may have been tortured. Hatidža worries that the ICTY may have destroyed the artefacts that belonged to her sons and husband and that she lost them forever:

> I have a piece of cloth and amulet from my older son and these are big things for me. I have nothing from my younger son. I have only one photo when he was a baby and one of his toys. That is what I keep with me in my house. I would never wish this to anyone, not even to Ratko Mladić to live from memories. And to kill memories is genocide on top of genocide.

The ICTY, 'genocide of memories' and *the right to destroy*

They [the Serb army] killed our children, and the court of justice [ICTY] killed memories of our loved ones.[16]

The ICTY was established in 1993 'for the sole purpose of prosecuting persons responsible for serious violations of international humanitarian law committed in

---

[16] Hatidža Mehmedović, above n 2.

the territory of the former Yugoslavia between 1 January 1993 and a date to be determined by the Security Council upon restoration of peace.'[17] The intention of the court was to bring only the perpetrators of the most serious crimes before the court, and once that task was completed, the ICTY would close down its judicial activities. All indictees for the statutory crimes, 161 in total, had been brought before the ICTY as of February 2013.[18]

Materials, such as bones, tissue parts, hair, blood sample, IDs and photographs, were used by prosecutors preparing for the largest trial before the ICTY for the so-called Srebrenica seven, indicted for genocide in Srebrenica which started in August 2006. In June 2010, all seven Serb defendants, former police and military officials were found to have played various roles in the 1995 Srebrenica genocide.[19] According to Hague officials, the evidence was destroyed just before the start of the trial of the 'Srebrenica seven'. The Office of the Prosecutor (OTP) spokeswoman, Olga Kavran, reportedly stated that such decision was made in accordance with standard court procedure:

> We are talking about artefacts that were disposed of at the end of 2005 and the beginning of 2006. The vast majority of these artefacts came from mass graves, were deteriorating, and presented a risk for health.[20]

The destroyed material consisted of approximately 1000 pieces of identification, photographs and articles of clothing belonging to the victims found in the mass graves (see for example Figs. 9.1 and 9.2).[21] I asked Hatidža what she and the Mothers thought about the OTP official position with respect to the destruction:

> We are aware that the evidence materials, artefacts were in a bad shape. Of course, they were. They had not been taken from our homes or boutiques but they had to be preserved to warn future generations and our children. We know they were in bad shape, but why they did not return them to Bosnia? There must be a way these days to preserve those things. They had to stay in a museum. I will never be happy again because they killed all of my family. Children have to know the truth and to me all of them are same. I don't make difference amongst them. What the Hague did is a crime. In Srebrenica, they killed our children and in the Hague, our memories.

Similarly, Amor Mašović, the head of the Bosnian Institute for Missing Persons reportedly stated:

---

[17] The UN Security Council, S/Res/827 (1993), 25 May 1993.

[18] The last indictee, former Bosnian Serb military leader Ratko Mladić, was arrested on 26 May 2011 and extradited to the Hague on 31 May 2011 to face trial for war crimes.

[19] *Prosecutor v. Vujadin Popović, Ljubiša Beara, Drago Nikolić, Ljubomir Borovčanin, Radivoje Miletić, Milan Gvero and Vinko Pandurević*, 'Srebrenica', IT-05-88, Judgement Summary, 10 June 2010.

[20] Kristin Deasy and Dzenana Halimović, 'After Hague Destroys Srebrenica Evidence, Survivors Feel Pain Of Lost Memories', *Radio Free Europe*, 3 September 2009.

[21] *Srebrenica Genocide Blog*, 'U.N. Tribunal Destroys Evidence of Srebrenica Genocide', 8 May 2009.

Fig. 9.1 Artefacts exhumed from Srebrenica mass graves. Courtesy of the International Commission on Missing Persons (ICMP), Sarajevo, Bosnia and Herzegovina

> If some of the skeletal remains have also been destroyed, then that is really unacceptable. Those remains should have been sent to Bosnia for DNA analysis, so that the identities of the victims could be confirmed, and then returned to their families. The Hague tribunal's explanation about the possibility of infection is extremely debatable. Why were they permitted to store these items in conditions that would cause them to disintegrate?[22]

Yet, the OTP maintains that there was nothing unusual about the ICTY decision to destroy artefacts and that such procedures are regarded as 'regular' explaining that in national judicial institutions, 'when the gathered materials are not needed for court proceedings, they can be destroyed, if, for example, they represent a threat to people's health.'[23]

Although destruction of artefacts did not raise any significant international discussion, it sparked bitterness and action from survivors and their associations. The Sarajevo-based 'Society for Threatened Peoples' called the destruction of the evidence a 'monstrous scandal', saying any similar attempt to destroy documents from the Nuremberg trials of the 1940s would have caused an international outcry.[24] Belma said that that the ICTY cannot explain why it did not return the artefacts to survivors, or at least inform them and asked for their consent to destroy them.[25]

---

[22] Ibid.

[23] *Balkan Insight,* 'Srebrenica Artefacts Destroyed in the Hague', 16 July 2010, http://www.balkaninsight.com/en/article/srebrenica-artefacts-destroyed-in-the-hague.

[24] Personal interview with Belma Zulčić, Sarajevo, 2 December 2011.

[25] On October 20, 2011 I sent an email to the ICTY Prosecutor office asking whether the ICTY has any policy on destruction of evidence. Although there are no clear policies about destruction either before the ICTY or any other international tribunal, I was asking for any help to understand the reasoning and authority behind the decision to destroy. I received a reply a day later that 'unfortunately, this issue is a part of an ongoing discussion with victims organizations' and that they are 'not able to assist me in this matter'. Email correspondence on file with author.

Hatidža also said that they had been told by Mr Brammertz, the ICTY Prosecutor, that the court and its staff 'were afraid of infection'. However, she said that the ICTY 'could send us a package with this stuff. This stuff belongs to the Memorial Centre. Can you imagine if artefacts from Holocaust were destroyed?'[26] Similarly, Sasa Madacki, the Head of the Human Rights Centre at the University of Sarajevo stated,

> Try to imagine someone destroying a part of artefacts kept in the Holocaust Museum or Yad Vashem or Auschwitz for hygienic reasons. This is nonsense and is extraordinary particularly today when we have various methods of disinfections, conservation and restoration.

These statements draw a link between the Holocaust and Srebrenica and are based on the fact that artefacts and archives from the Nuremberg Military Tribunal (NMT) were all preserved. The NMT was also a temporary institution set up by the four victorious powers to try the major war criminals of European Axis. After the end of trials, on 14 March 1950, film footage, written documents, printed materials and other exhibits were delivered to the International Court of Justice. As Acquaviva argues, in this case, it was decided that such records should be entrusted to the custody of the principal judicial organ of the UN due to fact that Germany had not fully recovered its sovereignty by 1950.[27] However, about 15,000 documents from private firms involved in the NMT proceedings, 5,900 documents from the Reich government and 3,500 documents from the Wehrmacht were subsequently given back to Germany.[28] It was regarded as important for countries to have objects which reflect their cultural heritage and national history preserved in their own museums.

The Security Council Resolution 1966 (2010), states that 'the archives of the ICTY, the ICTR and the Mechanism shall remain the property of the United Nations.'[29] The Resolution excludes any possibility to claim any of the materials preserved in the archives by either private or public subjects. While it is understandable that the ICTY and ICTR are custodians of these records as long as they need them for procedure, it is disputable whether their custody should remain beyond the trial process.[30] Rather than being seen as permanent custody, the artefacts should be in temporary custody for the duration of trial and evidence

---

[26] The official opening of the Srebrenica-Potočari Memorial Room and Cemetery for the Victims of the 1995 Genocide was on 20 September 2003. In the Room in Srebrenica-Potočari, the objects are accompanied by personal narratives of the human loss. The purpose of the Room is two-fold: preserving the memory of the dead, but also reminding people of those who survived the genocide. For extensive analysis of the Memorial Room, please see Olivera Simić, 'Remembering, Visiting and Placing the Dead: Law, Authority and Genocide in Srebrenica' above n 9.

[27] Guido Acquaviva, 'The Best before the date indicated': Residual Mechanism at the ICTY', in Bert Swart, Alexander Zahar and Goran Sluiter (eds.) *The Legacy of the International Criminal Tribunal for the Former Yugoslavia* (New York, Oxford University Press, 2011), 511.

[28] Telford Taylor, 'Final Report to the Secretary of the Army on the Nurnberg War Crimes Trials under Control Council Law No. 10', 15 August 1949, cited in Acquaviva, ibid.

[29] UN Security Council, Resolution 1966 (2010) Adopted by the Security Council at its 6463rd meeting, on 22 December 2010, S/RES/1966 (2010), Article 27.

[30] Guido Acquaviva, above n 28.

Fig. 9.2 Artefacts exhumed from Srebrenica mass graves. Courtesy of the International Commission on Missing Persons (ICMP), Sarajevo, Bosnia and Herzegovina

procedures. Once the trial is over and the artefacts are no longer needed, they should be returned to their owners and in the case of Srebrenica, survivors and its relatives. This is a procedure followed by some district courts in national jurisdictions, including Australia. Prosecutor Dzenita Balic with the District Court in Brisbane, Queensland stated:

> Certainly regarding criminal trials, when exhibits are used, they are tendered in trial. They are kept in the registry until the appeal period lapses. The exhibits are then returned back to the Crown at which time they are returned to the police by our office and they then distribute them back to their respective owners.[31]

The ICTY should have catalogued or stored the artefacts, and if this was not possible, returned them to the Bosnian authorities who could then return them to survivors. It is unclear why the ICTY did not ask survivors whether they wanted some of these to be returned to them. Possibly, this was because the artefacts are ICTY records and, as such, the UN may have considered them part of the UN archives, and thus determined that there was no need to consult anyone outside these institutions about their disposal.[32] Although the ICTY was not legally required to ask survivors about the destruction of the artefacts, just as it did not need to ask them about preserving the materials in its archives, it has been argued that it should have informed the Bosnian government about its intention to destroy

[31] The exhibits that would be destroyed would be those that are used in the commission of a crime and/or those where destruction orders are made (in case of weapons, drugs, perishable things). Email correspondence on file with author (April 24, 2012).

[32] UN Security Council, *Report of the Secretary-General on the administrative and budgetary aspects of the options for possible locations for the archives of the International Criminal Tribunal for the Former Yugoslavia and the International Criminal Tribunal for Rwanda and the seat for the residual mechanism(s) for the Tribunals*, S/2009/258, 21 May 2009, para 15.

the artefacts.[33] Still, the survivors found it disturbing that they were given no warning that the ICTY had decided to destroy the artefacts.

> No one informed us about the destruction. We found it by accident from people who work on exhumation sites and then decided to ask Brammertz [ICTY Prosecutor] about it in 2009. He told us it was a mistake, but no one bears responsibility for it. He told us that amongst destroyed artefacts there were hair, clothes, ID's, passports, photographs, even bones. However, last year [2010] he said here in Potocari that the things which the ICTY destroyed are not important and worthwhile. What is not important to him or others is piece of my child, and it is the most important to us. He should never say that, but I guess he had to under pressure that came from somewhere else.[34]

In *Prosecutor v Momir Nikolic*, the court determined there was looting and property destruction in Prijedor Municipality and that these acts amounted to crimes against humanity.[35] However, not all property destruction is serious enough to constitute a violation of Article 5 of the ICTY Statute. For example, destruction of clothing and wallets, according to the ICTY, was not deemed grave enough.[36] Perhaps the ICTY was led by a similar thought in the case of Srebrenica artefacts destruction that such destruction could not amount to a serious crime. Indeed, those artefacts were not deemed to be worthy of being permanently preserved by the ICTY for their 'administrative, fiscal, legal, historical or informational value'.[37] Yet, for the survivors, the artefacts had multi-dimensional and life value attached to them.

The Imperative to Remember: The Importance of Memories and Memorialization

The living owe it to those who no longer can speak to tell their story for them.[38]

Kazanjian and Nichanian suggest that genocide, understood in terms of the destruction of life, is not catastrophic.[39] Rather, genocide becomes catastrophic when understood in terms of the destruction of death: through denial, genocide dispossesses memory and precludes the very possibility of mourning.[40] By

---

[33] I am grateful to Mr Guido Acquaviva, for sharing his expertise on this topic. Email correspondence on file with author, 19 October 2011.

[34] Interview with Hatidža Mehmedović, above n 2.

[35] *Prosecutor v Momir Nikolic*, IT-02-60, Judgement, 2 December 2003.

[36] *Blagojevic and Jokic*, IT-02-60, Trial Chamber, Judgement, 17 January 2005, paras. 615 and 620.

[37] UN Security Council, above n 33, paras. 41 and 42.

[38] Czeslaw Milosz, *The Issa Valley* (Farrar, Straus and Giroux, 2000), 281.

[39] David Kazanjian and Marc Nichanian, 'Between Genocide and Catastrophe' in David L. Eng and David Kazanjian (eds.), *Loss: The Politics of Mourning* (University of California Press, 2003), 134.

[40] Ibid.

disposing of artefacts, the ICTY disposes memory and the process of mourning; it destroys the last effects of the dead and memory that these effects represent. As Minow argues, 'one of the goals of genocides has been the obliteration of the remembrance of individuals, their lives and dignity'.[41] Forgetting becomes then, as Lenz would argue, 'the second death'.[42] In so far as genocide destroys not only life but also death, Kazanjian and Nichanian argue that genocide destroys humanity.

Munira Subašić's 20-year-old son disappeared in Srebrenica genocide, and his remains have never been found. She has no old photographs, no old clothes and no remains, and her years as a mother could have been a dream. She cannot prove that her son ever existed. Munira reportedly stated:

> If you don't have photographs, if you don't have a mezar [Muslim grave], if you don't have anything that belonged to that person, it's like the person never existed. Those things put us in a position to prove that we did have our children.[43]

Thousands of pieces of clothing and small objects such as lighters, watches, tobacco boxes and glasses were found with the dead of Srebrenica when they were exhumed by a team of forensic criminologists.[44] These personal effects provide a narrative to the lives of the dead and rebuild a memory of what happened to Srebrenica and its people. Without this memory, the person as a unity, as having a life, 'the course of the life', drifts away.[45] It is important for survivors that they are able to have visible, tangible proof of their dead and missing and their past existence. They are concerned not only with remembering but also with documenting history by preserving the objects that belonged to their loved ones. Memorialization, thus becomes an important part of the process that satisfies the desire to honour those who died or suffered during the war and become a mean of examining the past.[46] In cases of genocide and mass killings, memorialization often revolves around human remains.[47] All activities that the Mothers support must acknowledge their suffering and their memories because they cling to the past, 'fight against the erosion of memory brought about the passage of time'; they simply refuse to let the 'past become the historical past, the past perfect.'[48] (2001), 777–790.

---

[41] Martha Minow, *Between Vengeance and Forgiveness* (Beacon Press Boston, 1998), 1.

[42] Siegfried Lenz, *Ü ber das Gedächtnis* (Munich: DTV, 1992), 10.

[43] Kristin Deasy and Dzenana Halimovic, 'After Hague Destroys Srebrenica Evidence, Survivors Feel Pain Of Lost Memories', *Radio Free Europe*, 3 September 2009.

[44] Suzanne Bardgett, 'Memorial Room for Battery Factory at Potocari, *The Muslim News*, Issue 195, 29 July 2005, http://www.muslimnews.co.uk/paper/index.php?article=2061. Accessed 7 June 2012.

[45] W. James Booth, *Communities of Memory: On Witness, Identity, and Justice* (Cornell University, 2006), 31.

[46] Judy Barsalou and Victoria Baxter, *The Urge to Remember: The Role of Memorials in Social Reconstruction and Transitional Justice* (The United States Institute for Peace, 2007), 6.

[47] Ibid, 6.

[48] W. James Booth, 'The Unforgotten: Memories of Justice,' *American Political Science Review* 95(4).

Fig. 9.3 Artefacts exhumed from Srebrenica mass graves. Courtesy of the International Commission on Missing Persons (ICMP), Sarajevo, Bosnia and Herzegovina

The Mothers want to find their missing, their remains, any piece that may identify them and acknowledged their loss and hopefully burial and final peace. Memory is the responsibility of living ones and is related to what Booth calls 'bearing responsibility', the way in which we assume the burdens of our past, acknowledge it as ours and not someone else's, and accept that this 'ours' persists through time and change.[49]

Memorialization is also an important reparation mechanism that can provide survivors with some solace in the transitional justice period. Reparations to survivors can be material or symbolic and individual or collective.[50] They are 'attempts to provide benefits directly to the victims of certain types of crimes'[51] and can be understood as 'acts or objects, as things done or given'.[52] According to the UN, reparations can include restitution, physical and mental rehabilitation, economic compensation, guarantees of non-repetition and a wide range of satisfaction including the recovery and reburial of remains, commemoration and memorialization.[53] Roht-Arriaza refers to these as moral reparations, and they

[49] W. James Booth, 'The Work of Memory: Time, Identity and Justice', *Social Research* 75 (1) 2008, 238.

[50] Naomi Roht-Arriaza, 'Reparations decisions and dilemmas', *Hastings International and Comparative Law Review* 27 (2) (2004), 157–219.

[51] Pablo de Greiff, 'Justice and Reparations' in *The Handbook on Reparations* (Oxford University Press, 2000), 453.

[52] Brandon Hamber and Ingrid Palmary, 'Gender, Memorialization, and Symbolic Reparations' in Ruth Rubio-Marin, *Gender of Reparations: Unsettling Sexual Hierarchies While Redressing Human Rights Violations* (Cambridge University Press, 2009), 325.

[53] General Assembly Resolution 60/147, *The United Nations Basic Principles and Guidelines on the Right to a Remedy and Reparation for Victims of Gross Violations of Human Rights Law and Serious Violations of International Humanitarian Law* (United Nations, 16 December 2005).

include, in addition to the above, finding missing bodies, assistance in reburials and appropriate rituals, and converting repressive sites into museums.[54] The Srebrenica survivors were hoping to open a museum and exhibit artefacts from their loved ones that would serve as a monument to the community's suffering and act as a catalyst for local political transformation as well as an educational tool and warning for future generations.

They initiated this process a few years ago when the Srebrenica-Potocari Memorial Room was opened containing twenty showcases aiming to shed light on the personal life stories of the dead boys and men. Each of the cases holds personal items found on or with the dead when they were exhumed from the mass graves[55], and the short texts about the dead can take the reader on a journey into the lives the men and boys once had. The personal stories of the dead have been researched and written about by Emir Suljagić, a survivor of the genocide who lost his father in a massacre. Emir has said that:

> The objects were exhumed along with the bodies, and have been recognised by the families. The idea is to make a personal portrait out of each object. When you tell someone that 10,000 people died, they cannot understand or imagine that. What I want to say is that these people were peasants, car mechanics or masons. That they had daughters, mothers, that they left someone behind; that a lot of people are hurt by this person's death (Fig. 9.3).[56]

The museum would serve as a reflection on a recent violent past and build a collective social memory and common legacy of suffering and trauma. The museum in the present would inform a relation between the living and the dead that would be marked and informed by loss.[57] As Perera argues:

> [Courtney Brkic who worked in the graves at Srebrenica] recounts how the clothing found among the bones and shattered skeletons—hand-sewn shirts, knitted socks and scarves—spoke of homes and families left behind in a way that anonymous bones could not. These broken scraps and remnants form a bridge between the living and dead and between what can and cannot be known, or counted as evidence.[58]

Thus, by transmitting memories to the new generation, survivors seek to keep memories of the past alive.[59] Refusal to bring the dead into the sanctuary of memory is to annihilate them for the second time.[60] Memory also occupies a vital

---

[54] Naomi Roht-Arriaza, 'Reparations decisions and dilemmas', above n 51.

[55] Suzanne Bardgett, above n 45.

[56] Ed Vulliamy, 'Srebrenica: genocide and memory, *Open Democracy*, 4 July 2005.

[57] Martine Hawkes, 'Containing Testimony: Archiving Loss After Genocide', *Continuum: Journal of Media and Cultural Studies* 26 (6) (2012).

[58] Suvendrini Perera, 'They Give Evidence: Bodies, Borders and the Disappeared', *Social Identities: Journal for the Study of Race, Nation and Culture* 12 (2006), 749. I would like to thank Martine Hawkes for bringing this quote and article to my attention.

[59] Lia Kent, 'Local Memory Practices in East Timor: Disrupting Transitional Justice Narratives', *The International Journal of Transitional Justice* (5) 2011, 444.

[60] W. James Booth, above n 49, 782.

place at the heart of justice and the struggle to keep the victims unforgotten.[61] As Rodrigo argues, it has been generally understood that 'memories can be encapsulated in solid objects, which come to represent memories…and preserve their life beyond their pure mental existence.'[62] Such objects may be texts, images or artefacts that have the potential to trigger the recollection of individuals, events and relationship from the past.[63] Their exhibition may ensure that 'private death is publicly present and transformed into public discourse and even into a communal commodity'.[64]

Conclusion

BiH is like a shopping centre. The people come here to take what they need, good or bad, to take some photos and spend some time in it to gain some political status. It is like a circus.[65]

So far, the Bosnian government has not made any official statement nor sent any request to the ICTY to explain why the court destroyed the artefacts, but according to survivors and their supporters, the government should have done so. Because the government officials sent the artefacts to the court, they are perceived to have a responsibility to follow up on what has happened to these objects. As discussed previously, it has been recognized that it is important for countries to have the objects which reflect their cultural heritage and national history in their own museums. Visiting such commemorative landscapes is a necessary act of witnessing that enables reverence, remembrance and reflection on the event and its victims.[66] More importantly, these objects often hold the key to the identification of dead bodies, as in Hatidža's case, since the identification of the missing and dead is done by matching information from the deceased, such as clothes and other personal items, with information from individuals who are missing or presumed dead.[67]

As I have argued in this chapter, artefacts which held a memory and remembrance of past lives were not deemed to have important value to the ICTY and

61 Ibid, 777.

62 Russell Rodrigo, 'Between Remembrance and Recreation: Containing Memory in Urban Landscapes' (1) (2011) *Memory Connection*, 273.

63 Ibid.

64 Philip Stone and Richard Sharpley, 'Consuming Dark Tourism: A Thanatological Perspective', *Annals of Tourism Research* 35 (2) 2008, 558.

65 Interview with Hatidža Mehmedović, above n 2.

66 Joy Sather-Wagstaff, *Heritage that Hurts: Tourists in the Memoryscapes of September 11* (Left Coast Press, 2011), 153.

67 PAHO, WHO, ICRC and IFRC 'Management of Dead Bodies after Disasters: A Field Manual for First Responders' (Washington, D.C. 2006), 13.

were not judged to be worthy of being preserved. Choices as to what is remembered and forgotten have massive moral implications for individuals, groups and communities, and they often influence the direction in which a country moves.[68] It remains unclear whether there is a mechanism to clearly identify which materials and records of the ICTY should be preserved and archived and why, and which items will be disposed of. Also, a question remains as to whose interests should be acknowledged in making such decisions. Survivors, researchers and governments may have an interest in accessing materials, documents and archives for various reasons: to preserve a memory but also to raise new challenges to old cases.[69]

While not relevant to the ICTY, the chapter argues that the artefacts were important to Srebrenica survivors for many reasons. As Belma stated:

> These artefacts are important since they give an identity to skeletons and bones found in mass graves. They mean a lot in the process of identification but also as the last pieces of memory and proof of the lives taken so abruptly.

By 'disposing them off', the ICTY denied the Mothers' claim to symbolic or moral reparation. As a consequence, the Mothers and their supporters signed a petition which gathered more than 4,000 signatures against the ICTY act of destruction. They have worked closely with a group of lawyers from London who are preparing the charges against the ICTY and Carla Del Ponte. They want to know, as Hatidža told me, 'who gave them [ICTY] the right to destroy.'[70] Ultimately, they want to prevent the ICTY and other *ad hoc* tribunals from destruction of artefacts in the future, without consulting survivors and the national governments. To Hatidža and the Mothers, this act has been unnecessary and even genocidal, 'The Serb army killed our children and the house of justice [ICTY] killed memories on our loved ones. They committed genocide of memories.'[71]

Acknowledgments I would like to thank Chef de Cabinet in the Office of the President of the Special Tribunal for Lebanon, Mr Guido Acquaviva, Associate Professor Peter Rush and Dr Martine Hawkes for their careful reading and useful comments on an earlier draft of this paper. I would also like to thank participants of the panel session 'Excavating the Truth in the Wake of Human Rights Atrocities' (Law and Society conference, Honolulu, Hawaii, June 5–8, 2012) for their valuable comments. I am indebted to Hatidža Mehmedović and Belma Zulčić for their participation in the research.

[68] Elizabeth Porter, *Peacebuilding: Women in International Perspective* (Routledge, 2007), 126.

[69] For discussion on this theme, see Trudy Huskamp Peterson, 'Temporary Courts, Permanent Records' (United States Institute of Peace, August 2006), Special Report.

[70] Interview with Hatidža Mehmedović, above n 2.

[71] Ibid.

Bibliography

1. Acquaviva, Guido. 2011. 'The Best before the date indicated': Residual Mechanism at the ICTY. In *The legacy of the international criminal tribunal for the former Yugoslavia*, eds. Bert Swart, Alexander Zahar and Goran Sluiter. New York: Oxford University Press.
2. Barsalou, Judy and Victoria Baxter. 2007. *The Urge to Remember: The Role of Memorials in Social Reconstruction and Transitional Justice.* The United States Institute for Peace.
3. Berjano, Marguerite. 1994. *Guzman revolutionizing motherhood: The mothers of the Plaza de Mayo.* Wilmington, DE: Scholarly Resources.
4. Booth, James. 2008. The work of memory: Time, identity and Justice. *Social Research* 75(1): 237–262.
5. Booth, W.James. 2006. *Communities of memory: On witness, identity, and Justice.* Ithaca: Cornell University.
6. Booth, W.James. 2001. The unforgotten: Memories of justice. *American Political Science Review* 95(4): 777–797.
7. Balkan Insight. 2010. Srebrenica artefacts destroyed in The Hague. http://www.balkaninsight.com/en/article/srebrenica-artefacts-destroyed-in-the-hague. 16 July 2010.
8. Czeslaw, Milosz. 2000. *The Issa valley.* Straus and Giroux: Farrar.
9. Cockburn, Cynthia. 1998. *The space between us: Negotiating gender and national identities in conflict.* Zed Books.
10. de Greiff, Pablo. 2000. *Justice and reparations. The handbook on reparations.* Oxford: Oxford University Press.
11. Deasy, Kristin and Dzenana Halimovic, After Hague destroys Srebrenica evidence, survivors feel pain of lost memories. *Radio Free Europe*, 3 Sept 2009.
12. General Assembly Resolution 60/147, *The United Nations Basic Principles and Guidelines on the Right to a Remedy and Reparation for Victims of Gross Violations of Human Rights Law and Serious Violations of International Humanitarian Law* (United Nations, 16 Dec 2005).
13. Hawkes, Martine. 2012. Containing testimony: Archiving loss after Genocide. *Continuum: Journal of Media and Cultural Studies* 26(6): 935–945.
14. Hamber, Brandon and Ingrid Palmary. 2009. Gender, memorialization, and symbolic reparations. In *Gender of Reparations: Unsettling Sexual Hierarchies While Redressing Human Rights Violations*, ed. Ruth Rubio-Marin. Cambridge: Cambridge University Press.
15. Huskamp Peterson, Trudy. 2006 Temporary Courts, Permanent Records. United States Institute of Peace, August 2006, Special Report.
16. Institute Research for Genocide Canada, Natasa Kandic-Eyewitness Testimony. http://instituteforgenocide.org/?p=1126.
17. Judan, Tim and Daniel Sunter, How video that put Serbia in dock was brought to light. *The Guardian.* http://www.guardian.co.uk/world/2005/jun/05/balkans.warcrimes.
18. Kent, Lia. 2011. Local memory practices in East Timor: Disrupting transitional justice narratives. *The International Journal of Transitional Justice* 5: 434–455.
19. Kumar, Krishna, *Women and Civil War: Impact, Organizations and Actions.* Lynne Rienner, 2001.
20. Leydesdorff, Selma. 2011. *Surviving the Bosnian genocide.* Bloomington: Indiana University Press.
21. Lenz, Siegfried. 1992. *Ü ber das Gedächtnis.* Munich: DTV.
22. Minow, Martha. 1998. *Between vengeance and forgiveness.* Boston: Beacon Press.
23. PAHO, WHO, ICRC and IFRC. 2006. Management of dead bodies after disasters: A field manual for first responders. Washington, D.C.
24. Perera, Suvendrini. 2006. They give evidence: Bodies, borders and the disappeared. *Social Identities: Journal for the Study of Race, Nation and Culture* 12: 637–656.
25. Porter, Elizabeth. 2007. *Peacebuilding: Women in international perspective.* London: Routledge.

26. Roht-Arriaza, Naomi. 2004. Reparations decisions and dilemmas. *Hastings International and Comparative Law Review* 27(2): 157.
27. Rodrigo, Russell. 2011. Between remembrance and recreation: Containing memory in Urban Landscapes. (1) *Memory Connection*, 272–282.
28. Sather-Wagstaff, Joy. *Heritage that hurts: Tourists in the memoryscapes of september 11.* Left Coast Press, 2011.
29. Simić, Olivera. 2009. Remembering, visiting and placing the dead: Law, authority and genocide in Srebrenica. *Law Text Culture* 13: 273.
30. Simić, Olivera. 2008. A tour to a site of genocide: Mothers, bones and borders. *Journal of International Women Studies* 9(3): 320–330.
31. Stone, Philip, and Richard Sharpley. 2008. Consuming dark tourism: A thanatological perspective. *Annals of Tourism Research* 35(2): 574–595.
32. Silber, Laura, and Allan Little. 1996. *The death of Yugoslavia.* Harmondsworth: Penguin Books.
33. Srebrenica Genocide Blog. http://srebrenica-genocide.blogspot.com/2008/12/update-8372-victims-of-srebrenica.html.
34. Srebrenica Genocide blog. U.N. tribunal destroys evidence of Srebrenica genocide. 8 May 2009.
35. Taylor, Diana (2001) Making a spectacle: The mothers of the plaza de Mayo. *Journal of the Association for Research on Mothering: Mothering, Fathering and a Culture of Peace.*
36. Taušan, Marija. 2012. Masovna stratišta of Kravice do Pilice. *BalkanInsight*, http://www.balkaninsight.com/en/article/masovna-stratista-od-kravice-do-pilice. 10 July 2012.
37. Turshen, Meredeth and Clotilde Twagiramariya. 1998. *What Women Do in War-time: Gender and Conflict in Africa.* Zed Books.
38. The UN Security Council, S/Res/827 (1993), 25 May 1993.
39. United Nations Security Council Resolution 819 (1993) on the situation in Bosnia and Herzegovina. See, S/Res/819/1993, 16 Apr 1993.
40. Vulliamy, ed. Srebrenica: genocide and memory. *Open Democracy*, 4 July 2005.
41. Wieten, Jesse. 2013. Mladic trial still expected to end in 2016. *News.* http://news.xinhuanet.com/english/world/2013-04/11/c_132301640.htm. 11 Apr 2013.
42. Williams, Daniel. 2005. Srebrenica video vindicates long pursuit by Serb Activist. *Washington Post.* http://www.washingtonpost.com/wp-dyn/content/article/2005/06/24/AR2005062401501.html. 25 June 2005.
43. Taylor, Telfordm. 1949. Final report to the secretary of the Army on the Nurnberg War Crimes trials under control Council Law No. 10', 15 Aug 1949.

Cases

44. *Prosecutor v. Radislav Krstic*, Judgement, Case No. IT-98-33-T, 2 August 2001.
45. *The Prosecutor v Ratko Mladic*, Case No. IT-09-92-I, 1 June 2011.
46. *Prosecutor v. Naser Orić,* Case No. IT-03-68-A, Appeal Judgment, 3 July 2008.
47. *Prosecutor v. Vujadin Popović, Ljubiša Beara, Drago Nikolić, Ljubomir Borovčanin, Radivoje Miletić, Milan Gvero and Vinko Pandurević*, 'Srebrenica', IT-05-88, Judgement Summary, 10 June 2010.
48. *Prosecutor v Momir Nikolic*, IT-02-60, Judgement, 2 December 2003.
49. *Blagojevic and Jokic*, IT-02-60, Trial Chamber, Judgement, 17 January 2005.

Chapter 10
(Mis)representations of Transitional Justice: Contradictions in Displaying History, Memory and Art in the Skopje 2014 Project

Despina Angelovska

Introduction

In February 2010, the Macedonian government for the first time officially presented its new plan for the reconstruction of the capital's city-centre, called "Skopje 2014" in reference to the year in which it was to be finished.[1] Presented as a revision of the totalitarian communist heritage and employing arguments of transitional justice such as nation-building, memory preservation and the rehabilitation of victims of communism, the government-funded project included the erection of numerous prestigious public buildings, museums, memorials, monuments and statues. Despite its transitional justice claims, the project has been criticized for radically reshaping the identity of the city and the nation.

This chapter considers the politics of public art and memorialization in relation to policies of transitional justice in the context of the Skopje 2014 project. The aim is to analyse the complex and contradictory relations between the Macedonian ruling party's project of symbolic demarcation from the communist past and the concepts of transitional justice employed to legitimize it. Focusing on the controversial display in public space of various architectural, artistic and memorial practices that are meant to illustrate the political will to reckon with the communist past and forge new public markers, this study questions the alleged dimension of the project as an initiative of symbolic reparatory transitional justice. Pointing out the dangers of certain instrumentalized applications of transitional justice in fledgling democracies and divided societies, it reflects on the complexities and contradictions of memory politics displayed in public spaces.

---

[1] "Macedonia's Timeless Capital, Skopje 2014", YouTube, last modified February 4 2010: https://www.youtube.com/watch?v=iybmt-iLysU.

D. Angelovska (✉)
University of Audiovisual arts, ESRA, Nikola Rusinski Street No. 1, 1000 Skopje, Republic of Macedonia
e-mail: adespa@yahoo.com; despina.angelovska@gmail.com

P. D. Rush and O. Simić (eds.), *The Arts of Transitional Justice*,
Springer Series in Transitional Justice 6, DOI: 10.1007/978-1-4614-8385-4_10,

In the first part of this study, I briefly review the measures of transitional justice adopted in Macedonia and introduce the Skopje 2014 project as embodying a broader symbolic politics of reckoning with the communist past. I argue that the policies of transitional justice adopted reflect the way in which the political elite interpret and confront the communist past. In the second part, I consider the politics of memory of the project displayed in the city's space, focusing on its contradictions. In the third part, I question the alleged symbolic reparatory dimension of the Skopje 2014 project, while in the fourth part, I analyse the narrative of communism as represented in the Museum of the Victims of the Communist Regime. In conclusion, pointing out the crucial deficiencies of the politics of memory displayed within the Skopje 2014 project, I reflect on the factors contributing to successful processes of transitional justice in city space. In this respect, I briefly consider the critical and creative reactions from citizens standing up in defence of the city and of justice in transitional society.

Although the Skopje 2014 project has already provoked numerous national and international reactions and a number of publications, its relation to policies of transitional justice has not yet been elaborated and there are no available studies on this subject. This chapter therefore draws principally on field research, relating it to relevant contemporary debates on transitional justice and scholarship. Seeking to embrace the particular complexity and breadth of Skopje 2014 in its connection to the politics of memory, this chapter employs an interdisciplinary approach in trying to relate different fields such as architecture, art, urban studies, memory studies and museum studies to the scholarship on transitional justice.

Initiatives and Measures of Post-Communist Transitional Justice Adopted in Macedonia

Transitional Justice and Lustration

In a broad and commonly accepted sense, transitional justice refers to how societies address legacies of widespread and systematic abuses of human rights, mass atrocities or other forms of severe social trauma, in order to build a more democratic, just and peaceful future.[2] The term "transitional justice" emerged in the late 1980s and early 1990s with reference to the transitions from authoritarian rule in Eastern Europe and Central America.[3] It is often used interchangeably with terms

[2] Carlos Closa Montero, *A Study on how the Memory of Crimes Committed by Totalitarian Regimes in Europe is Dealt with in the Member States* (Madrid: CSIC, 2010), 13; Lavinia Stan, "Transitional Justice, a Definition", *Lavinia Stan's blog* (blog), May 11, 2010 (10:54 a.m.), https://laviniastan.wordpress.com/2010/05/11/transitional-justice-a-definition/.

[3] Christine Bell, "Transitional Justice, Interdisciplinarity and the State of the 'Field' or 'non-Field'", *International Journal of Transitional Justice*, Vol. 3 (2009): 7.

and concepts such as "the politics of memory", "reckoning with the past", or "de-communisation".[4] The repertoire of methods and instruments adopted by different governments is diverse,[5] while the adopted models and objectives of transitional justice are historically conditioned and still evolving.[6] In general, transitional justice has been categorized either as retributive (perpetrator-oriented) or reparative (victim-oriented).[7]

Following the collapse of the Communist bloc in Europe between 1989 and 1991, lustration has been the most commonly adopted instrument of retributive transitional justice, used for "screening and 'prosecuting' former communist leaders, candidates for office, and selected public employees".[8] It was only after the coming to power of a new political coalition, presided over by the right-wing party VMRO-DPMNE,[9] that the Macedonian Parliament adopted a law on lustration in 2008. The controversial applications and amendments to this law still continue to inspire virulent reactions and criticisms in Macedonian society. VMRO-DPMNE, the party proposing the latest amended law, has been accused of politically manipulating and selectively applying lustration for dealing with political opponents.[10]

Symbolic Transitional Justice Policies

As often stated in contemporary debates on transitional justice, while retributive justice measures play a crucial role in addressing past human rights abuses, their efficacy in promoting a democratic transition to civil society remains questionable when they are not supplemented by further initiatives supporting social reconciliation and recovery.

While the Macedonian conservative government has been deeply engaged in the use of retributive instruments of transitional justice and the lustration of public

[4] Stan, "Transitional Justice".

[5] Lavinia, Stan (ed.), *Transitional Justice in Eastern Europe and the Former Soviet Union: Reckoning with the Communist Past*, London: Routledge, 2009, 1.

[6] Montero, *Memory of Crimes*, 14.

[7] Jon Elster (ed.), *Retribution and Reparation in the Transition to Democracy*. (Cambridge: Cambridge University Press, 2006); Mano Gabor Toth, *Symbols in Transitions: Public Places, Reparatory Justice, and the Statue Park,* Master's Thesis (Budapest: CEU, 2011), 15; Mark S. Ellis, "Purging the Past: The Current State of Lustration Laws in the Former Communist Bloc", *Law and Contemporary Problems*, 59/4 (1996):181–196.

[8] Ellis, "Purging the Past", 181.

[9] VMRO-DPMNE, the Internal Macedonian Revolutionary Organization and the Democratic Party for Macedonian National Unity, is a Macedonian Christian-Democratic party.

[10] Despina Angelovska, "The Failure of Macedonian Post-Communist Transitional justice: Lustration, between Cleansing and Parody", in *Transitional Justice and Civil Society in the Balkans*, edited by Olivera Simić and Zala Volčič, New York: Springer, 2013.

officials, it has neglected to adopt measures of reparation or compensation for victims has been neglected. Even though the Parliament in 2006 approved a *Declaration of Apology to the Victims of Repression by the Regime Between 1945 and 1990*, and although the Albanian partner in the governing coalition, DUI,[11] announced a draft-law for the rehabilitation of victims of communism in spring 2012, no such law has yet been adopted.

Despite this deficiency in the institution of justice for victims, VMRO-DPMNE embarked upon an ambitious symbolic project of reckoning with the communist past and rebuilding national identity—with the additional aim of giving wider pedagogical support to retributive processes of transitional justice. In 2006, the new government commissioned a plan for the reconstruction of the capital's centre. Presented to the public for the first time in February 2010 under the name Skopje 2014, the project was also promoted as a symbolic gesture of reparation for the victims of communism, since it consisted amongst other things of erecting monuments, memorials, and museums to honour those persecuted.

Symbolic Representations of Post-Communist Transitional Justice: Contradictions in the Politics of Memory in the Skopje 2014 Project

The (Re)construction of Post-Communist Identity: Skopje 2014, a Nation-Building Project

After 1989, the new political elites of Eastern European countries based their legitimacy primarily upon the rejection of the communist experience[12] and the adoption of instruments of transitional justice. The forms of transitional justice that have emerged in post-communist countries are associated with the rise of nation-building,[13] since the historical production and construction of an alternative history are fundamental to the building of a state's political identity.[14] In recent decades of accelerated transition, as noted by Ruti Teitel, the concept of transitional justice has remained closely associated with diverse nation-building projects, involving the construction of identity politics through a range of diverse

[11] DUI, the Democratic Union for Integration, is the largest Albanian political party in Macedonia.

[12] Csilla Kiss, "We are not Like Us. Transitional Justice: The (Re)construction of Post-Communist Memory", in *History and Judgement*, edited by A. MacLachlan and I. Torsen, Vienna: IWM Junior Visiting Fellows' Conferences, Vol. 21, (2006): 3–4.

[13] Ruti G. Tetel, "Transitional Justice Genealogy", *Harvard Human Rights Journ*al, Vol. 16 (2003): 71.

[14] Ibid., 87.

local approaches.[15] It was in such a context of "heightened democratic transition"[16] that the Macedonian Government conceived Skopje 2014 as a post-communist nation-building project. The project, displayed by means of urbanism, architecture and art, joins the broader policy of eastern post-communist countries of re-branding their nations as (western) European ones, while orientalizing[17] their communist past.

The Europeanization of Post-Communist Macedonia and the Orientalization of Communism

As argued by Tatiana Zhurzhenko, the politics of memory in post-communist countries have been employed to (re)position these nations within the European space. The new democracies in Europe have created new national historical narratives founded on externalizing the communist past, often presenting that past as an alien phenomenon imposed by a foreign force (i.e. the Soviets) against the nation's will. What makes this narrative even more powerful, adds Zhurzhenko, is its underlying dichotomy of "Occident" and "Orient", civilization and barbarism. Communism is presented as an oriental and barbaric force threatening European civilization. This kind of orientalization of communism has further served to facilitate its externalization.[18] Moreover, the enlargement of the European Union has created an additional need in post-communist countries for a common narrative of European history.[19]

Thus, prolonging a broader post-communist politics of memory, Skopje 2014 strives to (re)build a European identity of the nation via the reconstruction of its capital. What is interesting to note is that Skopje had already been entirely rebuilt with the help and solidarity of the international community after the catastrophic earthquake of 1963. It was the famous Japanese architect Kenzo Tange who won the competition for the new master plan of the city-centre. Due to seismic risks, the riverbanks of the Vardar were kept free of construction. After Macedonia's independence in 1991, the city square, the reconstruction of which had long been postponed, remained an empty transitional place, the old Stone Bridge linking the two parts of the city naturally divided by the River Vardar. As argued by Mijalković and Urbanek, it was only in 2006, for the first time since the 1960s, that the post-communist government adopted political decisions to reshape the urban space and turned towards reinventing Macedonia's separate and glorified

[15] Ruti G. Teitel, "Transitional Justice in a New Era", *Fordham International Law Journal,* Vol. 26, no. 4 (2002): 893.

[16] Ibid.

[17] *Cf.* Edward Said *Orientalism*, (London: Vintage, 1979).

[18] Tatiana Zhurzhenko, "Geopolitics of Memory", *Eurozine* (May 10 2007): http://www.eurozine.com/articles/2007-05-10-zhurzhenko-en.html.

[19] Ibid.

identity.[20] It is precisely in the "void" left by the communist era—in the spaces by the riverside and in the city square—that the new Skopje 2014 project is being implemented. The project consists of erecting a building to house the National Archives, a new building for the Foreign Ministry, a Constitutional Court, an Electronic Communications Agency, a triumphal arch, an Orthodox church, a National Theatre, monuments, memorials, museums and over fifty statues in the centre. Symbolically (re)positioning Macedonia as a European country, the project is intended to embody the continuity of the Macedonian nation since antiquity—and even since the Neolithic Age—to the present day. Stressing discontinuity with the orientalized communist past while emphasizing its European affiliation, grandiose public buildings have been erected in neo-classical, neo-romantic and neo-baroque styles. These serve a dual purpose as a counter-narrative both to the city's socialist egalitarian, functional and modernist architecture and to its oriental Ottoman heritage.

Reinventing the bourgeois identity of the city, Skopje 2014 even proposes to reconstruct various projects of the pre-communist past, such as the National Theatre, the orthodox church of St. Konstantin and Elena, and the Officers' Club—all of which were destroyed by the earthquake in 1963. Paradoxically, these buildings in bourgeois nineteenth-century style that are intended to stand as testimony to an authentic European identity were in fact first constructed during Serbian rule before the Second World War and are thus embodiments of Serbian colonialism. When those buildings were erected in 1930, furthermore, they constituted the new city-centre, which was thereby shifted from the northern Ottoman part of the city to the southern side of the river. Already in that period, these buildings were meant to show the western European orientation of the city following liberation from Ottoman rule.[21] As noted by Mijalkovic and Urbanek, again today the resurrection of the old pre-communist centre of Skopje strives to establish the city's identity as European, Christian and bourgeois, while to a great extent denying its oriental, Islamic and communist past.[22] At the same time, contrary to the goal of sustainable social reconciliation called for by transitional justice, the Skopje 2014 project's aim of Europeanization to the detriment of the Oriental and the communist past rejects the idea of the inherited hybridity of the city which is essential to its constitutive multiculturalism.[23]

[20] Milan Mijalkovic and Katharina Urbanek, *Skopje, the World's Bastard:Architecture of The Divided City* (Klagenfurt: Wieser Verlag, 2011), 10.

[21] Ibid, 83.

[22] Ibid.

[23] Majrola Rukaj, Milan Mijalkovic and Katharina Urbanek, "Skopje, the Bastard City", *Osservatorio Balcani e Caucaso*, (September 9, 2011), http://greengopost.com/skopje-the-bastard-city/.

Antiquization

Building an alternative politics of memory to the communist past is one of the main arguments employed to legitimize Skopje 2014. The project also consists of filling the core of the city with imposing monuments of reinvented national heroes, amongst whom especially dominant is a centrally situated 22-m-high monument to Alexander the Great. This is accompanied by other monuments from the antique period, such as the statue of Alexander's father Philip II, and of his mother Olympias II of Epirus, as well as the nine muses on the colonnade called "Independent Macedonia", a number of historical figures from the Byzantine era. Already when VMRO-DPMNE came to power in 2006, antique sculptures and artefacts were placed in front of and inside the government building in order to "fill the empty and sterile socialist-era building".[24] This effectively began the process that has been described by some as "antiquization".[25] Antiquization is intended to support Macedonia's international legitimation as a sovereign and ancient European nation and its positioning within a continuous and glorious history of civilization. By emphasizing an antique Macedon heritage, the government additionally intends to overshadow the premise of the Slavic origin of the Macedonians that was emphasized in communist historiography. The Slavic aspects of Macedonia's history, according to the new revision, "can only be considered as a small parenthesis in the millennial history of Macedonia".[26]

Antiquization is an essential part of the process of post-communist nation-building. With the reconstruction of the capital, the new political elite is seeking to complete the transition from communism, to confirm Macedonia as an authentic and ancient European nation, thereby additionally demonstrating "natural evidence" of the necessity of the country's integration within the European Union.

The Beautification of the Post-Communist City: Art versus Ideology

Art is another essential aspect of the Skopje 2014 project, which includes the display of over fifty statues within the city-centre. A variety of artistic practices are often used in support of processes of transitional justice. Within the transitional politics of Skopje 2014, the use of art serves a dual purpose. The first, as expressed by the spokesman of the Ministry of Culture, is "to prettify the city and give it the

---

[24] Macedon, "Паско Кузман-Скулптурите во владата раскажуваат Македонска историја стара 7.000 години", *Macedonian Civilization* (blog), August 1, 2007, (12:02:21 am). http://my.opera.com/ancientmacedonia/blog/show.dml/1207581.

[25] The term *antiquisation* is used by historians to refer to the Renaissance practice of giving a city the appearance of ancient Rome or Athens.

[26] Macedon, "Паско Кузман".

look of a genuine metropolis"[27]; the second is to reckon with the previous communist practices of ideological aesthetics. In this respect, the allegedly purely artistic motivation of this project is meant to clearly mark the shift to a new order in which art is used solely to adorn public space rather than being abused for political purposes. The Deputy President of the Macedonian Artists Association, Resat Ameti, praising the Ministry of Culture's sculpture project initiative, stated that the sculptures should have a "humanist character".[28]

It was in this "humanist" spirit and in order to propose a counter-narrative to the "political art" of the communist era that numerous smaller sculptures such as "The Shoe Cleaner" "The Beggar" and "Šmizla"[29] were placed beside monumental works. For this purpose, the government has published an open nationwide call for artists, affording priority to young artists who are not yet established.[30] The choice of engaging inexperienced artists in such an important and complex project as that of reshaping the capital's public space has been criticized by many as irresponsible and as tending to produce amateurism and kitsch.[31] The choice of young and unknown but professional artists to re-imagine the city was again meant to express the government's desire to turn a new page and to erase any possible relation with the established communist artistic heritage while at the same time allegedly professionalizing and democratizing the initiative. Another important aspect of demarcation from the communist aesthetic in this project is the proliferation of figurative monuments. While most propaganda monuments and sculptures during communism were abstract, intended to express the ideals of industrial society and of modernism, almost all the sculptures and monuments displayed as part of Skopje 2014 are figurative. Finally, as argued by the historian and theoretician of art, Nebojša Vilić, this project reflects the government's idea of "re-branding Skopje as a city of public sculpture".[32] This re-branding should also give a commercial value to art and depoliticize public space, thus reflecting the government's desire of expressing what Mijalković and Urbanek analyse as the "end of politics".[33] However, as argued by Mijalković and Urbanek, this alleged

---

27 "Конкурс на Министерството за Култура—На Скопје му Недостасуваат Скулптури", *Culture Republic of Macedonia*, accessed September 10 2012, http://www.culture.in.mk/story_mk.asp?id=23415&rub=54.

28 Resat Ameti, quoted by Mijalkovic and Urbanek in *Skopje*, 78.

29 Meaning a complacent and superficial girl obsessed with physical appearance.

30 Nebojša Vilić, *Силувајте so Скопје, кн.1* (Skopje: 359 °, 2009).

31 Vilić, *Скопје,* 56; Jasna Koteska, "Troubles with history : Skopje 2014", *ArtMargins,* December 29 2011, http://www.artmargins.com/index.php/2-articles/655-troubles-with-history-skopje-2014; Nikola Gelevski, "Споменициите и кичот", *Okno.mk*, 4 October 2011, http://okno.mk/node/13998.

32 Vilić, *Скопје*, 30.

33 Mijalkovic and Urbanek, *Skopje*, 79.

professionalization rather camouflages the project's "originally intended amateurism"[34] whereby every citizen can be an artist and suggests an "underlying crisis of competence".[35]

Ironically, one of the main criticisms directed at Skopje 2014 and the statue project is exactly that of their politicization and instrumentalization. The main financier, commissioner and even designer of this top-down initiative are the Government of the Republic of Macedonia. Moreover, although the Skopje 2014 project was already commissioned in 2006, it was kept secret until 2010. The lack of public debate or consultation with experts and citizens in the preparation phase, as well as the lack of transparency concerning the cost of the project financed by the tax-payers, has provoked virulent criticism and polemic. The project was even declared partly illegal by the Constitutional Court.[36] Rather than being perceived as the promised de-politicized and democratic artistic reshaping of Skopje, this top-down (re)construction of the city has been denounced as a "a scary and totalitarian display of power".[37] Instead of contributing to social reconciliation, the project has additionally been accused of creating new ethnic, class and gender divisions and exclusions.[38] Creating a new politics of memory that reflects the government's identification with antiquity, the project Skopje 2014, as analysed by Koteska, forced Macedonian citizens to "choose between being Slavs or being descendants of Ancient Macedonians".[39] Displaying nationalistic symbols and monuments meant solely to glorify the Macedonian nation, it creates segregation within the city and between communities. In this respect, there is a deep division between Macedonians and Albanians in their attitudes towards the project. In order to divert attention from this problem, a second city square is being constructed around a monument of Skanderbeg in the part of the city with an Albanian majority. The construction of two parallel city squares, one for Macedonians and another for Albanians, is again being financed entirely by the government, while the country's other ethnic minorities remain underrepresented. By erecting monuments mainly of male heroes or patriarchal rulers, moreover, the Skopje 2014 project obliterates the representation of woman. Finally, the class division is visible in the clear hierarchy expressed in the contrast between the huge monuments of great rulers or military governors and the small "humanist" sculptures of ordinary people.

---

34 Ibid., 78.

35 Ibid., 79.

36 "Владата Нема да го Запре Скопје 2014", *Utrinski Vesnik*, June 2 2010, http://www.netpress.com.mk/mk/vest.asp?id=73809&kategorija=7.

37 Koteska, *Troubles with History*.

38 Ibid.

39 Ibid.

(Mis)representations of Reparative Justice in the Skopje 2014 Project

Commemorating Victims of Communism

Another important dimension of Skopje 2014 is the commemoration of victims of communism. Monuments to the memory of those persecuted during communism have been erected and a Museum of the Victims of the Communist Regime has been inaugurated as a symbolic gesture of reparation. Very recently, an initiative has been adopted by the city authorities to change the names of the city's streets, boulevards and bridges. As recognized by scholars of transitional justice, the renaming of streets can be a powerful expression of political change.[40] This initiative is the first of its kind in the twenty years since Macedonia's independence in 1991. It has been promoted as a nation-building initiative, but also as having a commemorative function. In this respect, as a form of symbolic reparation, the renaming of streets can assist in restoring dignity and public recognition to victims. Teitel argues that reparations of this kind serve to rehabilitate victims.[41] Hence, some of the Skopje's new street names directly address the victims of the communist regime, such as "Goli Otok" or "The Victims of Communism", while Metodija Andonov-Čento, Macedonia's first president after the Second World War and a victim of the Communist regime, has also been honoured with a large marble statue on Skopje's central square.

This renaming initiative has provoked huge public reactions within Macedonian society. As argued by scholarship on transitional justice, the changing of street names also has the function of constructing a politicized version of history. This function being prone to manipulation, it should be viewed with caution.[42] Indeed, the strongest reactions have been provoked by the erasure of an important part of recent Macedonian history related to the struggle against fascism and to the socialist period, and the replacement of most of the names connected to these with the names of antique kings and rulers such as Amyntas III or Philip II of Macedon. Some of the streets, furthermore, have been renamed after precursors or founders of VMRO, a nineteenth-century Macedonian revolutionary organization of which the governing party VMRO-DPMNE considers itself the successor. Additionally, a monument to the founders of VMRO has been elevated in the city-centre, further illustrating the governing party's use of transitional justice policies for the glorification of its own ideology. What has been perceived as especially problematic, however, is the naming of a street and a bridge after one of the most controversial personalities from recent history, Todor Aleksandrov, a most notorious historical

---

[40] Mia Swart, "Name Changes as Symbolic Reparation after Transition: the Examples of Germany and South Africa", *German Law Journal* Vol. 9, no. 2 (2008): 106.

[41] Ruti Teitel, *Transitional Justice* (New York: Oxford University Press, 2000), 125, 137.

[42] Swart, "Name Changes": 106.

leader of VMRO whose figure continues to provoke virulent polemics and sharp divisions among historians and citizens.

The initiative of renaming streets and building monuments, conceived without any public consultation, seems only to have deepened the divisions already existing in the society. As pointed out by scholars and practitioners of transitional justice, it is vital that discussions on the design and implementation of mechanisms of transitional justice reach out to the broadest possible population in order to avoid further societal fractures.[43] Commemorating controversial and disputed historical figures and events about which no broad consensus in the society has been reached may exacerbate tensions and polarization in an already divided society rather than serving efforts towards reconciliation and peace-building as part of transitional justice. As argued by the director of the Macedonian Institute of National History, the historian Todor Čepreganov, "Memorials and street naming should reinforce the unification of citizens, not their division".[44]

As mentioned earlier, the politics of memory embodied within the Skopje 2014 project additionally serve the political interests of the power-holders. Transitional justice in divided societies must thus be considered carefully with all its potential and limits and as a reflection of political and social tensions.[45] In that regard, monuments and memorialization practices can be also used to force a specific ideology upon society and to sanction a particular version of history, becoming an instrument for the glorification and legitimization of power-holders.[46]

The Museum of the Victims of the Communist Regime: Displaying the "Communist Other"

Representing History and Commemorating the Victims of Communism in a Wax Museum

As claimed by Artemis Christodoulou, "remembrance lies at the centre of a network of transitional justice goals central to survivors of mass atrocity and human rights abuses, such as truth-seeking, prevention of future abuses, reparation and

[43] "Transitional Justice", *Topic Guide*, GSDRC, accessed September 10 2012, http://www.gsdrc.org/go/topic-guides/justice/transitional-justice.

[44] Mirjana Spasovska, "Нова влада, нова историја - нови поделби?", *Radio Slobodna Evropa*, June 23 2012, http://www.makdenes.org/content/article/24623301.html.

[45] Suzanne Buckley-Zistel, "Transitional Justice in Divided Societies—Potentials and Limits". Paper presented at the 5th European Consortium for Political Research General Conference, Potsdam University, Germany, 10–12 September 2009: 16.

[46] B. Hamber, L. Ševčenko, and E. Naidu, "Utopian Dreams or Practical Possibilities? The Challenges of Evaluating the Impact of Memorialisation in Societies in Transition", *International Journal of Transitional Justice*, vol. 4, no. 3 (2010): 397–420.

reconciliation".[47] It is in this sense that the Museum of the Victims of Communism, built to commemorate those who suffered under communism, is meant to embody these central goals of transitional justice. Claiming to honour the memory of the victims, it emphasizes its value of symbolic rehabilitation.

The Museum was inaugurated on 8 September 2011, the twentieth anniversary of the declaration of Macedonian independence. It is in fact only a department of the Museum of the Macedonian Struggle for Sovereignty and Independence, which presents the striving for Macedonian statehood from the time of Ottoman occupation until the declaration of independence in 1991. The museum is situated in an imposing and bourgeois neo-classical building constructed especially for the purpose. It has been conceived as having additional commercial and touristic value. As I have already argued, commercialization has been an important element of Skopje 2014 as another marker of alleged de-politicization. In this regard, the Museum of the Victims of the Communist Regime joins a number of European museums devoted to the memory of communism, such as The House of Terror in Budapest, Grutas Park in Lithuania, the DDR-Museum in Berlin. The vindicated constitutive commercial and entertainment value of the Museum of the Victims of the Communist Regime, however, could also appear to contradict its purpose of being a symbolic reparative instrument for victims.

The Museum of the Victims of the Communist Regime constitutes a part of the Museum of the Macedonian Struggle which is dedicated to contemporary national history. Thus, it serves a dual function as a history museum and as a site of memory. As to its historical dimension, even though the museum presents authentic historical documents and items, it is conceived mainly as a display of figurative realist paintings and wax figures representing important historical events and personalities. The entire museum complex currently exhibits some 109 wax figures, 69 paintings of historical scenes and 16 portraits.[48] The idea of a history museum placing the main emphasis on artistic paintings and even more so on wax figures may also seem contradictory. A history museum as an educational institution bears the responsibility of presenting eruditely and factually supported information to those who visit with the intention of learning and understanding, expecting an objective presentation of history.[49] If a carefully documented presentation of history with facts and elaborated analysis enable visitors to develop a critical reflection on the past, then I argue that the Museum of the Victims of the Communist Regime has just the opposite effect. Exhibiting national history is already a controversial issue, especially in divided society, and this can become even more problematic in the case of this museum where the main emphasis is placed on artistic interpretations of the national past while the few authentic

---

[47] Artemis Christodoulou, "Appendix 4, Part 1: Memorials and Transitional Justice", Sierra Leone Truth and Reconciliation Commission, accessed 9 September 2012, http://www.sierraleonetrc.org/index.php/appendices/item/appendix-4-part-1-memorials.

[48] Музеј на Македонската Борба-Скопје, accessed September 2, 2012, http://mmb.org.mk/w/

[49] Brianne Hwang, *Constructing the Communist Other: A Comparative Study of Museum Representations of Communism*, Master's Thesis (Budapest: CEU, 2009), 100.

historical exhibits are used mainly as background scenery. On the one hand, such "artistic representation" seems to blur the frontier between history and fiction, between "nation and narration"[50] and could have a positive, deconstructive effect; on the other hand, it could open even wider the possibility for reinventing national and nationalist history and its political instrumentalization and manipulation.

Analysis of the Museum Exhibition and Visit: A Guided Tour through a Frozen Past

In this section, I draw my theoretical conclusions from my personal field experience as a visitor to the museum. Interestingly, individual visits to the museum are not permitted—only guided group tours. The guide, a trained historian, determines the rhythm, trajectory and content of the visit. Furthermore, the tours are scheduled within a highly compressed time-frame which leaves no time and space for personal research and reflection. Nor does the layout of the museum encourage an exploratory and interactive experience for the visitor. The exhibition catalogue offers only scarce general information, while taking photos is not allowed, which reinforces the secretive aspect of the museum's policy. As the focus of the exhibition is on wax or painted representations of history, without sufficient supporting facts or explanations and without enough time for individual exploration, it is the guide who holds the key of the represented scenes. He transmits what seems a unique and unmitigated historical truth. This truth, moreover, in the Wax Museum, has been embodied in order for the visitor to see with his own eyes and to be persuaded.

On this strictly guided tour, the visitor to the Wax Museum of history is thus confronted with what seems to be a resurrection of the past. He has the unique privilege of catching a glimpse of a frozen past, exactly as it was. As stated by the employees of the museum, all the wax figures represent the historical figures in their precise height. They embody the past in such an obvious and palpable way that there can be no room for doubt about it.

The Theatre of History: An Analysis of the Museum's Visual Narrative

Instead of putting the emphasis on elaborated factual, documentary and analytical support, the Museum of the Victims of the Communist Regime chooses to reinforce the affective power of its narrative by creating an atmosphere of veracity, employing various resources to reinforce the emotional experience of the visitor.

---

[50] Cf. Homi K. Bhabha (ed.), *Nation and Narration* (London: Routledge, 1990).

At the moment of entering the exhibition rooms, the dimmed lights immediately immerse the visitor in a world of illusion. The effect is reinforced by various props and audio-visual means. Positioned in front of the scene of history, the visitor becomes a captivated spectator-voyeur for whom the "fourth wall" has been broken. Glimpsing the frozen past, the visitor has no opportunity, however, to (inter)act, becoming merely a passive receptor of what is displayed.

Valentin Svetozarev, a famous theatre scenographer, designed the set of the museum. Using theatrical display techniques, he has created a scary and claustrophobic atmosphere to tell the story of the victims of communism. For example, the room consecrated to the memory of Goli Otok—an island to which political prisoners in the Socialist Federal Republic of Yugoslavia were sentenced to hard labour—displays a wall covered with small shovels, barbed wire, reflectors, and stones, sounds of alternately terrifying and sad music and firing squads, while the visitor discovers wax figures and paintings representing the persecuted, such as the suffering of Čento, the execution of the 52 prisoners from Veles, the bloody gauntlet at Goli Otok. Interestingly, the socially engaged realist aesthetic of most of the paintings resembles precisely that of Soviet socialist-realism.

Thus, the museum presents the atrocities committed by the former regime, and in so doing, it acknowledges a very painful and traumatic truth about the sacrificial costs of communism in Macedonia and makes a gesture of public recognition of the victims. On the other hand, displaying this important repressed truth with wax figures or figurative paintings and using theatrical techniques of display serves to fictionalize, fabricate and even—as we shall see later in this chapter—caricature that past.

The Victims versus the Victimizers

One of the key challenges of memorialization is to determine how to address the narrative of past atrocities.[51] Skopje's new museum employs the narrative of victimization, opposing the "evil communists" to their victims. Rather than engaging with the topic of atrocities committed by the communist regime by addressing the ideological and contextual circumstances, the museum treats the issue at a moralizing and sentimental level at which the ideology and the perpetrators are generally classified as "evil". And while the victims are mostly identified, the victimizers are abstractly represented as communist Others. This victimization crystallizes a narrative that provokes feelings of pity for the victims and fear of the communist Other, while passing to this Other all the responsibility for the crimes. The narrative is rendered even more persuasive by theatrical display. Emotionally and physically immersed in what has been designed to be a deeply moving experience, confined within this "dark tourism" and claustrophobic

[51] "Transitional Justice", Topic Guide.

space, the visitor is neither invited nor facilitated to create a necessary critical distance. With the proposed narrative of victimization offering a moral alibi and discouraging reflection and dialogue, the debate on Communism can apparently be closed.

Waxy Victimization

The museum's binary narrative, displayed by means of wax figures, sometimes seems so extremely simplified and overly pathetic that it approaches caricature. As I have already pointed out, within the chosen display policy, the exhibition narrative is conveyed through embodied replications with almost no accompanying written information. The corresponding need to display exhibits with unequivocal affective meaning dictates that the chosen visual narrative is most often a frightening or pathetic one. For illustration, in the museum are displayed the wax figures of a famous Macedonian actor, Risto Šiškov, and a distinguished poet, Jovan Koteski, who were persecuted and imprisoned by the communist regime. The two men are represented sitting next to each other at bar tables, looking completely deceived and ruined, surrounded by bottles of alcohol. Šiškov is banging a heavy fist on the table, breaking the glass on a portrait of Tito. The message conveyed, as also pointed out by the guide, is that this was communist repression which morally destroyed Šiškov and drove him to alcoholism. This reduction of the actor and the poet to wretches and alcoholics (though both in fact achieved fame and recognition during the communist period) must make one question whether they are also being used as props in this melodramatic and victimizing representation of communism—and whether this representation really contributes to the restoration of their dignity.

The Political Manipulation of the Museum's Goal of Symbolic Rehabilitation

As mentioned above, the Museum of the Victims of the Communist Regime, together with the Museum of VMRO, constitutes the national Museum of the Macedonian Struggle, which has been entirely financed by the government. What must be stressed is that while the Museum of VMRO has 12 exhibit subdivisions, the Museum of the Victims of the Communist Regime has only one. Moreover, being much smaller than the VMRO Museum, and conceived of as its chronological continuation, the Museum of Victims can easily be perceived as a simple extension of the first. This is further indicated on the website of the museum itself, which includes the following text:

> The Museum of the Victims of the Communist Regime represents a continuation of the idea and struggle of the Macedonian people for their own independent and democratic Macedonian state, of the ideals and program goals of VMRO for an independent Macedonia that continued also after the Second World War…[52]

The Museum of VMRO in presenting the history of this organization in fact glorifies the governing party that not only considers itself to be the natural inheritor of VMRO but has also adopted its name. Another contradictory choice in the display of the Museum of VMRO is that it starts with the period of the Karpoš insurrection against the Ottomans, an event which took place in 1689, while VMRO was only created at the end of the nineteenth century. What the visitor could and is meant to conclude from this choice is that VMRO constitutes the sublimation and continuation of the preceding heroic liberation movements. What can further be deduced is that the ideology defended by VMRO (by its right wing), as taken over by VMRO-DPMNE, is the only true patriotic option because it fights for the independence and sovereignty of the country, while on the opposite side, there is the socialist and communist ideology that has betrayed those ideals and provoked the tragedy displayed in the Museum of the Victims of the Communist Regime. In this respect, within the museum's narrative, the communist Other is represented as a traitor to the Macedonian nation and state.

In this manner, instead of serving the alleged symbolic reparation aims of achieving a symbolic rehabilitation of the victims of communism, the Museum employs transitional justice legitimation to glorify and sanction the ideology of the governing party and discredit its political opponents. Instead of commemorating the victims of communism, the museum in fact glorifies those who suffered for defending the idea of an independent Macedonia—an idea to which the governing party VMRO-DPMNE pretends to be entitled.

Conclusion on the Museum of the Victims of the Communist Regime

As Brianne Hwang notes, "a 'harmful' exhibit is one in which a narrative is presented and received as the complete and unmitigated truth without acknowledgement of alternative interpretations and unascertainable complexities".[53] Even if contemporary historiography has put into question the traditional conception of an objective and unique historic truth, I argue that the Museum of the Victims of the Communist Regime within the Museum of Macedonian Struggle pretends to recreate the historical truth, proposing a continuous and unequivocal reconstruction of the past. Moreover, it employs a moralizing narrative of victimization, appealing to emotions in order to reinforce the truth it delivers. It also uses

---

[52] Museum of the Macedonian Struggle, accessed September 2012, http://mmb.org.mk/w/.

[53] Hwang, *Communist Other*, 22.

theatrical and cinematographic techniques that absorb and completely immerse the spectator, discouraging critical thinking or interaction. Offering a reconstruction of a frozen past, it leaves no room for alternative interpretations. And finally, by externalizing and demonizing communism and thus avoiding the painful task of self-examination, the Museum of the Victims of the Communist Regime shirks confrontation with the past and thus fails to achieve the goals of transitional justice.

Conclusion: Citizens Reshaping Transitional Justice in the City

> "We are raising our voice today to protect the right to speak and to think, the right to the city understood as freedom!"[54]

In this chapter, I have considered the contradictions in the policies of symbolic transitional justice displayed in the artistic and memorial practices of the Macedonian government's Skopje 2014 project. I have approached the politics of memory embodied in Skopje 2014 as reflecting the broader struggle of post-communist political elites for control over collective memory and the creation of a new nation-building narrative—a struggle which, as noted by Artemis Christodulou, lies at the heart of post-authoritarian accountability policies.[55]

As argued by scholarship on transitional justice, the instruments of transitional justice can easily become objects of political manipulation in fledgling democracies and divided societies.[56] In this regard, I have considered the instrumentalization of transitional justice policies represented in Skopje 2014, arguing that their reparative dimension has been diverted in order to promote the government's political agenda and ideology. This highlights an important aspect of transitional justice which must be taken into consideration in contemporary debates, i.e., that transitional justice in post-conflict societies is always a political process and that we thus have to maintain a critical stance towards the political implications of its applications.[57] Another important aspect that has been outlined when reflecting on applications of policies of transitional justice in particular contexts is that of the "unintended consequences"[58] and further divisions such policies can provoke in post-conflict societies.[59] In this sense, I have also considered the limits and

[54] "Плоштад Слобода: Го Шириме Гласот", *Okno.mk*, April 8 2009, http://okno.mk/node/401.

[55] Christodoulou, "Memorials".

[56] Zistel, *Transitional Justice*, 2.

[57] Ibid.

[58] Alexander Laban Hinton, (2010) Introduction:"Towards an Anthropology of Transitional Justice", in A. L. Hinton (ed.) *Transitional Justice: Global Mechanisms and Local Realities after Genocide and Mass Violence.* (New Jersey: Rutgers University Press, 2010), 17.

[59] Zistel, *Transitional Justice*, 15.

distortions of symbolic policies of transitional justice in Skopje 2014 as promoting a segregating politics of memory excluding different groups. Moreover, I have outlined one of the principal deficiencies of the policies of transitional justice embodied in the project, i.e., the lack of public debate, transparency and legitimacy in the conception and realization of the project. Skopje 2014 remains a top-down initiative designed by the government and imposed on the citizens, excluding them from designing the capital's transitional (re)construction. This crucial participatory deficiency in the politics of Skopje 2014 highlights an important issue which emerges in contemporary debates, and that is whether transitional justice should privilege a top-down or a bottom-up approach.[60] The example of Skopje 2014 seems to confirm the argument of Patricia Lundy and Mark McGovern that traditionally dominant top-down interpretations of transitional justice can provoke difficulties in post-conflict societies and should consequently be revised. To achieve longer-term sustainability, transitional justice needs to adopt a participatory approach.[61] As Skopje 2014 has shown, transitional justice programmes that do not have local ownership and genuine participation are far less likely to have legitimacy or to be effective.

Furthermore, by abusing the argument for memory preservation, the Skopje 2014 project has overloaded the public space with monumental and petrified vestiges of the past, entrapping the town in history, transforming the living city into a museum of frozen memory. As noted by Siobhan Kattago, the past becomes a burden when it prevents the individual from living in the present and when it eclipses the future.[62] In this respect, a blogger from Skopje posted the following relevant reflection on the "museification" of Skopje: "With the erection of those monuments in the city-centre, the square will be transformed into an ally of the great figures of Macedonism—and Macedonia will continue for a long time to be preoccupied with (selective) history which has too big consequences for Macedonian society (…) bringing us back into history, it will exacerbate the division of the already too much divided society".[63] While too little memory engenders ignorance and the possible falsification of history, too much memory, as displayed within Skopje 2014, can lead to endless conflict and mythification.[64]

Skopje 2014 has also been criticized for its inclusion of many symbolic and non-functional buildings.[65] As noted by architects Mijalkovic and Urbanek, the purpose of the new governmental buildings with greatly decorated facades is to

---

[60] Patricia Lundy and Mark McGovern, "Whose Justice ? Rethinking Transitional Justice from the Bottom Up. Journal of Law and Society", vol. 35, no. 2, (June 2008): 265.

[61] Ibid., 267.

[62] Siobhan Kattago, "Agreeing to Disagree on the Legacies of Recent History" in *Memory and Representation in Contemporary Europe : The persistence of the Past*, (Farnham: Ashgatu Publishing, 2012), 30.

[63] Aleksandar Dimitrijević, "Восочна Историја", *Volan* (blog), January 14, 2010, http://volanskopje.blogspot.com/2010/01/blog-post_14.html.

[64] Kattago, "The Slippery Slope of Memory", in *Memory* , 23.

[65] Rukaj, Mijalkovic and Urbanek, *Skopje*.

celebrate a glorious nation. These buildings are mainly to be seen from the outside—to be admired principally as symbols of power, neither to be lived in nor to function as democratic spaces. The lack of functionality, as argued by Mijalkovic and Urbanek, reflects an "intentional avoidance of spaces where democracy would be practiced and developed".[66] This deficiency in the transitional reshaping of the city highlights another relevant issue related to the responsibility and complexity of designing transitional justice policies for (re)constructing public space: with its authoritarian top-down approach, Skopje 2014 has missed an opportunity to create essential spaces for citizens to determine, shape and develop shared solutions for their capital.

On the other hand, the non-participatory dimension of Skopje 2014 has also provoked significant public counter-reactions and creative forms of resistance within civil society. For the first time in Macedonia, a public debate has been opened regarding the transitional politics of public art, which, as outlined by the theoretician and historian of art, Suzana Milevska, can also be seen as "a potential for a deliberative and participative democracy which is precisely founded on the opening of the public sphere where all the citizens can take part in public debates and express their discontentment or admiration related to the Government project".[67]

It is thus as a reaction to the government's project of autocratic and ethnocratic (re)construction of the city that an informal grass-roots movement has been born, the first of its kind in independent Macedonia, called "The First Archibrigade", mainly consisting of architecture students. On 28 March 2009, the archibrigadiers organized their first protest against Skopje 2014 and the construction of an orthodox church on the city square. Following this event, various additional informal grass-roots movements and NGOs have been created in reaction to the top-down reconstruction of the city, such as "Square Freedom"[68] and the "Singing Skopjeans".[69] Using new social media to communicate their views, those grass-roots movements have organized a range of protests, petitions, public debates and artistic performances related to Skopje 2014, claiming the citizens' "right to the city".[70] The participants of the ad hoc choir "Singing Skopjeans", in this respect, have decided to express their right to the city and their protest by singing engaged songs on selected building sites and locations of Skopje 2014, regularly publishing their performances on YouTube. Re-appropriating the city with their committed artistic performances, the "Singing Skopjeans" also stand up in defence of the preservation of the erased city memory. In particular, I could quote one of their

[66] Ibid.

[67] Suzana Milevska and Jasna Frangovska, "Етика и Естетика", *Okno.mk*, March 18, 2010, http://okno.mk/node/4932.

[68] "Плоштад Слобода", *Okno.mk*, last modified February 10, 2012, http://okno.mk/node/16977.

[69] "Plostad Sloboda's Channel", *YouTube*, accessed September 10, 2012, https://www.youtube.com/user/PlostadSloboda.

[70] Henry Lefebre, *Le Droit à la Ville* (Paris: Anthropos, 1968).

music video performances, held on 27 December 2010, interpreting the song "Under Pressure" by Queen and David Bowie, recorded in a basement, denouncing the government's authoritarian occupation of public space and violation of freedom of expression.[71]

Raising thus their voices against the abuses of the post-communist government policy displayed in the Skopje 2014 project, reshaping and correcting the imposed politics of memory and placing the citizens at the core of transitional justice processes, those grass-roots movements and engaged artistic initiatives highlight what a just politics for the city in transition should be.

Bibliography

1. Angelovska, Despina. 2013. The failure of Macedonian post-communist transitional justice: Lustration, between cleansing and parody. In *Transitional justice and civil society in the Balkans*, ed. Olivera Simić, and Zala Volčič. New York: Springer.
2. Bell, Christine. 2009. Transitional justice, interdisciplinarity and the State of the "Field" or "Non-Field" in the. *International Journal of Transitional Justice* 3: 5–29.
3. Bhabha, Homi K. (ed.). 1990. *Nation and narration*. London: Routledge.
4. Buckley-Zistel, Suzanne. 2009. Transitional justice in divided societies—Potentials and limits. Paper Presented at the 5th European Consortium for Political Research General Conference, vol 16. Potsdam University, Germany, 10–12 Sept 2009.
5. Christodulou, Artemis. 2012. Appendix 4, Part 1: Memorials and Transitional Justice. Sierra Leone Truth and Reconciliation Commission. http://www.sierraleonetrc.org/index.php/appendices/item/appendix-4-part-1-memorials. Accessed 9 Sept 2012.
6. Ellis, Mark S. 1996. Purging the past: The current state of Lustration laws in the former communist bloc. *Law and Contemporary Problems* 59(4): 181–196.
7. Elster, Jon. 2006. *Retribution and reparation in the transition to democracy*. Cambridge: Cambridge University Press.
8. Gelevski, Nikola. 2011. Спомениците и Кичот. in *Okno.mk*. http://okno.mk/node/13998. 4 Oct 2011.
9. Hamber, Ševčenko, Naidu. 2010. Utopian dreams or practical possibilities? The challenges of evaluating the impact of memorialisation in societies in transition. *International Journal of Transitional Justic*e. 4(3):397–420.
10. Hinton, Alexander Laban. 2010. From the Introduction to *Transitional Justice: Global Mechanisms and Local Realities after Genocide and Mass Violence,* ed. A. L. Hinton, 1–22. New Jersey: Rutgers University Press.
11. Kattago, Siobhan. 2012. *Memory and representation in contemporary Europe: The persistence of the past*. Farnham: Ashgate Publishing.
12. Kiss, Csilla. 2006. We Are not Like us. Transitional Justice: the (Re)construction of Post-Communist Memory. In *History and Judgement*, ed. A. MacLachlan, I. Torsen, IWM Junior Visiting Fellows' Conferences, Vienna, vol. 21:3–4.
13. Koteska, Jasna. 2011. Troubles with history: Skopje 2014. *Art Margins*. http://www.artmargins.com/index.php/2-articles/655-troubles-with-history-skopje-2014. 29 Dec 2011.
14. Lefebre, Henry. 1968. *Le Droit à la Ville*. Paris: Anthropos.
15. Lundy, McGovern. 2008. Whose Justice ? Rethinking Transitional Justice from the Bottom Up. *Journal of Law and Society* 35(2): 265.

[71] "Under Pressure Raspeani Skopjani", *You Tube*, last modified December 27, 2010.

16. Mijalkovic and Urbanek. 2011. *Skopje, the World's bastard: Architecture of the divided City*. Klagenfurt: Wieser Verlag.
17. Milevska, Frangovska. 2010. Етика и Естетика. *Okno.mk*. http://okno.mk/node/4932. 18 Mar 2010.
18. Montero, Carlos Closa. 2010. Study on how the Memory of Crimes Committed by Totalitarian Regimes in Europe is Dealt with in the Member States, Madrid: CSIC.
19. Плоштад Слобода: Го шириме гласот. *Okno.mk*. http://okno.mk/node/401. 8 Apr 2009.
20. Плоштад Слобода. *Okno.mk*. http://okno.mk/node/16977. 10 Feb 2012.
21. Quinn, Joanna R. 2008. Transitional justice. In *Human rights: Politics and practice*, ed. Michael Goodhart. London: Oxford University Press.
22. Rukaj, Mijalkovic, Urbanek, Skopje. 2011. The Bastard City. *Osservatorio Balcani e Caucaso*. http://greengopost.com/skopje-the-bastard-city/. 9 Sept 2011.
23. Said, Edward. 1979. *Orientalism*. London: Vintage.
24. Spasovska, Mirjana. 2012. Нова Влада, Нова Историја—Нови Поделби? *Radio Slobodna Evropa*. http://www.makdenes.org/content/article/24623301.html. 23 June 2012.
25. Stan, Lavinia (ed.). 2009. *Transitional justice in Eastern Europe and the former Soviet Union: Reckoning with the communist past*. London: Routledge.
26. Swart, Mia. 2008. Name changes as symbolic reparation after transition: The examples of Germany and South Africa. *German Law Journal* 9(2): 106.
27. Teitel, R.G. 2000. *Transitional justice*. New York: Oxford University Press.
28. Teitel, Ruti G. 2003. Transitional justice genealogy. *Harvard Human Rights Journal* 16: 69–94.
29. Teitel, Ruti G. 2002. Transitional justice in a new Era. *Fordham International Law Journal* 26(4): 893–906.
30. Toth, Manor Gabo. 2011. *Symbols in Transitions: Public Places, Reparatory Justice, and the Statue Park*. Master's Thesis, Budapest: CEU.
31. Vilić, Nebojša, *Силувајте so Скопје, кн.1*, Skopje: 359, 2009.
32. Zhurzhenko, Tatiana. 2007. The Geopolitics of Memory. *Eurozine*, last modified. http://www.eurozine.com/articles/2007-05-10-zhurzhenko-en.html. 10 May 2007.

Index

P. D. Rush and O. Simić (eds.), *The Arts of Transitional Justice*,
Springer Series in Transitional Justice 6, DOI: 10.1007/978-1-4614-8385-4

MIX
Papier aus verantwortungsvollen Quellen
Paper from responsible sources
FSC® C105338

If you have any concerns about our products,
you can contact us on
ProductSafety@springernature.com

In case Publisher is established outside the EU,
the EU authorized representative is:
Springer Nature Customer Service Center GmbH
Europaplatz 3, 69115 Heidelberg, Germany

Printed by Libri Plureos GmbH
in Hamburg, Germany